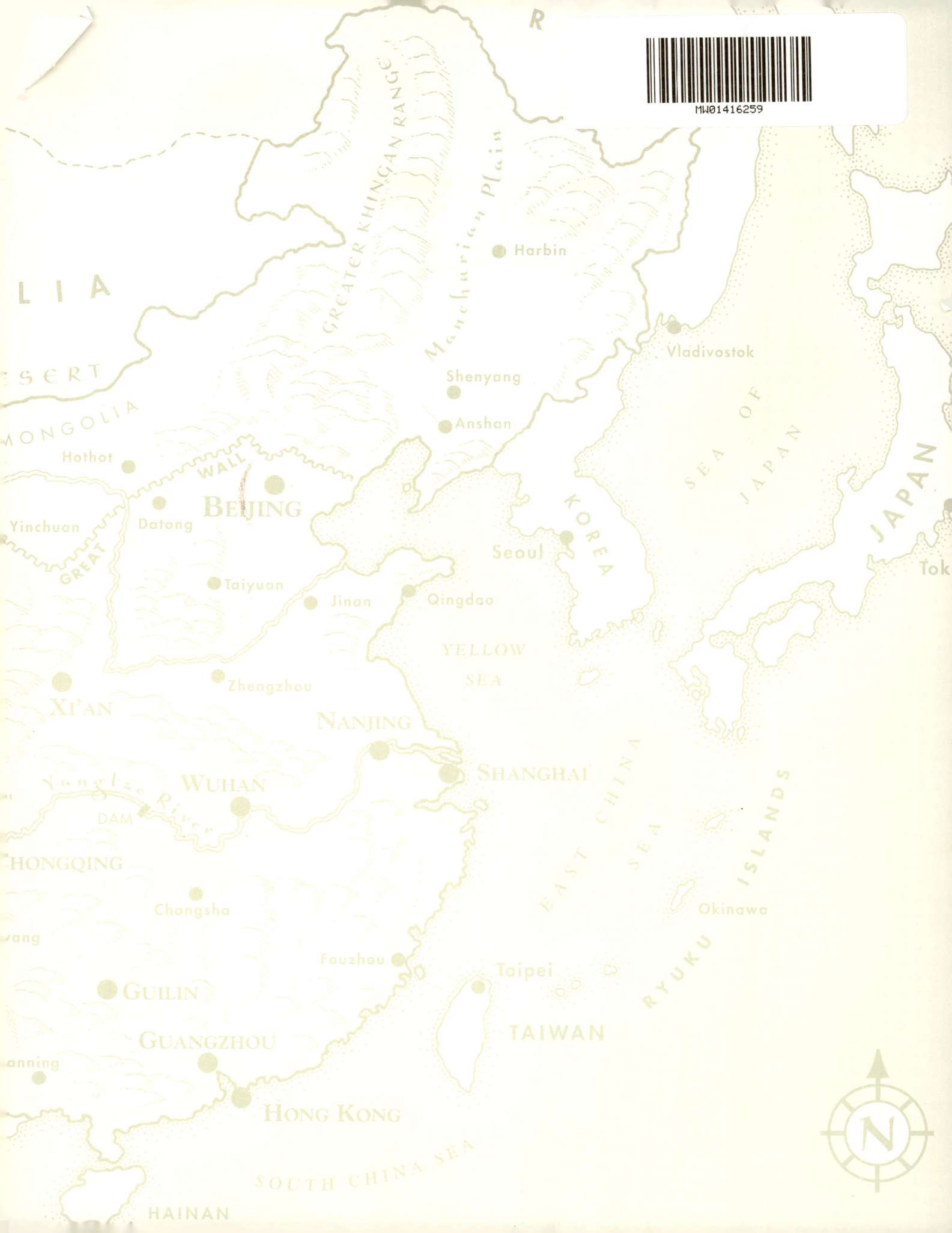

Discovering China

To Jean and Frank Popoff —
Enjoy exploring China with
Mac & I
   Nelson [signature]
                    8/2000

Yes, We Can Cook

Souvenirs Of Tuscany

by Helen Dow Whiting

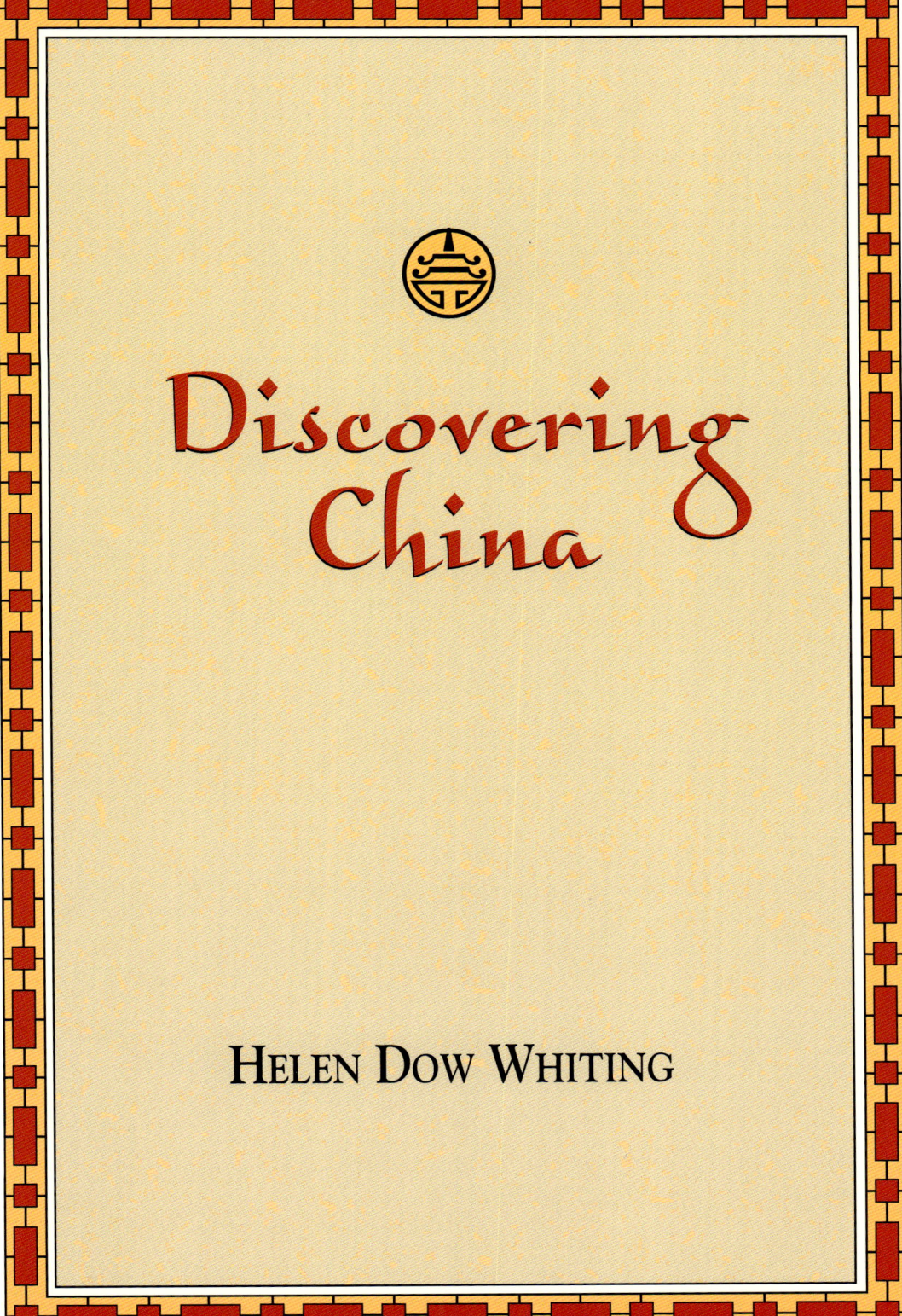

Copyright ©1999
Printed in the United States of America by Express Printing, Hailey, Idaho

All rights reserved. No part of this book may be reproduced or transmitted in any form or by any means, electronic or mechanical, including photocopying, recording, or any information storage and retrieval system, without permission in writing from the publisher.

Book design and production by Typographics, Hailey, Idaho

This book is dedicated to Mac's and my Grandchildren—

Mack and Corey Whiting, Cameron and Chessye Collette,
Castine and Noah Dow, Brandon and Meghan FioRito.

We hope you will sprinkle your lives with
exciting adventures such as these.

"An emperor knows how to govern—when poets are free to make verses, people to act plays, historians to tell the truth, ministers to give advice, the poor to grumble at taxes, students to learn lessons aloud, workmen to praise their skill and seek work, people to speak of anything, and old men to find fault with everything."

Lecture by the Duke of Shao to King Li-Wang in 845 BC

Prologue

Deng's China

> "WHAT DOES IT MATTER WHETHER THE CAT IS BLACK OR WHITE AS LONG AS IT CATCHES MICE."

So said Deng Xiaoping who emerged in 1978 as China's president, premier and party general secretary after Mao Zedong's death. "To get rich is Glorious!"

This was the philosophy Deng wished to instill in the people. To get China moving again, he set about to rejuvenate and build a robust economy. While holding on to the same political system, Deng would try both ways to invigorate it, as well as introducing new ideas. He had seen the chaos of the Cultural Revolution. This system had sponsored the "Great Leap Forward" movement (1959-1961) that brought about the collapse of Chinese agriculture. Some 30 million people starved to death or died as a result, although this famine was concealed from the outside world until 1980. Chaos on this scale would not be tolerated again. Deng keenly felt he could maintain the allegiance of the people by bettering their lives economically.

He was four feet ten inches tall, with his feet barely touching the floor when he sat, but he projected a giant figure and dominated any room he was in. He was very quick, had a great sense of humor and called himself a "country bumpkin" because he came from the interior of China. He liked to eat "hot pot," a northern Chinese dish of vegetables, mutton and rice cooked in a pot of hot water, then seasoned with spicy sauces. He chain smoked and used the spittoon often. He was one of very few Chinese leaders who would go out to dinner with a foreigner.

He had made the Long March when 100,000 Chinese Communists set out and marched for a full year to defeat Chiang Kai-shek's Nationalists. This march revealed to some 200 million people in 11 provinces that the Red Army was their only way to liberation. They covered a distance on foot equivalent to New York from San Francisco and back, while fighting the entire way. Only 10,000 of them completed it. Deng was one of those.

What made him a leader was his ruthlessness and lust for power, having a good support system in place, and his vision for the future of China. He lived to the age of 92, when in February of 1997 he succumbed to respiratory failure after a long battle with Parkinson's disease and lung infection.

It is to this China which Deng created that we are going.

Contents

CHAPTER 1
Hong Kong   1

CHAPTER 2
Pondering, Proposing, Preparing   17

CHAPTER 3
Approaching the Mainland   27

CHAPTER 4
Guangzhou   41

CHAPTER 5
Guilin   67

CHAPTER 6
Shanghai   89

CHAPTER 7
Nanjing   135

CHAPTER 8
Wuhan   155

CHAPTER 9
The Yangtze River Trip   167

CHAPTER 10
Chongqing   201

CHAPTER 11
XI'AN   231

CHAPTER 12
THE SILK ROAD (WESTERN CHINA)   251

CHAPTER 13
BEIJING   297

FINAL POSTSCRIPT   328

Appendix

A   UPDATE OF CHINESE LEADERS   333

B   LOG OF POLITICAL HAPPENINGS
    IN CHINA 1993-1997   337

C   BIBLIOGRAPHY   354

ACKNOWLEDGEMENTS   359

I HOPE YOU WILL ENJOY TRAVELING

THROUGH CHINA WITH US…

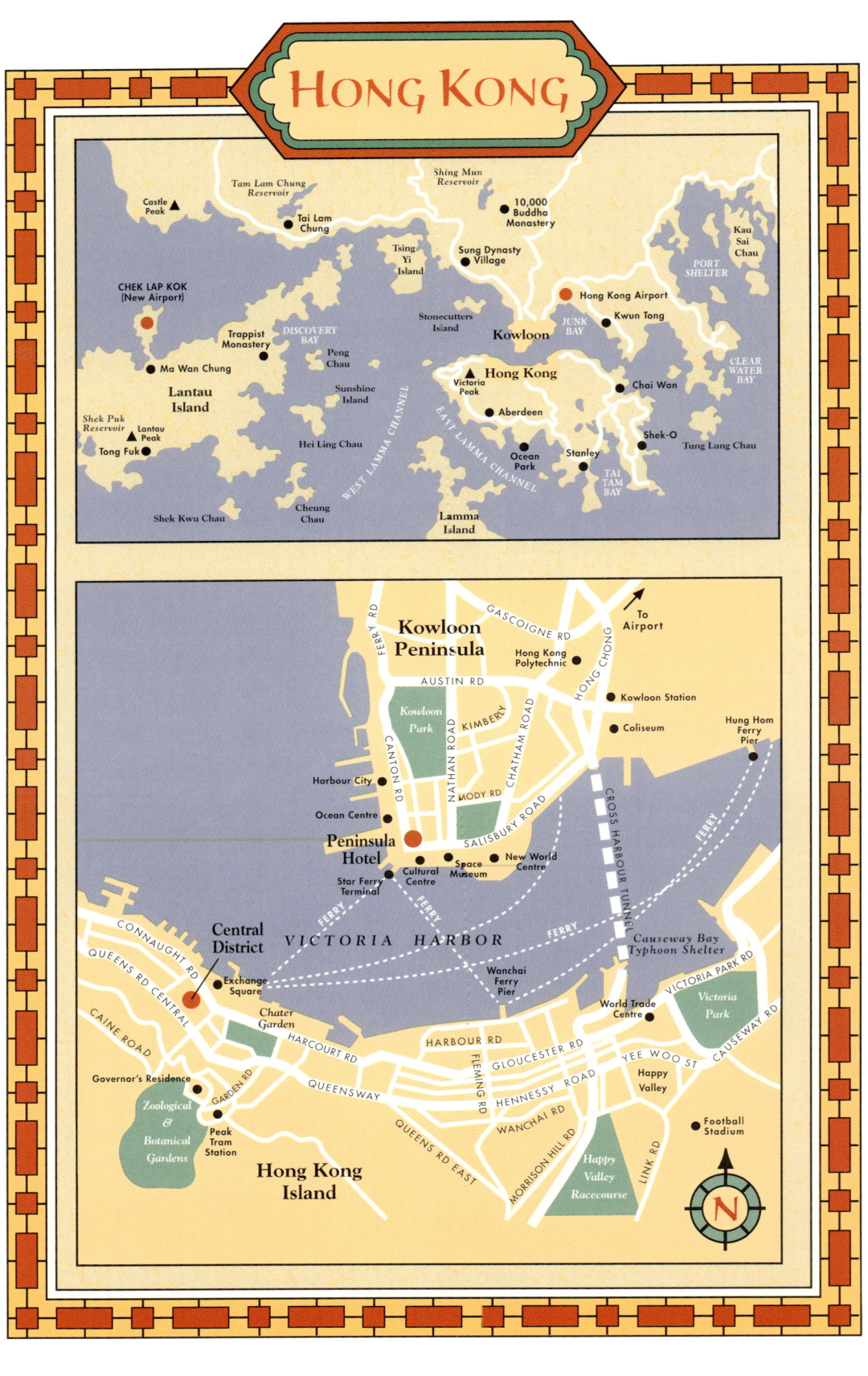

 Hong Kong

In a happy mood, we boarded United Airlines flight #805, non-stop from San Francisco to Hong Kong. While stowing away our carry-ons, we noted there were four other people in our row—all males. One sat with his laptop open, ready to work, the second was reading James Clavell's "Noble House," the exciting novel about Hong Kong, the third was daydreaming, and the fourth, nearest to us, was blowing his nose. All lit cigarettes the minute we were airborne so we rang for the stewardess to check if anyone up front would trade seats.

No one was interested so we settled back. Perhaps the smoking would not be too annoying. As we cruised along, we noticed the passenger beside us must be developing a cold. He alternately sneezed, coughed and then lit a cigarette. Finally my curiosity about his incessant smoking was aroused as he lit an inordinate amount, more than any of the other men in the row. I casually checked my watch and was startled to learn 15 minutes seemed to be the maximum time between each one. Except when napping, his heavy dependency on tobacco lasted the entire 13 hours of the flight. Unbelievable!

Somehow the hours passed. After eating, reading, talking, napping, strolling around the cabin and trying to sleep, there still were five hours to go. Three food services were offered. We participated each time for something diverting to do rather than to soothe any hunger pains. We drank as much water as we could manage. This refreshed our spirits and cleared our heads. Two movies were offered, but neither interested us when the stewardess positioned the screen in front of the cabin for viewing. It reminded passengers to pull down their window shades. For a while the cabin was pleasantly dark—a quiet time—and we napped. The trip continued on uneventfully.

Then captain announced we were making our approach to Hong Kong. At last. What a spectacular landing we experienced at Kai Tak International Airport. Flying the westward flight approach path, the airplane descended downward toward the concrete landing strip. We thought we could see the site of Dow Chemical's huge new plastic manufacturing plant. We almost touched the skyscraper apartment buildings of Kowloon passing on either side of us. Every balcony seemed adorned with the family washing, strung on clotheslines and fluttering in the breeze. The people whose homes were in these buildings must live with constant noise aggravation. Every three or four minutes another huge aircraft was scheduled to land at Kai Tak. Down, down we went until the tires finally touched the narrow runway lying parallel to the sparkling, dark blue waters of the busy Hong Kong harbor. It was an exhilarating experience. Kai Tak is one of the busiest airports in the world. Taxiing toward our assigned disembarking slot we passed aircraft from dozens of countries.

The time was exactly 13 hours since taking off from San Francisco, leaving us stiff from sitting and groggy from breathing stale air. We passengers were in such haste to disembark that everyone almost forgot to say goodbye to the stewardesses. How good it felt to be on solid ground and to inhale fresh air. We walked briskly toward Passport Control.

Mac and I stood in one of several long lines. We watched groups of young Asians being carefully checked by the officer in charge. When it was our turn, he passed us through quickly. I found a trolley for the luggage while

Mac pulled it off the baggage carousel. We pushed the trolley into the line at Customs Control. With a curt nod, the inspector waved us toward the exit gate. By prearrangement, there was an American Express representative waiting with a car and driver to deliver us to the Peninsula Hotel in the urban center of Kowloon. After seating us in the car, he started to give a tourist lecture about Hong Kong. Then, he took a breath and asked if we had been here previously. When we told him, "Yes, many times," he immediately turned his back and spent the rest of the ride to the hotel gossiping with the driver. We did not even have a chance to say how exhilarating it was to be back.

Our assigned rooms at the Peninsula comprised a large living room/bedroom suite overlooking the bustling Hong Kong harbor. The view was somewhat obscured by the enormous, modern Space Dome Museum and Cultural Center. This building, constructed entirely of reinforced concrete, was architecturally interesting, but unfortunately blocked a clear view of the moving panorama in the harbor. Watching the heavy traffic and identifying the different varieties of ships was the obvious reason to request a waterfront suite at the Peninsula. Then we reminisced: When we first visited Hong Kong in the early '60s, we could do this. We also recalled that, during that same period, the hotel maids were instructed to fill the bathtub with water each morning before leaving the room. Mainland China controlled the water supply coming into this British colony, and no one knew if or when the supply might be cut off.

The Kadoorie Dynasty

The Peninsula Hotel is owned by the Kadoorie family whose present spokesman is Michael Kadoorie. He was born in 1941, the same year Hong Kong fell to the Japanese. The surrender took place at the Peninsula Hotel, and it became the Japanese headquarters for the duration of World War II. They also commandeered China Light & Power for the duration, Hong Kong's only power company and a Kadoorie holding.

Michael's grandfather, the late Sir Elly Kadoorie, knighted by Queen Victoria, originally came to China from Baghdad in the 1880s by way of Bombay and Shanghai. He made fortunes in each place before coming to Hong Kong. In Hong Kong, he bought the site of what is now the St. George's building in the central business district. This is where the family still works. Recently, they sold a large block of their China Light & Power stock to Citic Pacific, Ltd., a Mainland Chinese concern, as a move to appease China when Hong Kong was no longer under British control. Sir Elly helped build the Sephardic synagogue where the family worships. His two sons were Lawrence, Michael's father, and Horace. A man now in his fifties, Michael says, "We had a home in Shanghai called Marble Hall with an 80-foot Greco-Roman ballroom and English-style lawns, where my grandfather lived most of the time. Not in Hong Kong. Hong Kong was then a backwater place while Shanghai was the third-largest city in the world."

During World War II, Sir Elly died in a prison camp in Japanese-controlled Shanghai, and in 1949, when the Chinese Communists captured Shanghai, the family's properties, the Astor House and Palace Hotels, as well as Marble Hall, were confiscated.

At the end of World War II, Lawrence Kadoorie returned to Hong Kong wearing a borrowed GI uniform to claim the family's ruined buildings and, with his brother, Horace, to rebuild the family's fortune. It was their idea to construct a traffic tunnel under the harbor. Lawrence, a domineering type, was the first Hong Kong man to earn a British peerage and had seats on many corporate boards. He also had ties to Deng Xiaoping.

Michael credits his father as having had a large hand in resurrecting the colony from a population of around 600,000 after the World War II to its present six million. He was a considerable influence in the colony's business community. His family's money started the growth of Kowloon and the New Territories when those places were only a railroad link to China. As the chairman of China Light & Power, Lord Kadoorie persuaded Shanghainese silk manufacturers to come to Hong Kong, promising them all the power they needed for their factories. This was the start of the huge textile trade which eventually developed. A previous exodus from the Mainland to Hong Kong had occurred in 1937 when the Japanese first bombed Shanghai. Today the Kadoories remain a considerable influence in the colony's business community and want to protect and preserve their legacy of the past. They still own the Peak Tram, once used only by Hong Kong's elite to reach their homes, but now shuttling tourists for a glimpse of Hong Kong from the top. The family spends millions to protect Pak Ngau Shek from developers. It is a mountain overgrown with beautiful orange orchids and some 156 different rare species of butterflies.

The Kadoories are a part of a group of families whose assets, connections and confidence are the foundation of Hong Kong's commerce. The Kadoories started one of the first brokerage or trading houses, known as "hongs," more than a century ago. Their firm is called Sir Elly Kadoorie Continuation, Ltd. They join with Jardine Matheson and Butterfield & Swire as members of the elite who dominate Hong Kong business.

Hong Kong's Past

When the Peninsula Hotel, now part of a world-wide chain, opened in 1928, life in this British colony was good. Business flourished and even the poorest European had at least two servants, a sizeable house, plus a gardener, a houseboy, and a car driven by a chauffeur. Weekends were filled with golf, tennis and swimming. Nights were spent on white-tie dinners and charity balls. Then, in December of 1941, things drastically changed. The Japanese, who were already at war with the Chinese, invaded Hong Kong, beginning with an air raid on Kai Tak airport. They destroyed five uncamouflaged aircraft which was the entire British air fleet. A land invasion followed, and the Japanese, who many of the colony's British thought of as "small and weak," believing one Englishman was worth three of them, soundly defeated the British after an 18-day battle. The colony was not liberated until 1945 and endured three years and eight months of brutal Japanese occupation.

By 1948, when the Communists seized power and controlled all industries in China, the textile industry, which was the base of Shanghai's wealth, moved to Hong Kong. Bringing along any equipment that could be salvaged, the textile tycoons fled the Mainland en masse from 1949 to 1952. Those businessmen were responsible for giving Hong Kong its worldwide reputation in the textile and garment businesses.

In the 1950s and 1960s, the Communists closed the Mainland to all foreigners. They wanted Hong Kong to be their only window open to an outside world. This city was to be China's port for foreign trade rather than any of the coastal cities like Canton (Guangzhou) or Shanghai. Foreigners were especially to be kept away from Beijing, just as they had been in the past when the imperial dynasties ruled the nation. Beijing insisted on being aloof from the rest of the world.

In 1978, when Deng Xiaoping succeeded Mao Zedong, his "opening up to the outside world" made a new economic miracle possible for Hong Kong. This was a chance for the industrialists to shift their operations back onto the Mainland where there was more space to expand their factories. An estimated 25,000 factories now operating in China were owned by or producing for Hong Kong companies. They employed over three million people.

Today, Hong Kong is a thriving colony with beautiful hotels and restaurants, excellent highways and air services, plus shopping facilities for numerous varieties of items. Whatever anyone could possibly dream of wanting is there to buy. Starting with simple little souvenirs to silk clothing to valuable antiques, jewelry, furniture and household goods, as well as foods of all kinds, if one has the patience to look, undoubtedly "it" will be found in some shop somewhere. The fun is in the search.

The New Territories

In the '60s, we were allowed inland only to a certain rural area in the New Territories. Those were lands leased to the British by China. At the highest peak was a lookout called Lok Ma Chau. Standing there, we could gaze over at the collective farms in Communist Canton. We saw beautifully terraced rice paddies with red Communist flags flying in the fields while the Hakku people, each wearing a wide rimmed, black coolie hat with black fringe around the edges, hand tilled the soil with hoes. There was an observation tower too. Manned by a guard with powerful binoculars, its presence discouraged coming any closer. In those days, Mainland China was a tempting but forbidden enigma for citizens of the United States. Today there are some 650 villages existing in the New Territories.

Late in the 1800s, the British agreed Ch'ing (also called "Qing") law, not British colonial law, would rule these territories. The Ch'ing Dynasty was the era of the Manchus which had begun in 1644 and finally collapsed in 1911, but still dominates the lives of the 700,000 villagers who reside in the territories today. To quote a villager who runs a small acupuncture clinic, Cheng Lai-sheung, "It is very common that women have no rights in the villages. You're not supposed to speak out because it is against filial piety and tradition. That's the way it's been since the Ch'ing Dynasty was established."

The *International Herald Tribune* in April 1995 reported the results of elections for the village heads held in the Territories. In many of the villages, women were not allowed to vote. In some, husbands voted for their wives, and in others, male relatives voted for widows—another Ch'ing tradition. The village leaders said that while they welcomed the women to vote, most women were not interested because they did not care who won. Controlling women's voting rights may be the last remnant of imperial tradition.

We understand that last year another legacy was legislated out of existence. This was the practice of denying women inheritance rights. Only after a vigorous, if not vicious, debate led by a legislator named Christine Loh Kung-wai did this come about. She is a businesswoman who was an appointed member of the Hong Kong Legislative Council. Said she, as quoted in the same April 1995 *International Herald Tribune* article, "Under Ch'ing Law even if your parents wanted to give you something after they died, they could not if you were a female." Of course many village leaders were unhappy to see Ch'ing traditions crumbling, but times have changed as women asserted themselves for their rights. How these changes would be furthered when China took over Hong Kong and its territories in 1997 can only be guessed.

On this very short visit to Hong Kong in 1993, we were extremely pleased to find the Peninsula Hotel's new construction activities did not interrupt any of the excellent services always offered to its guests. Greeting one's arrival, Welcoming Tea was quickly brought to the room. It was presented in a lovely oriental teapot encased in a silk brocade-lined tea caddy to keep it hot. The floor waiter serving the tea took much pride in making "his" guests comfortable. He offered other niceties like rich chocolates to nibble, bars of special soap to use and a large supply of current newspapers from several different countries. We were asked if we needed clothing pressed for dining that evening. We knew when we returned from dinner, our beds would be turned down, the curtains in the rooms drawn and the lights dimmed. A very proficient staff has been thoughtfully trained to be concerned for the comfort of each guest. These attentions to amenities were impressive for travel-weary, jet-lagged guests like ourselves. It was the hallmark of the hospitality offered at the Peninsula.

Literature in our room said that during May of 1995 a new wing would be opened at the Peninsula. It will encompass 132 new, big guest rooms with high ceilings. An all-weather pool will have a view of the harbor. There will be a spa, a state-of-the-art communication system and a new Philippe Starck restaurant. This restaurant was open while we were there, but was fully booked when we tried to make a dinner reservation. The Peninsula's fleet of Rolls Royce limousines will be replaced with two heliports on the roof, making guests only seven minutes away from Hong Kong's new airport currently being built on Lantau Island. Mac and I read all this with a smile. We realized when we looked out our windows and saw scaffolding still around the front entrance, none of the wonderful plans were quite in place as yet.

As we started to unwind from the flight, we two felt more exhausted as each hour passed. A single day to recuperate in this relaxing suite, while beneficial, was hardly enough time to catch our breath. An extra day would be most welcome. What interfered was the scheduled early morning train trip to Canton. Mac decided to telephone our American Express representative, a Mr. Wu, to inquire whether we might reschedule to another day or perhaps drive over there in a private automobile. Driving would take only about four hours. Mr. Wu politely listened to Mac and promised to call back.

The Rail System

Since it was first opened in 1911, there has been continuous railroad service between Hong Kong and Canton. The railroad station in the '60s was just below the Peninsula Hotel. I remember watching people board the once-a-day service. Since our country had no diplomatic ties with China, no one from the United States was allowed on that train. We citizens could not obtain the required visa. Every American in Hong Kong was warned never to stray into any area controlled by China. Especially when boating in the waters around the harbor, a popular recreation, great care was taken not to drift into the waters controlled by Communist China. One would be arrested if caught by a Chinese patrol ship.

How dramatically different things were now! There were streamlined, high-speed trains, with a capacity of some 775 passengers, running from the

Kowloon Station to Canton every day. The railroad station was at Hunghom beside the cross-harbor tunnel. Starting at six in the morning

until eleven at night, four express trains were scheduled daily. Tickets had to be purchased before departure.

Mr. Wu returned Mac's telephone call. Politely he listed his objections to Mac's requests: Driving to Canton was impossible. First, his driver probably could not pass through the border. He had no papers. Second, if the driver could pass through, probably his car could not. It had no papers. Third, rescheduling seats on a later train was absolutely impossible. He had obtained for us the only seats available this entire week, and they were the ones on the early morning train. He strongly urged us to keep these

confirmed seats. With more than a little amusement at this long dissertation, we certainly knew that we would be on the early morning train to Canton.

And, we learned a lesson in tactfulness, or about not "losing face" from an expert.

Losing face

Losing face is an integral part of the Chinese attitude toward life. It is more than a feeling of guilt. The loss of face can be a slight, a missed opportunity, a family shame, a regional shame, or a failure to perform a duty according to expectations of one's peers, particularly in front of foreigners. Chinese people do not like to say "no." They will go to great lengths to find a tactful way of expressing the negative. Not having to say "no" is part of the Chinese notion of politeness. They feel it is not right to deny a visitor's request so they really extend themselves to find a discreet way to suggest something cannot be done. Hopefully the ignorant foreigner recognizes this.

Later, we will recall this discussion with Mr. Wu more comprehensively. It was a basic lesson in learning that any travel plan changes were virtually an impossibility. Change threw everything off balance in China. In contrast, we Americans thought nothing of rescheduling travel plans. Spoiled by our capable travel agents, who often worked miracles to accommodate complicated requests, we forgot the communication ability they had at their fingertips with computers. China does not have this technology as well developed. Their booking offices were very often confused and inefficient. Since every transaction was checked through Beijing, no matter where one made the request, this was time consuming for local travel offices, as well as frustrating for the tourist. Mac and I soon realized an early arrival anywhere worked to our advantage. Settling reservation problems with a hotel's staff took time and patience. The earlier one arrived at each new destination, the faster the inevitable problems could be solved.

On Becoming Mainlander Chinese

At the time of our trip, there were exactly two years before this British colony fell under the domination of Communist China. This provided much conversation, speculation and worry among its citizens, for at midnight on June 30, 1997 the Union Jack would come down, and the Chinese flag would go up.

The Union Jack was first planted at Possession Point, a waterfront site just off Wing Lok Street, by Captain Edward Belcher at 8:15 AM on January 26, 1841. Possession Point, now known as Hollywood Road Park, was a place where coffin makers played chess while awaiting new customers. Thus will end 155 years of the British presence in the territory and 99 years of British colonial rule. Henceforth Hong Kong will be known as the Special Administrative Region of the People's Republic of China. Two flags will be flown, one with the five yellow stars of China and the other with the single, five-petaled Bauhinia blossom, a type of orchid, representing the Hong Kong Special Administrative Region.

The region will be governed by China's Basic Law that states: 1) The economy of

Hong Kong will be more controlled by the Mainland imposing tight restrictions. 2) Politically, the executive and legislative councils will not be able to exercise any independent actions. 3) The courts will try to maintain independence and will do so in commercial cases. They will have difficulty enforcing judicial decisions of the Mainland courts. In any decision, the Communist Party will always come first. 4) Mandarin will be the official language. The second will be English. 5) Academic freedom will be gone.

Freedom of religion was supposed to be protected by the Basic Law, but religious groups realized they must consult with Chinese officials to avoid offense. These five laws were making people very pessimistic. Television stations and newspapers were turning into propaganda tools for Beijing. Those who did not kowtow to Beijing would be shut down and their editors jailed.

The current governor of Hong Kong and the last English appointee, Chris Patten, urged Beijing to start reassuring Hong Kong and the rest of the world that it intended to trust Hong Kong. As he saw it, bolstering the sagging confidence of the Hong Kongers was essential to the success of the transfer of its sovereignty.

There were many signs of the coming change. On the cliffs of Chung Hom Kok, the giant satellite dishes that gathered information from China for British intelligence agencies have been dismantled and shipped to Australia. Civil servants were being taken to Beijing to be harangued about the evils perpetrated by the British during the Opium Wars in the mid-19th century. The Royal Hong Kong Jockey Club and the Royal Yacht Club decided to omit the term "royal." Newspaper satire was not immune. The cartoon, "The World of Lily Wong," a political and social strip carried in the *South China Morning Post* that both amused and outraged Hong Kongers, suddenly ended. The papers called it an "economy measure," but its cartoonist author, Larry Feign, insisted it was for political reasons. Hong Kong was an information hub for all of Asia. *Time, Newsweek, The Wall Street Journal* and CNN were just some who staffed offices. The *International Herald Tribune* and *The Washington Post* were printed here. There were news bureaus for publications all over the world. Many had begun censoring themselves before Beijing took over.

When Prime Minister John Major of Great Britain announced British passports would be issued to those Hong Kongers who wished them, a line one mile long formed at the Embassy. Counting the number of people in the long lines, at the end of the final week some 130,000 people had applied, more than had petitioned for passports over the past four years.

The British National Overseas passport, while not conferring British citizenship, did allow residents of current and former British territories to travel without a visa to Britain and about 80 other countries. The Special Administrative Region passport that will be issued here by China allows its holder entry into only Britain and Singapore. So far, they are the only two countries that have agreed to grant visa-free entry to its holders.

About half of Hong Kong's six million residents are eligible by birth for British overseas passports. Those applying the last Sunday in March of 1996 were among the two million Hong Kong residents who were not born here and were mostly immigrants from China. They were its taxi and bus drivers, clerks and secretaries, vegetable sellers and waiters, plumbers and road workers. They did not hold British, Canadian or American passports, nor had they purchased citizenship from Mauritius or any other small country offering passports for a price. Their fate remained in Hong Kong.

Other concerns reflected Hong Kong's past: There was a colonial cemetery at Happy Valley where many British taipans and seafarers, missionaries, pirates, opium smugglers and scoundrels had plaques on a towering monument that symbolized the past. Would they be left? There were street names and building names that honored past governors, navy captains, military personnel and British royalty. Queen's Road ran through the heart of Central and Wanchai. There was Prince Edward subway station. The Prince of Wales barracks which housed the British garrison would soon be home to Chinese troops. Roads with such names as Macdonnell, Kennedy, Bowen, Caine and Robinson were named for former governors. Would the Chinese change these?

The Escape Route

Now it is public knowledge that there was a Hong Kong escape route for Chinese dissidents who wished to leave the Mainland. It ended as of June 30th, 1997. Approximately 500 defectors since the 1989 incident at Tiananmen Square have made use of it. Through the years, virtually every Western consulate in the territory has had to confront the problem of accepting political refugees. When using the escape route, the dissident would receive a coded message to travel quickly to one of the many fishing piers along China's southern coastline. There he would board a junk, a nondescript Chinese fishing boat, one of the many that plied the South China Sea. The dissident hid below deck while the boat's captain crossed several miles of rough sea to a Hong Kong shore, always being careful to evade any Chinese patrol boat. If all went well, the dissident arrived on a deserted beach and scrambled ashore. He was an hour away from central Hong Kong. Once there, he received temporary resident and travel papers. These were a passport to freedom for him.

Hong Kong's Bright Future

One promising sign in Hong Kong's future was currently under way, as reported in an October 1995 article in the *International Herald Tribune*. This is the $20 billion new airport development at Chek Lap Kok island. The vastness of this project is staggering. It contains five square miles of land, and initially involved the flattening of Chek Lap Kok island and reclaiming the airport site from the sea. That work was predicted to take 42 months, but was finished ahead of schedule. The land will support newly planned highways, office buildings and apartment blocks. Currently in progress were the following: A brand new town called Tung Chung with schools, police stations, fire houses and shopping centers to accommodate some 20,000 people; two suspension bridges—one, the Tsing Ma having the longest center spans in the world, carrying six lanes of traffic on the upper decks and enclosed railways on the lower decks; a high speed rail system to whisk travelers the 21 miles from Hong Kong to Chek Lap Kok island in 23 minutes; a six-lane highway running from Hong Kong's center right to the airport; and, finally, a third tunnel under Hong Kong's harbor. With the possible exception of the Three Gorges Dam project on the Yangtze River, this is the world's largest infrastructure project. More startling is the fact there were no delays or overruns, with everything going along on schedule and under budget. The government of Hong Kong financed the bulk of these projects. There will be no new taxes for its citizens. The entire project was expected to be mostly completed in 1997. This huge development reshaped Hong Kong. No more will it have one of the world's busiest airports in the middle of the city.

This entire project seemed a very exciting vote of confidence for the future. The Chinese Mainlanders might learn a lot from the Hong Kongers.

The Handover Ceremonies

I watched the Handover ceremonies on television from our home in the United States. When they ended, I had a large lump in my throat and tears in my eyes, for they were very moving. These were the random notes I made from the report in *The International Herald Tribune*:

Monday, June 30th, 1997 about 500 troops from the People's Liberation Army streamed across the border into Hong Kong, just hours ahead of the British colony's Handover to China.

At 9:00 p.m., a convoy of Chinese soldiers from the Mainland rolled into the rural New Territories in the north. The troops, armed with automatic rifles, crossed the border, seated in buses or standing in open trucks. The early deployment of these troops had been agreed on with Britain in advance of the formal Handover. An additional 4,000 troops, accompanied by armored vehicles, helicopters and warships, were to arrive later by land, sea and air. Beijing saw the troop movement as a symbol of Chinese sovereignty over Hong Kong. The troops were expected to be stationed at Sek Kong, the major military and air force base used by the British garrison during colonial rule.

The symbolic end of British rule began Monday afternoon at 4:30 when the doors of Government House, home for British governors since 1855, opened and Hong Kong's 28th resident of the house, Chris Patten, his wife, Lavender, and their three daughters walked down the steps. At attention in the circular drive was the police band, in snow white tunics with polished silver buttons. Mr. Patten stepped onto a small dias. The band broke into "God Save the Queen" and eight officers from the Royal Police Training School, bearing ceremonial World War II Lee Enfield 303 rifles, snapped through a drill of flipping rifles, abrupt turns and slow-step marching, in a salute to the last governor. Mr. Patten then walked slowly down a line of representatives of each of the territory's services, from the Correctional Service Department to the Auxiliary Medical Services, all dressed in white uniforms. As a single bugler played "Last Post," a drizzle of rain started to fall, and the Union Jack was slipped down the flagpole. The police band struck up Mr. Patten's favorite song, the "Highland Cathedral." After being presented with the folded flag on a royal blue pillow, Mr. Patten stepped into a 1961 Rolls Royce. The car, flying the governor's ensign, circled the courtyard three times, a Chinese ritual meaning, "We shall return," and a ritual always performed by all previous governors. The governor's car went out the gates, and a small contingent of police in their brown uniforms swung the gates closed for the last time. Thus ended 122 years of British residency.

Tuesday, July 1st, 1997 at Tamar, the Royal Naval base, as "God Save the Queen" billowed forth, British soldiers lowered the Union Jack for the last time in Hong Kong. "God Save the Queen" was played by a band of Scots Guards wearing tall, bearskin hats. Seconds later, with the playing of China's national anthem, "March of the Volunteers," China's flag with five gold stars was raised solemnly along with the new flag of Hong Kong, a stylized white Bauhinia flower on a red background. It was pouring rain, a good omen according to the Chinese.

The drizzle turned into showers, then to a downpour of monsoon rains. With the rains pelting him, Governor Patten delivered his last speech. "Our own nation's contribution here was to provide the scaffolding that enabled the people of Hong Kong to ascend: The rules of law. Clean and light-hearted government. The values of a free society. The beginnings of representative government and democratic responsibility. Hong Kong's values are decent values. They are universal values. They are the values of the future in which the happiest and the richest communities, and most confident and most stable too, will be those that best combine political liberty and economic freedom as we do today."

Prince Charles of England spoke briefly. "The United Kingdom," he declared, "has been proud and privileged to have had responsibility for the people of Hong Kong, to have provided a framework of opportunity in which Hong Kong has so conspicuously succeeded and to have been part of the success which the people of Hong Kong have made of their opportunities."

Declared Jiang Zemin, President of all China, who was in Hong Kong for the ceremonies, "The return of Hong Kong to the motherland after going through a century of vicissitudes indicates that from now on the Hong Kong compatriots have become true masters of this Chinese land and that Hong Kong has now entered a new era of development."

Hong Kong with its six million people had returned to China.

This was the first time a capitalist country had been turned over to a Communist one.

A Sense of Humor

Hong Kong merchants have a sense of humor about the Handover. "One country, two systems" was what China promised Hong Kong, so it became the logan for selling all sorts of merchandise. "One price, two dresses! One store, two sales! One party, two hangovers! Hurry, only a few shopping days left under British rule!" There were Handover watches and Handover jewelry, Handover umbrellas, Handover top hats and baseball caps, Handover underwear, Handover commemorative coins and stamps, Handover coffee mugs, pocket diaries, T-shirts, postcards, lighters and even a Handover Barbie doll with long black hair wearing a Chinese empress dress. Reebok made commemorative shoes in red and yellow, the colors of the Chinese flag, with the Chinese characters for "97" embroidered on the tongue. A can of authentic Hong Kong "colonial air" was available with a label that read "the last gasp of an empire." Restaurants and bars all were offering some kind of Handover specials for the night of June 30th. These savvy merchants knew how to make the best of a selling opportunity.

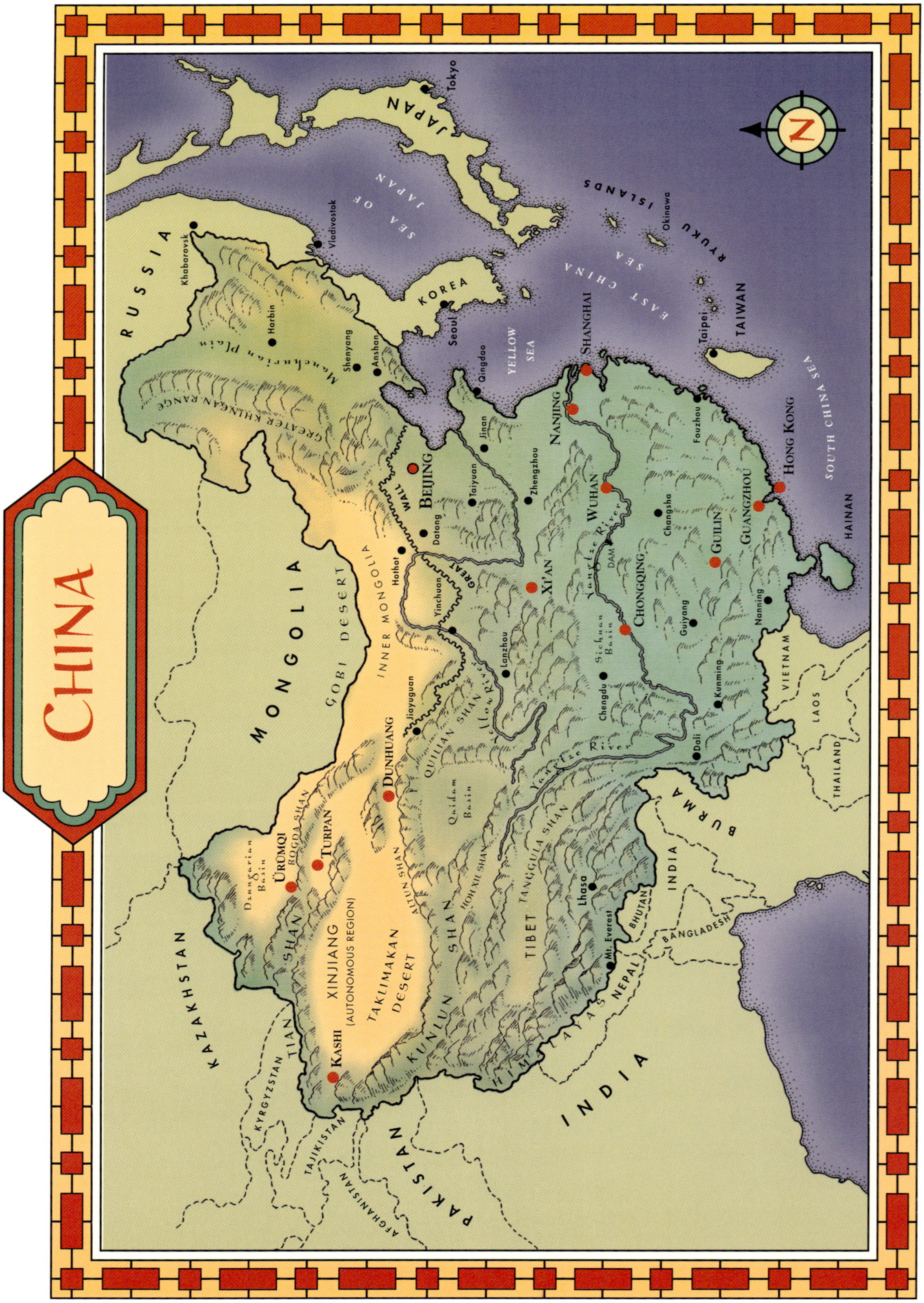

CHINA
N
RUSSIA
Khabarovsk
Vladivostok
SEA OF JAPAN
JAPAN
Tokyo
KOREA
Seoul
YELLOW SEA
EAST CHINA SEA
RYUKU ISLANDS
Okinawa
TAIWAN
Taipei
SOUTH CHINA SEA
HAINAN
Harbin
Manchurian Plain
GREATER KHINGAN RANGE
Shenyang
Anshan
Qingdao
Jinan
BEIJING
GREAT WALL
Datong
Taiyuan
Hohot
Zhengzhou
SHANGHAI
NANJING
WUHAN
Yangtze River
DAM
Changsha
Fouzhou
HONG KONG
GUANGZHOU
GUILIN
Guiyang
Nanning
XI'AN
CHONGQING
Sichuan Basin
Chengdu
Kunming
Dali
Yinchuan
Lanzhou
Huang He
MONGOLIA
GOBI DESERT
INNER MONGOLIA
Jiayuguan
DUNHUANG
QILIAN SHAN
Qaidam Basin
TURPAN
ÜRUMQI
BOGDA SHAN
Dzungarian Basin
TIAN SHAN
XINJIANG
(AUTONOMOUS REGION)
TAKLIMAKAN DESERT
KASHI
ALTUN SHAN
KUNLUN SHAN
HOH XIL SHAN
TANGGULA SHAN
Yangtze River
TIBET
Lhasa
Mt. Everest
HIMALAYAS
NEPAL
BHUTAN
BANGLADESH
INDIA
BURMA
VIETNAM
LAOS
THAILAND
KAZAKHSTAN
KYRGYZSTAN
TAJIKISTAN
AFGHANISTAN
PAKISTAN

chapter 2

Pondering, Proposing, Preparing

For a long time, Mac and I wished to explore Mainland China. Our interest stemmed from many visits to Hong Kong, starting in 1962, and especially from a visit to Taiwan. This island was the most like Mainland China of any place we were allowed to visit in 1962.

Although the atmosphere of Hong Kong was British, mostly it was an outlet for the Mainland Chinese to sell their products. It was governed by England and most citizens, whether born from Chinese parents or not, thought of themselves as more British than Chinese. No American could buy anything with a Chinese label or origin unless there was written proof the object was over a hundred years old. It was frustrating for us to see interesting works of art, furniture, jade and porcelain and not be allowed to bring any of it back into the United States.

Taiwan was a different matter. It felt Chinese from the moment one arrived. One hundred miles from the Mainland, this was the island where the Kuomintang government of Chiang Kai-shek took refuge when they left Mainland China. Later they claimed it "The National Republic of China." The Mainlanders refused to acknowledge it as an independent state. The United States had diplomatic relations with Taiwan in 1962 when we first visited, but not very many Americans had been there, even though they could obtain visas. We flew into its capital, Taipei, from Hong Kong and were greeted at Immigration by uniformed Chinese police. One was a woman. All were armed with guns. They carefully checked our passports and unsmilingly allowed us into the terminal. Once through Customs, we were cheerfully greeted by the Chinese business people, the M.C. Changs, whom we had come to meet. Mrs. Chang handed me a bouquet of roses she had cut that day from her garden. I remember one blossom was a dark, almost black red which was a different variety than I had ever seen. She had wrapped the stems in heavy wax paper. Luckily she did, for those roses had many thick, prickly thorns.

We were whisked to the Grand Hotel, situated on a hill overlooking the city of Taipei and the Tamsui River. It looked huge. Very Oriental in design, with a bright red pagoda-shaped roof, it dominated the hillside. The drive up to its entrance twisted around a hill. We instinctively felt immersed in Chinese culture.

An outstanding event happened on that visit to Taiwan. It was a formal reception for Mac and our party to meet representatives of the government and local business people. We dressed in cocktail attire for this occasion. As we stood in the receiving line shaking hands with dozens of Chinese men and women, a hush fell over the crowd. A pathway was cleared, and a very elderly gentleman appeared. He was plainly dressed in trousers with a long Chinese, high-neck cotton jacket. His head was shaved, but he had the longest white beard either of us had ever seen. He walked holding a long staff. By his presence, this man commanded respect from all. He greeted Mac and me with typical Chinese "he-hees" for he spoke not a word of English, but he was aware of the company we represented. We both bowed and Mac touched his outstretched hand. He was the head of the Control Yuan, the Supreme Court of Taiwan. We were very honored by his presence. Our company was selling granular plastic to the Taiwanese. They became the world's leading injection molders of plastic.

Knowing that Taiwan was on military alert and heavily armed, we were not surprised to find many men in military dress at that reception. All the men who lived there were trained by the military for an immediate attack, should it come, from the Mainland. The United States had a large base there too. When I was taken sightseeing by Mrs. Chang the next day, one of the women in our party was the wife of the United States Army Commander. She was a jolly person and not at all fearful for her family's safety. We women had a great time.

Several years later, we took our six children, ages six to sixteen, to Taiwan during a trip around the world. They remember a Chinese dinner. We had asked our guide to direct us to an authentic restaurant where the children would be welcome. When we arrived, we were shown to the upstairs dining room and seated, without a word spoken by the attendant. The eight of us sitting at a round table were an eyeful for the rest of the diners. Never had some seen such a large American family at dinner. Soft drinks were served. Then we proceeded to sit and wait and wait and wait. No waiter approached us with menus. The children finished their soft drinks and began wiggling in their seats. We must have been sitting a good half hour or more when a young man appeared. Mac said to him, "Where have you been? We've been here a long time." The man looked at Mac and said, "Well, I don't know. I was just walking along the sidewalk outside this restaurant when one of the waiters grabbed me. 'Do you speak English?' he asked, and when I said I did, he pulled me inside this restaurant 'to help these poor foreigners.' Here I am. What can I do for you?" We all laughed and explained what we wanted to eat, as he interpreted the menu for us. He repeated this in Chinese to our hovering waiter. It turned out to be one of the best meals we had on the entire trip. All eight of us ate with chopsticks which caused nods of appreciation from the rest of the diners.

In May 1980, at the time of soaring oil prices and the world energy crisis, Mac and a team of scientists and engineers were sent to Taiwan by the National Academy of Sciences. They were to consult with the government on energy conservation. At the conclusion, Mac and the group talked for two hours with the prime minister about effective measures. Within weeks, their recommendations were made into law. It took years before most other governments acted on this urgent measure. Mac found it very gratifying to be of assistance to such an alert government. Taiwan continued being on military alert and threatened with a takeover by the Mainland during all these times. It still is today.

Mac and I continued traveling throughout the Orient after those business times in the early '60s, but ordinary citizens from the United States like ourselves were not allowed the necessary visas to enter Mainland China. During the '60s and '70s, the United States had no diplomatic relations with Beijing. Suddenly in 1983 the Bamboo Curtain lifted, and we Americans could obtain visas.

We hesitated. China was only beginning to pull itself together from the miseries of its Cultural Revolution. The people had endured 30 years of harsh restrictions under the rule of Mao Zedong. Now with their government mandating a completely different philosophy, they were coping with an about-face under Deng Xiaoping's leadership. Imagine being a 30-year old Chinese who from birth had been told what to think, how to dress, where to work, not to believe in one's family values, and instead to subscribe to the teachings of Mao, then suddenly one day being advised those ideas would no longer be tolerated. Or suppose the person was 30 years old when the Revolution started and 60 years old when it ended. How did that individual cope with yet another abrupt philosophical change at an advanced age? Change is stressful for everyone.

In the '80s, very few Americans visited China, and certainly not the general public. In 1991, when we ventured briefly into Shanghai and Suzhou, we realized conditions were favorable for planning an ambitious trip throughout the country. For various reasons, it was not until 1993 that we were able to start an extended tour.

The political atmosphere of Deng's government made visiting China more secure for us. This country with its 5,000-year old history had survived many a political turmoil and continued to grow through all those times. We thought China, with its ancient history and continued growth, should be recognized and understood, even though the United States government took its time establishing diplomatic relations. In spite of China's size, which is larger than all of the Soviet Union and Europe combined, the United States seemed to have no great interest in being friendly with this nation during our trip in 1993.

China's History

It is awesome to realize China's cultural history is older than most nations in the world. We have utter respect for this civilization's accomplishments. We knew for instance that China had developed a global trade that extended from the Indian Ocean to the Arabic Sea and around the South China and East China Seas long before Christopher Columbus set his sails toward the American continent in 1492. This involved many countries of diverse cultures and religions. China had trade with the Africans, Mediterraneans, the Islamic Middle Eastern people, Indians and others along the costal areas of Asia as early as the eighth and ninth centuries. In the 11th and 12th centuries, before Europe even entered this network, Chinese junks were reaching Calcutta and other Indian ports on the Bay of Bengal. It was not until the 15th and 16th centuries that the Venetians, Spanish, Portuguese, Dutch and English merchants began to participate in this same global trade. Compared to the Chinese merchants they were late-comers more interested in importing luxury Asian goods for the European nobility and the upper classes than in becoming international tradesmen in commodities.

In 1993, we needed to make many decisions on how to accomplish a fulfilling trip. In such an enormous country, we had to decide which regions to visit as well as to define what our other priorities would be.

We both enjoyed studying history, and China's was especially fascinating. Through visiting architectural temples and monuments and ambling through museums displaying relics from the past, we would put its history into perspective.

Beautiful landscapes and gardens have always been foremost in our mind's eye when visualizing the country. How many different ones would we view? Were the actual Chinese landscapes what we had visualized they would be? Gardens have been an avid interest of ours too. In Suzhou, we had enjoyed walking through formal Chinese ones in their authentic settings. Now, as we visited various cities, would walks through their gardens be allowed? Would we be able to understand their layout or see unusual qualities that we could appreciate? Maybe no garden except those in Suzhou survived the Cultural Revolution.

The most fun would be people watching. To see how the Chinese lived, where they worked, or whether communication with us was possible would be interesting. Hopefully we could be with children too. The Chinese are a very family oriented society. We share with them the importance of family structure in one's life.

Certainly a camera was a vital necessity to record whatever we saw.

Even in 1993, China was very new to tourism. Citizens from the United States who traveled to the Mainland were usually large groups. Enticing literature showed how simple the sightseeing would be if we chose to join one. If we were truly up for a challenge, we could be part of a group of trekkers, a current fad with younger people. Our friends urged us to cruise on an ocean liner which they particularly enjoyed. What appealed to them was the fact one could sightsee inland by day and sleep aboard each night in a familiar bed. Much as we appreciated everybody's excellent ideas, none of them really intrigued us. Full of other notions and many questions, we contacted Ugo Baldassari, a professional travel agent, formerly with

American Express and currently associated with All Travel in San Francisco. Together we developed an ambitious, interesting itinerary with plans to stay entirely in the Mainland. English-speaking native citizens would meet us at each stop to help us browse through their city and its surrounding areas.

As planned, our journey involved sightseeing in eight cities plus a five-day river boat cruise on the Yangtze River as it wound through the Three Gorges. Because we understood the weather might be quite warm and would grow warmer as summer approached southern China in May, we chose to start there, then travel northward where temperatures should be cooler. Purposely, we wanted to approach the Mainland slowly to ease ourselves into Asian culture. We planned to leave Hong Kong by train to Canton, then by air to Guilin. From Guilin, we would fly to Shanghai. Afterwards, we would take an express train to Nanjing. From Nanjing, we needed to overnight in Wuhan because it would be at the harbor in Wuhan where we would board the ship to cruise up the Yangtze River. Passing through the famous Three Gorges, its final destination would be the port of Chongqing. After taking time to sightsee in Chongqing, we would fly to Xi'an, and go on to Beijing, our final stop. Then, it was back to the United States. Mac estimated the total miles of this trip would be around 3,000, not counting the miles of driving with our guides in and around the cities. This six-week trip would be a long time for Westerners to be in an Asian culture.

Had we allowed enough time to assimilate the many, many new sights, sounds and impressions which lay ahead? Probably not, but we shall be absorbing everything like two thirsty wanderers searching for water.

China Travel Services whose headquarters are in Beijing confirmed our carefully planned itinerary months ahead of the May departure date. This was a must. As a condition for visiting the Mainland, all itineraries must be reviewed by those authorities. Everyone's travel plans needed to be made far in advance, as sometimes confirming took months. Thankfully Ugo had no trouble getting ours through this bureaucracy.

It also was the official job of the Chinese travel industry to aid tourists visiting the country. In China, group travel was customary and expected. Suddenly two individuals, a man and a woman, called "Whiting" planned to sightsee all over the country but not as part of a tour. Why were they coming without an organized group, like most tourists? Were they not business oriented, or perhaps, members of the diplomatic corps? Curious barbarians these Whitings. Difficult to understand their motives, but like all the other tourists, they too will be tolerated. In 1993, China was fully open for all visitors to move quite freely about the country. The only exception, of course, was in viewing military sites.

Just as our itinerary was confirmed, a serious business problem occurred. Its solution demanded our immediate participation. The time we needed to fix this upset the scheduling of the trip. Ugo, Mac and I studied the itinerary carefully. If we stayed a briefer time in Hong Kong only the departure date needed to be re-booked. That would keep our previously confirmed timetable intact. Since this was such an inauspicious beginning for a major undertaking, we crossed our fingers and undoubtedly Ugo did too.

With a calmness we did not feel, Ugo gamely searched flight schedules on his computer and found a single flight to re-book us on to Hong Kong. These seats on United Airlines were the only remaining pair available on any airline leaving from San Francisco to Hong Kong on our particular departure date. They allowed us to sit together in the first class section. Were we ever lucky! Knowing we were non-smokers, Ugo warned us 4E and 4F were in the smoking section, the only row in first class where it was allowed on this flight. He suggested if the person seated across the aisle indulged, possibly one of the stewardesses could switch our seats with someone up front in the non-smoking section. We told Ugo not to worry, and thanked him profusely for his excellent service. Elated to be confirmed on any flight, why should we worry about trivialities?

Thus, in May 1993, two very excited individuals began a challenging six-week trip into Mainland China. We crossed our fingers that the itinerary would proceed as planned. At the trip's conclusion, undoubtedly we would feel like Old China Hands but that would remain to be seen. Generally Old China Hands are those individuals who have lived on the Mainland for years and, having done so, quite rightfully earn the recognition.

With all plans in place and with very high expectations, we began a stroll through a wonderfully mysterious land.

Discovering China
MONGOLIA
GOBI DESERT
INNER MONGOLIA
KOREA
Seoul
YELLOW SEA
EAST CHINA SEA
TAIWAN
Taipei
Harbin
Shenyang
Anshan
Manchurian Plain
BEIJING
GREAT WALL
Hothot
Jinan
Zhongzhou
NANJING
SHANGHAI
WUHAN
DAM
Yangtze River
XI'AN
CHONGQING
Yinchuan
Lanzhou
Chengdu
Sichuan Basin
Guiyang
GUILIN
GUANGZHOU
HONG KONG
Fouzhou
Nanning
Kunming
VIETNAM
LAOS
BURMA
INDIA
BANGLADESH
BHUTAN
NEPAL
HIMALAYAS
Mt. Everest
Lhasa
TIBET
TANGGULA SHAN
HOH XIL SHAN
KUNLUN SHAN
ALTUN SHAN
Qaidam Basin
QUILIAN SHAN
Yellow River
Jiayuguan
DUNHUANG
TURPAN
ÜRÜMQI
BOGDA SHAN
Dzungarian Basin
TIAN SHAN
XINJIANG (AUTONOMOUS REGION)
TAKLIMAKAN DESERT
KASHI
KYRGYZSTAN
Whiting route through China
Whiting route on Silk Road
N

chapter 3

Approaching the Mainland

Our seats on the train to Canton, presently known as Guangzhou, were the first two front ones on the left side. Mac stowed the carry-ons in the overhead rack. I placed one of his briefcases against the side of the car with my purple leather tote on top. Mac rested his other briefcase in the aisle alongside his seat. This was not a bad arrangement for maximizing leg room. The train pulled out of the station promptly at 8:30. As it slowly gathered speed, we felt excited. We were on our way! The schedule said we would be arriving in Guangzhou a little before noon.

I sat back and let my mind wander. The occurrence with the American Express girl who was our escort to the train station in Hong Kong was a puzzling bit of unpleasantness. Clearly she was confused how to accomplish this job so she was edgy and unfriendly. Maybe we were her first clients. Who knows? The problem was she did not know exactly what to do. Her superiors at the American Express office insisted we must be in the lobby promptly at 7:30. So, although more than groggy from jet lag, there we were—breakfasted, checked out of our rooms, hotel bill paid and luggage stacked by the front door, but no one from American Express greeted us. In fact, there were very few people around at that hour. Finally we observed a young Chinese woman frantically dashing through this huge lobby. We suspected she was our contact and hoped she would join us. Within a few minutes she approached Mac. "Are you Whitings?" she asked. Affirming we were, she introduced herself as the American Express representative and said she would go find "my driver. Okay?" The "finding" took so many minutes that we wondered if we would miss our train. When she did reappear, she announced she could not find her driver, but had called for another. At this moment, an assistant hotel manager came up and inquired if he might be of service. Before we could answer, the young woman interrupted to ask him if we could meet her car at the back door of the hotel. This was an easier location for her driver to park, she explained. Haughtily, the young assistant manager drew up all five feet six inches of his body, looked down his nose and informed her in no uncertain terms that hotel guests always departed from the front of the hotel. Only from the front door. We turned aside so they could not see our amusement at this exchange. Within a few minutes, a small old model, well-worn and dusty Mercedes appeared at the entrance. It hardly measured up to one of the Peninsula's fleet of Rolls Royce limousines. The assistant manager hastened his bellboys to place our luggage in its trunk. Then he personally escorted us to the car and promptly bid us a good journey. Obviously he wanted this car out of sight as soon as possible. It was not up to the Peninsula's livery service standards.

The ride to Kowloon Railroad Station took ten minutes. Needless to say there was no conversation between either driver, agency girl or the two backseat passengers.

Passengers tried to get to the railroad station early to avoid standing in a long line while passing through Customs Control. Since we were now later than planned, we stood in a long line, and it was moving at a snail's pace. "Was this how touring in China will be?" we wondered aloud. We fervently hoped not. Having fulfilled her assignment to bring us here, the American Express girl bid us a curt farewell and left. We were on our own en route to Mainland China, excited, but somewhat apprehensive, not knowing exactly what lay ahead.

We read that in 1978 when China first welcomed tourists, but not American ones, a total of 10,000 came. Ten years later, in 1988, four million arrived, including some Americans. To accommodate this mass of visitors, China had to build about 1,500 hotels and train a million or so people to run them. The biggest tourist group was from Japan, followed by those from the United States, then Europeans, and lastly southeastern Asians. In 1989, when the tanks moved in on Tiananmen Square, the Chinese tourist industry came to a crashing halt. Undoubtedly when Premier Deng died, visitors might again hesitate, but currently there was a healthy tourist business. This was an ideal time to be visiting the Mainland.

We stood in another line to be checked through Passport Control. We watched a cluster of elderly Chinese women. There were about a dozen of them. Truly tiny in stature, each one was just about four feet tall by our estimation. All had grey hair tightly pulled back from their faces and pinned securely in buns at the nape of their necks. Their skin was light, almost parchment white in color with no yellow cast. Obviously they were all old friends on a special outing. They laughed and chatted loudly back and forth in the joy of being together. They were having a wonderful time. They did not complain about standing in line. Each passenger was passed individually through Passport Control. Then a railroad employee pointed the direction for boarding the train. This involved riding down a steep, extremely fast-moving escalator. At the bottom, a train attendant who was a smiling older woman looked at our tickets and pointed to the car where our seats were located. It was directly in front of us. The efficiency of all the railroad personnel was impressive. As we walked onto the train, we noted it was very clean.

Watching out the window as the train gathered speed, I began to think: What did we really know about this country called China? We had browsed through what travel books we could find, hoping they were up-to-date. Mostly these talked about what a huge country China was. Geographically, they pointed out, it was the third largest in the world with over a fifth of the world's population living there. They omitted any political discussion about the entire country being controlled by a restrictive government residing in Beijing. We learned that the number of cities with populations as great as those of London, New York or Tokyo was astonishing. Most had names unfamiliar to us. Occasionally we were able to find a few novels by a Chinese author who lived outside China. We were shocked to find our bookstores as well as our libraries lacked any up-to-date information on China. We found many more books and up-to-date data in London than we did in either New York or San Francisco. This was startling. What little information our newspapers printed was sent to them by the Xinhua News Agency in Beijing, the official news organ of the Chinese government, and it was usually found in the back pages. No wonder most Americans were ill-informed. Luckily, while traveling I began to read and later subscribed to *The International Herald Tribune*, which carried many interesting Chinese articles, but generally in 1993, other than that newspaper, there was very little data to be found elsewhere. I was constantly on the lookout.

One day, in an issue of *Vogue* magazine, a review of a book called "Wild Swans" caught my eye. Its content so intrigued me that I wanted a copy of the book to read. None were available in the United States. None of our bookstores knew of its existence. Later we happened to be at London's Heathrow Airport, and there at one of the bookstalls was a paperback copy which I hastily bought.

A Book Called "Wild Swans"

"Wild Swans—Three Daughters of China" was written by a young Chinese woman named Jung Chang. Jung sentimentally talks about three women. They were her grandmother, her mother and herself. It was the story of how each grew up facing completely different lifestyles as China's government changed its philosophies during their three generations. From her grandmother's life as a concubine during the Ch'ing Dynasty, to Communism in her mother's time, and on to capitalism in her own era, the book pictured the differences in lifestyles that happened to her family. A particularly poignant episode told of her mother's experience trying desperately to become a Communist Party member, and of her father, who was an established member of the Communist Party, vividly describing how Communism affected Jung and her family. This incident occurred around the middle of Mao's Cultural Revolution and was told to Jung by her mother:

"One day they had to walk over 30 miles in the heavy rains. The temperature was well over 90° and my mother was soaked to the skin with rain and sweat. They had to climb a mountain, only about 3,000 feet high but my mother was completely exhausted. She felt her bedroll weighing her down like a stone. Her eyes were clogged with sweat pouring from her forehead. When she opened her mouth to gasp for air, she felt she could not get enough in her lungs.

"After they had crossed the mountain, there were several deep, fast-moving rivers in their path. The water level rose to her waist and she found it almost impossible to keep her footing. In the middle of one river, she stumbled and felt she was about to be swept away when a man caught hold of her. She almost broke down and wept, particularly since at this very moment she spotted a friend of hers whose husband was carrying her across the river.

"My father was not carrying my mother. He was being driven along in a jeep with his bodyguard. His rank entitled him to transportation, either a jeep or horse, whatever was available. My mother had often hoped that he would give her a lift or at least carry her bedroll in his jeep, but he never offered. After she almost drowned in the river, she had it out with him. Could he not let her travel in his jeep occasionally? He said he could not because it would be taken as favoritism since my mother was not entitled to the car. He felt he had to fight against the age-old Chinese tradition of nepotism. 'It's for your own good,' and he reminded her that her application for full Party membership was pending. 'You have a choice: either you get into the car or you can get into the Party, but not both.'

"He had a point. The revolution was fundamentally a peasant's revolution, and the peasants had an unrelentingly harsh life. They were particularly sensitive about other people enjoying or seeking comfort. Anyone who took part in the revolution was suppose to toughen themselves to the point where they became inured to hardship.

"My mother understood the theory, but that did not stop her thinking about the fact my father was giving her no sympathy while she was sick and exhausted the whole time, trudging along, carrying her bedroll, sweating, vomiting, her legs like lead.

After 40 days of marching they reached the city of Nanjing. One day my mother and her unit had to run several miles on the double, fully laden, to the tomb of the founding father of the republic, Sun Yat-sen. When they returned, my mother felt an ache in her lower abdomen.

"That evening she walked five miles with her comrades in file to a performance of the Peking Opera, which she was eagerly looking forward. My father went in his car. On the way, my mother felt more pain in her abdomen and contemplated turning back, but decided against it. Halfway through the performance the pain became unbearable. She went over to where my father was sitting and asked him to take her home in his car. He looked around to where his driver was sitting and saw him glued to his seat, open-mouthed. He turned back to my mother and said, 'How can I interrupt his enjoyment just because my wife wants to leave?' My mother was in agony and turned abruptly away.

"She walked all the way back to the barracks in excruciating pain. When she got back, the barracks was deserted. Everyone except the guards had gone to the opera. She managed to drag herself on her bed and by the light of a lamp saw her trousers were soaked with blood. She fainted as soon as her head hit the bed. She had lost her first child and there was nobody near her."

I had heard the Chinese family structure was purposely undermined by the Communists during the Cultural Revolution. This was the first reading of its consequences I had been able to find. We knew, however, the core of Chinese life had always been the solidness of the family. Therefore nothing could be more devastating for its people and the nation as a whole than to be told and indoctrinated with the belief that the family as a unit would no longer be tolerated. Families Mao could not control. People he could, thus this strategy. Fortunately the importance of the family structure is once again recognized in Deng's China. It was, and always has been, the spark which drives the nation.

Our train passed through Mongko, Shatin, the Chinese University, Tai Po Kau, Tai Po and Sheung Shui, but none of these places could we identify for certain. This journey had interesting views across Tolo Harbor and glimpses of the New Territories rural life. We noted the scenery was both mountainous and tropical and always very green. We saw banana trees, tea trees, rice paddies and many areas of farmland. The crop planted appeared to be grain of some variety. Every inch of ground was utilized for agriculture or construction. We observed huge apartment complexes. There were superhighways being built, as well as roadbeds for new railroads. From time to time in the distance, there was the outline of clusters of tall buildings. We were impressed that so much construction was being undertaken and by how totally modern the cities appeared to be. We had not realized at what speed the Chinese were developing their nation. The train stopped briefly at the border into the Mainland. Although there were men milling around, no official came on board.

In preparation for this trip, we had studied our atlas to pinpoint where we would be traveling. We observed China's borders touched many countries. Looking north, its border was with Russia. Moving west were Kazakhstan, Kirghizia, Tadzhikistan, Afghanistan and Pakistan. At the southern border were Nepal, India, Bhutan, Burma, Laos and Vietnam. On the east were Macao, Hainan Island, Hong Kong and Taiwan. This area covered some four million square miles. As the sun rose over Shanghai, dawn was four hours away in Kashgar 3,000 miles to the west. What a huge land mass China was!

To establish China in a land relationship with the United States and the rest of the world, we studied latitudes on the globe. Stretching from its northern boundary to it southern-most point, China was the same distance as Toronto, Canada to Panama. The city of Shanghai at the mouth of the Yangtze River was the same latitude as New Orleans, Louisiana or the Suez Canal. The city of Guangzhou, our present destination, was the latitude of Havana and Calcutta. We noted the latitude of the capital of the United States and the capital of the Republic of China, Washington, D.C. and Beijing, was similar, an interesting coincidence.

Provinces

China is divided into 22 provinces and five autonomous regions with special status for national minorities. (Those were Inner Mongolia, Ningxia, Xinjiang, Guangxi and Tibet. There also are three directly administered towns, Beijing, Shanghai and Tianjin. They are the country's main industrial areas.) Following is a chart which I found in a library in Scotland naming them all. It showed their surface area in square miles as well as the population of each:

Province	Surface Area In square miles	Population In millions
Anhui	52,800	57.61
Fujian	46,125	30.79
Gansu	171,380	22.85
Guangdong	75,430	64.39
Guizhou	64,600	32.15
Hainan	13,064	6.74
Hebei	72,200	62.2
Heilongjiang	178,220	35.75
Henan	63,460	87.63
Hubei	68,400	55.12
Hunan	79,800	62.09
Jiangsu	38,760	68.44
Jiangxi	63,080	38.65
Jilin	71,060	25.09
Liaoning	55,366	39.96
Ch'inhai	273,600	4.54
Shaanxi	74,100	33.63
Shandong	58,254	85.7
Shanxi	59,280	28.42
Sichuan	215,460	108.97
Yunnan	149,720	37.82
Zhejiang	38,684	42.02
Guangxi	89,680	43.24
Neimenggu	456,000	21.84
Ningxia	25,230	4.8
Xinjiang	627,000	15.55
Xizang (Tibet)	466,640	2.2

Directly Administered Towns
Beijing	6,386	10.94
Shanghai	2,350	13.4
Tianjin	1,625	9.09

Special Administrative Region (1997)
Hong Kong		6.0

The province of Guangdong, the size of our state of Kansas, had a population of 60 million people. The Sichuan province, the source of the Yangtze River, ontained more people than the combined populations of Canada, Australia, New Zealand, Malaysia, Austria, Guatemala, Holland, Portugal and Greece. (The choice of these countries is from the reference in Scotland, not my imagination.) The Xinjiang province with 12 million people was larger than all of Western Europe. Hainan Island was humid and tropical with rice paddies. Northern Heilongjiang had a frigid tundra forest. In January, there are coconut palms growing on the beaches around Sanyain while in Mongolia the temperature is 25° below zero with the Siberian winds coming over the northern steppes. Two thirds of China's territory is hills, mountains and plateaus. The highest mountain peak is Mt. Everest, which the Chinese call Qomolangma. It is just under 28,000 feet, but this mountain is only one of hundreds which are more than 22,000 feet in height. What diversification this nation has!

Rivers

China has two long east-west rivers, the Yellow River (Huang He) in the north and the Yangtze River (Chang Jiang—Long River) in the south. Both were vital factors in contributing to making China Chinese almost from the very beginning of its recorded history. The Yellow River is 3,500 miles in length and runs from the plateaus of the Ch'inhai province carrying yellow soil downstream through the loess lands of the broad North China Plain as it meanders toward the Gulf of Bohai. The Yangtze River is over 4,200 miles long, the third longest river in the world after the Amazon and the Nile. With its headwaters in Tibet, it flows from west to east through eight provinces, dividing China into northern and southern halves. For over 2,000 years, the Yangtze has been China's major transportation route. It forms a broad muddy highway from Shanghai directly into the heart of China. At one time, the Yangtze could be crossed only by ferry boats. Today there are huge, steel bridges at Chongqing, Wuhan and Nanjing. A quarter of the country's agricultural land lies within the vicinity of this river. Ships up to 10,000 tons can easily navigate the 2,100 miles straight up river to Nanjing. The ancient Chinese established canals between these two rivers, facilitating north-south exchanges that led to the early cultural, political and linguistic unification of China. One other significant river is the Pearl, which flows through the south. Its tributary is the Li, which runs through Guilin. The Pearl is just over 1,400 miles in length.

Population

The population of China, counted at over one billion, is officially made up of the Han people plus some 55 other nationalities. The Han comprise 91 percent of the population. Included are the Hakka, Fujianese, Cantonese and a few other groups. They are united by a common history, culture and written language. Writing was perfected in North China. From there it spread and preempted and replaced any other system. It evolved into the writing that is still used in China. Differences in dress, diet, customs and dialects are minor and unimportant. The 55 other nationalities in China live mostly along its borders, like the Mongolians and Uigurs in the north and the Zhuang Yi and Bai in southern China near southeastern Asia. Other groups, such as the Hui and Manchu, are scattered throughout the country.

The Han people differ in many ways. They speak eight different linguistic tongues, and none can necessarily understand each other. With the economic rise of South China, southerners have begun to assert their cultural and political differences. Cantonese rock music, videos, movies and television programs, all heavily influenced by Hong Kong, are now popular throughout China. Comedians used to make fun of the southern ways and accents, but southerners now scorn northerners for their lack of sophistication and business ability. Most of these southern groups regard themselves not as Han, but as Tang people or descendants of the Tang Dynasty (618-907 AD).

Dynasties

Chinese history always refers to the Imperial Dynasties. Here is a simplified chart showing the major ones with their dates and a few concurrent world events:

DYNASTY	YEAR BC	EVENTS HAPPENING IN THE WORLD
HSIA	2100 -1776	
• Copper metallurgy		
	1800	Stonehenge in England built
SHANG	1776 - 1122	
• Built and inhabited towns		
• Possessed a script		
• Cast bronze		
CHOU	1122 - 221	
• Age of philosophy		
• Teachings of Confucius	760	First Olympic games held in Greece
• Development of irrigation and drainage projects		
• Anarchy and wars		
• Used bronze to make weapons		
CH'IN	221 - 206	
• Qin Shihuangdi unites empire		
• "Museum of Terra Cotta Warriors"		

DYNASTY	YEAR	EVENTS HAPPENING IN THE WORLD
	AD	
	1	Jesus Christ is born
WESTERN HAN	24 - 206	

- Silk industry is developed
- "Silk Road" trade route established

EASTERN HAN	25 - 200	

- Establishment of schools
- Development of porcelain
- Invention of paper

	79	Pompeii buried when Mt. Vesuvius erupts

Beginning of 350 years of disunity

	476	Goths depose last Roman emperor
SUI	518 - 618	

- Developed code of laws
- Competitive exams for jobs
- Canal building to link north and south China

TANG	618 - 907	

- Enlarged Sui code of laws
- Capital, Changan, was largest city in the world with two million population
- Golden age of poetry and ideas

	710	Nara is first Japanese national capital
	800	Charlemagne unites all of Europe for his lifetime

FIVE DYNASTIES AND TEN KINGDOMS

- Period of civil wars, discontent and rebellion

	907 - 960	
SUNG	960 - 1289	

- Northern China becomes part of Manchurian Ch'in Dynasty
- Southern China develops separately
- Time of prosperity
- Roads, canals and irrigation systems best in world
- Development of cities

	1095	Crusades begin
	1100	Hindu temple Angkor Wat is built in Cambodia

DYNASTY	YEAR AD	EVENTS HAPPENING IN THE WORLD
YUAN	1289 - 1368	
• Kublai Khan inaugurates this dynasty	1275	Marco Polo travels to China from Venice
	1320	Black Plague epidemic in Europe and China
MING	1368 - 1644	
• Period of restoration and reorganization	1492	Christopher Columbus discovers America
• Capital is moved from Nanjing to Beijing	1517	Reformation of the Christian Church
	1607	First colony in America at Jamestown, Virginia
CH'ING (Ch'in)	1644 - 1911	
• Manchus reign		
• Control Manchuria, Mongolia, Tibet, Influence Nepal, Burma, Korea, Vietnam Military successes lead to political decline		
	1648	Taj Mahal built in India
• Open foreign trade concessions in Canton	1700	Start of Industrial Revolution
	1776	American Revolution and Declaration of Independence
REPUBLIC OF CHINA	1912 - 1949	
• Sun Yat-sen		
• Chiang Kai-shek	1945	Atomic bomb dropped on Hiroshima, Japan
MAO ZEDONG	1949 - 1976	
• People's Republic of China		
	1969	United States launches Apollo II to land on the moon
DENG XIAOPING	1976 - 1993	
• Land reform and family values re-established		
• Opened foreign investment and trade		
JIANG ZEMIN	1993 -	

The Dynasties ended when revolution broke out and the infant emperor Henry P'u-i of the Ch'ing or Qing Dynasty was deposed. (In the United States, we were treated to a movie called "The Last Emperor," Hollywood's interpretation of his life.) After the Ch'ing Dynasty ended, the Republic of China was established under Sun Yat-sen who would be followed by Chiang Kai-shek. In spite of various uprisings, China remained a republic from 1912 to 1949. During the Cultural Revolution from 1949 to 1976, it was under the leadership of Mao Zedong, who, after his death, was succeeded by Deng Xiaoping. Upon Deng's death in February of 1997, Jiang Zemin became his successor.

As we rode along mulling over these various facts, several passengers stood up, gathered their belongings from the overhead racks and headed toward the front of the train. Even though no loud speaker or conductor had announced our arrival, we were approaching Guangzhou. We could see the outskirts of the city. We waited until the train completely stopped at the station before assembling our bags for departing. At the terminal, we were required to show a female uniformed official our health certificates. Two male immigration officials waved us along. They were not interested in seeing any documents. There was no trouble finding where to retrieve checked luggage. Everybody's various suitcases and parcels were now piled unceremoniously on top of an old wooden wagon. With large, tireless steel wheels screeching on the cement platform, the wagon was hand-pulled by a couple of old men. We could hear it coming before we saw it. All passengers might claim their pieces in an area which was roped off. There were no baggage trolleys to use nor were there any porters to help carry luggage. Getting our things into the passenger terminal was going to be an interesting proposition. The American Express helper/guide assigned to meet us, where was he? It certainly would be nice to have his assistance.

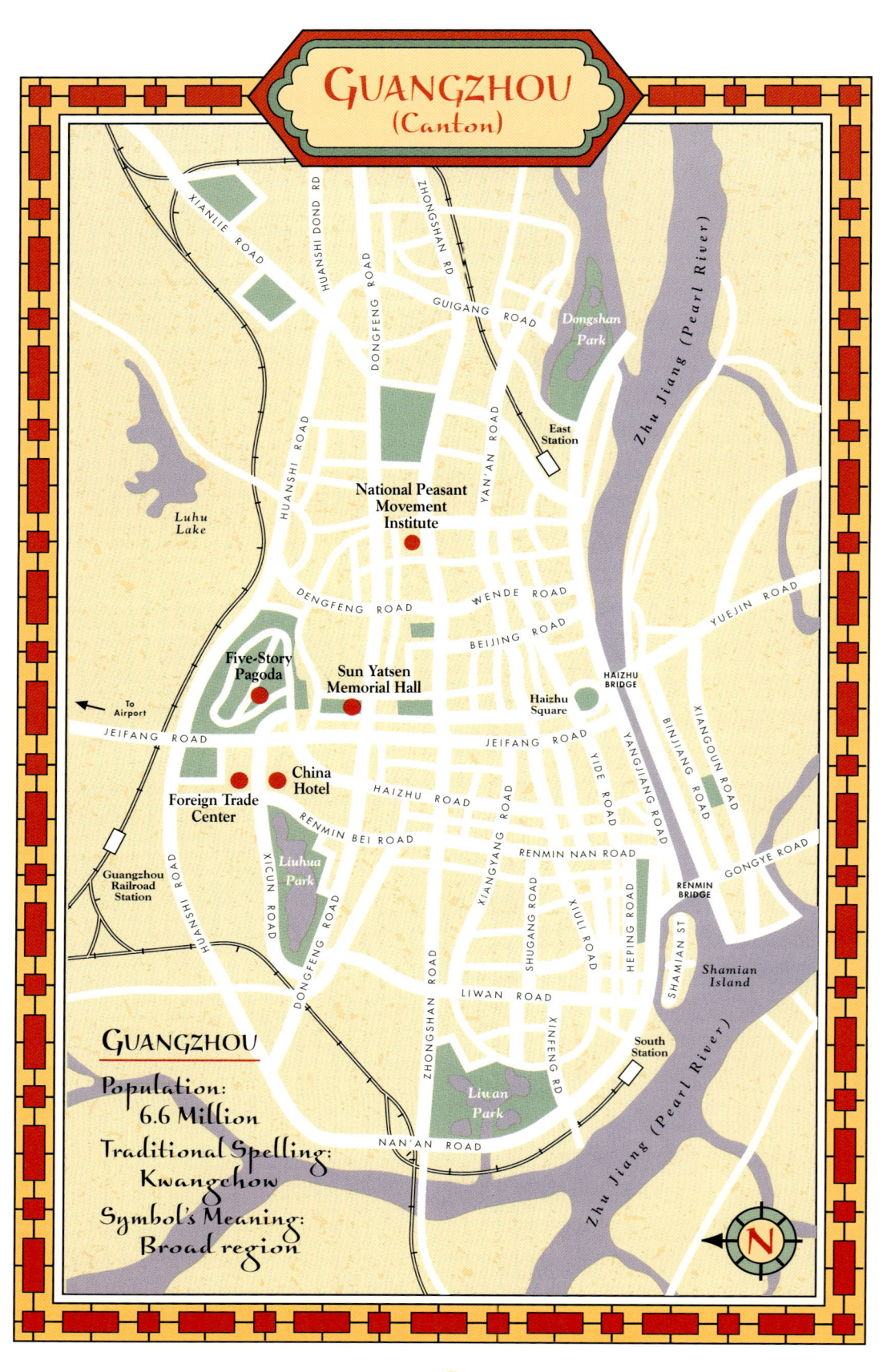

Guangzhou
(Canton)

Guangzhou
Population: 6.6 Million
Traditional Spelling: Kwangchow
Symbol's Meaning: Broad region

40

chapter 4

廣 GUANGZHOU

Through a swinging door into the concrete plaza of the passenger terminal poured a throng of noisy people. The din of their chatter filled the air. Everyone was looking for someone. We saw a person holding a placard printed "MrMrs Whitin." Then we saw Her and realized our guide was a female. She stood in the front row, along with a multitude of others who were watching for friends and relatives coming off the train. She was a tall, slim girl with a face as round and shiny as a full moon and pitch black hair bluntly cut the same length and hanging absolutely straight from the middle of her neck all the way around to her face. Long bangs over her eyes covered her high forehead. We guessed her age was somewhere in the twenties. We waved to her. She dashed around people to meet us. Non-passengers were not allowed to go through the swinging door onto the concrete platform beside the train.

"Hello, Mr. Whitin, you are? I help you luggage." She danced around me and grabbed for the handle of one of the two large suitcases Mac was pulling. He politely brushed her aside with his shoulder. "No, no, I'm fine. Please help Mrs. Whiting." Ignoring me, she continued to reach for a handle. This threw Mac off balance. He was annoyed because he could not progress down the ramp with this interference. Thinking quickly, I said to her, "Please, take these," and shoved into her arms both of the briefcases I was struggling to carry in addition to balancing a tote bag on my shoulder. She had no choice except to take them. "Oh," she squealed, "they so heavy!"

We reached the front of the terminal. She unceremoniously dumped the cases against a fence separating passengers from taxis and other vehicles. "You okay?" she asked, nodding toward me. "Yes, thank you, I'm fine," I answered, "but, please help Mr. Whiting." "Yes, okay," she replied and bounced off, half skipping, half running to meet Mac. He was almost to the bottom of the ramp with our two big suitcases when she caught up with him. She insisted on helping. This time he deliberately let her carry one. She complained loudly how heavy it was, but he paid no attention and brought his over by me. Struggling with the other, she heaved it into the pile with the rest. Irritated by the rough way she was handling our bags, Mac asked her to go and find our car. Mac left me to watch our things while he went back inside the terminal for our smaller luggage. As she skipped off, I pondered what sort of a character China Travel Services had assigned us as our guide. She certainly was a flighty individual.

Luckily the agency provided a small van, a wonderful vehicle for sightseeing. Since it was big and roomy as well as air conditioned, we were not only comfortable, but could easily see out of the windows. This was especially nice for Mac, whose eye level is generally higher than the top of most vehicles' windows, thus blocking his view. When we opened the sliding door to get in, we were shocked to find all our luggage scattered haphazardly inside. Some bags were on the seats while others were on the floor. We rearranged almost every piece to make spaces to sit. By now we were too hot and sticky to complain about the rough handling. Our mood was testy at best. We needed time to cool off and regain our composure. The very talky, ever-smiling guide certainly did not comprehend our sullenness. She was busily talking about the wonders of Guangzhou as we headed toward The China Hotel.

While never formally introduced to each other, we never heard nor asked this guide's name. She apparently forgot to present us her card, and we forgot to ask for it. As we began to know her, we found she was full of exuberance and had a real sense of humor. She loved being teased and would laugh at a joke with great glee, whether she understood it or not.

All Chinese laugh uproariously at things we Westerners sometimes find silly. The sight of someone falling down a flight of stairs could be a funny notion, for example. Sometimes a laugh covered embarrassment too. People smiled a lot. Why they were smiling, no one knew. They smiled and nodded when it was not appropriate to smile and nod. Perhaps inwardly they were, as the Chinese say, "throwing stones" at us. One wonders.

Since the Guangzhou airport was some distance from our hotel, we proceeded slowly through very heavy traffic. This gave us our first look at the city, our first glimpse of the Mainland.

The City They Called Guangzhou

Canton, now called Guangzhou, is the capital of the Guangdong province in the southern part of China. It lies on the Pearl River and has been a major trading port as long ago as the second century. Initially it was the only port where Peking (Beijing) would allow any foreign trader to be received. These early traders were Arabs, Persian and Hindu people, coming here centuries before anyone else. The Portuguese arrived in the 17th century to trade for silk and porcelain. The British followed a century later, then, the Dutch and the French. Now merchants come from around the world twice yearly for the major International Export Fair.

Our first impression of Guangzhou was being overwhelmed by the mass and variety of humanity moving along the highway, plus breathing damp, polluted air under an overcast, grey sky. The traffic was clogged with every sort of vehicle from automobiles, buses, heavy trucks, taxicabs, horse and buggies, bicycles and tractors. Many of those with gas motors spewed smelly black fumes. People were everywhere. There was no privacy anywhere. An endless sea of people walked along the sidewalks and some dodged between vehicles to cross to the other side of the highway. It was slow progress all the way.

Our driver needed to be careful not to run into a person or anything else moving. He was alert for pedestrians, particularly old folk. If an elder suddenly leapt in front of the car and missed being hit by six inches or so, this would be a sign of great good fortune. The driver had cut the string of demons that follows old folks about so that person will have lost his band of bad spirits. Having been cut off from the nimble pedestrian, the bad spirits are now firmly on the driver's tail. Tough luck. Bad joss! Such is the folklore. Fortunately no one hurled himself at our car.

"Have More Babies," said Mao

At the beginning of the Cultural Revolution some 30 years ago, Chairman Mao told the people that the more Chinese babies they had the better it would be for China. He said the imperialists are afraid of the Chinese hordes. People believed what he said, and we now see some of the results. With a population over a billion strong, China has the problem of feeding all of them. Mao never solved this, but left it for his successor, Deng Xiaoping, to resolve.

After a long, slow drive, we made a left turn into a driveway. This began the grounds surrounding the hotel. Rounding a corner we stopped at the entrance. The doorman rushed forward to open the van's sliding door. "Welcome to The China Hotel," he said with a big smile. Seeing our many pieces of luggage, he signaled a bellboy to bring a trolley. With our guide leading the way, we followed her inside.

The lobby was a huge, multi-functional room with marble flooring and flashy art deco wall decorations. Its ceiling was at least two stories high. We headed toward the right side and walked around a piano and two empty chairs residing on a teal blue round of carpet. Soon a female flutist, a male violinist and an elderly male pianist appeared. A large bouquet of fresh flowers in a tall vase was positioned on the rug opposite this grouping. The other side of the lobby was divided into two sections. One side had chairs for those who waited. The other part had chairs with tables for those who waited and wished refreshment.

The piano player was adjusting himself on his bench as we walked up to the reception desk. Mac gave our name to the clerk. We waited. Looking through a stack of papers, the clerk lifted his head and told Mac he had no reservations for us. Mac sighed and reached for his briefcase. In it was our confirmation slip, which he handed to the clerk. Our guide, who was hovering close by, asked if we would like to sit down while she worked with the clerk. The clerk agreed this was a good idea. We re-crossed the lobby, past the piano player, flutist and violinist, all making music which was very loud, to the waiting section with the tables for refreshments. "A drink, perhaps?" our guide asked. "We will just wait, thank you," answered a tight-lipped Mac. "Please check what is happening to our room reservations." As she skipped off, we sat down. Neither of us was happy with this situation. The blaring clatter of piano, flute and violin music compounded the lack of grace in the atmosphere of this huge room.

We noted a desk nearby, manned by a hotel official who was wearing a very formal day suit. He eyed us. Then he stood and came over. "Mr. Whiting? Very sorry. We mixed up your name. We have very nice suite for you. Will you come this way, please?" Signaling to our guide, whom we agreed to meet at nine the next morning, we followed the manager. An elevator whisked us up to the tenth floor. There was a nice, quiet bedroom/living room suite awaiting us. We breathed a sigh of relief and relaxed.

An itinerary had been prearranged by the China Travel Service for our two-day visit in Guangzhou. Looking it over, we decided to minimize their suggestions to fewer attractions. Thus we passed up visiting the Five-Story Pagoda, as we were certain there would be other opportunities to see pagodas during the trip, the Trade Fair Center which was just across the street, and a look at the Pearl River front. Seeing that was tempting because someone told us the color of its waters was as yellow as mustard. We could visualize the sampan homes of those citizens who did not want to live on shore. Some years ago, we saw this kind of colony in an area of the Hong Kong harbor. We did want to explore the neighboring town of Foshan.

To begin sightseeing on our first day, we drove to a group of buildings known as the Ancestral Temple of the Chen Family. To our surprise, it seemed only around a few corners and very near The China Hotel. Built between 1890 and 1894, it was now a Folklore Museum, displaying arts and crafts from Guangzhou. We were not told who the Chen Family was, nor did we ask.

Since this temple initiated our first look at any antiquity in the Mainland, we scrutinized each room minutely. The entire place was a series of four large rooms with an open side facing onto a lovely courtyard. Each room had a display of a different Chinese art, and some rooms had a few antique pieces. The first held ceramics, the next Chinese paintings, a third contained metal works in iron and brass, and the last was full of ivory carvings. It was in this one that we particularly noticed a huge, single ivory ball whose insides contained many more ivory balls, each ball inside the proceeding one.

This piece was intriguing because it was hand carved from one piece of ivory. Reading the literature concerning how it was created we learned the craftsman worked from the inside carving a single ball first, then the next ball inside the first to be followed by one inside the second one. He continued in this way, carving as many balls as the material would allow. No single ball was ever carved outside the piece, then placed inside. It was fun to guess just how many balls there might be altogether. The more balls made the whole piece more valuable. (One might speculate how many of these pieces broke before the carver learned his technique too.) A small piece made like this (from plastic or wood) could be bought in any curio shop. Those in ivory were expensive.

As we slowly ambled through other exhibition rooms, the sky got very dark. A sudden rainstorm poured straight down in a blinding sheet. Luckily we were inside. We looked up and watched a China Airline airplane descending toward the Guangzhou airport. Apparently this temple was on the glide path for today's instrument landings. We counted three separate airplanes making approaches within 12 minutes. This seemed a lot in stormy weather. Mac said three were about the right timing to be expected. How interesting to watch modern technology while we stood inside an old Chinese temple with its beautifully curved roofline which was ornately decorated with colorfully painted wood carvings. They were varieties of mythical animals and birds.

As quickly as it started, the rain let up. We continued our walk through the rest of the exhibits. At the ceramic display, we noted that the pieces in this collection were animals such as chickens, tigers, camels and birds. All were fired with wonderful glazes. Their artists had wonderful senses of humor about their work.

One particularly nice piece was a model of a horse, perhaps four feet tall. Glazed in a greenish brown, he was a sturdy beast with three legs. The two back legs were combined. His neck proudly arched upward holding erect a saucily poised head with great big ears. Half teasing, we told the guide we would like to buy it. "Not for sale!" she exclaimed in a horrified voice. "This is antique for museum, you know." It looked too modern to be an antiquity. Our exuberant guide's pronouncements were exclamations in a very loud voice that everyone around us could hear distinctly. Speaking in a loud voice apparently was a Chinese trait, for neither of us was deaf. We soon learned quietness was not a cultivated quality.

Freedom of Expression

China is a nation of poets. "Unless you study poetry," said Confucius to his son, "you will not be able to converse." Poetry can inspire emotion, help one observe, make a person fit for company and help one express grievances. It is a way of telling someone how much he means to you. To receive a poem from someone is a precious gift. Unjust rulers always try to stamp out any form of communication, especially one that is not easily understood, such as poetry. A poet possesses three essential things that a dictator lacks: The intellect to decipher the symbolism in a poem, the imagination to interpret its meanings, and the inclination to do either. A dictator immediately assumes the poem is a protest against him and his regime and will likely jail the poet whom he suspects is writing subversively.

In China, free speech was denied on and off through the regimes of many different emperors. Early emperors burned books and buried scholars alive. Today, the Communists are still afraid of free speech. During the Cultural Revolution thousands of writers died for uttering a single sentence. Poetry disappeared from the public but not from the private eye, and Chairman Mao suppressed all voices except his own. The best selling book was Mao's "Little Red Book of Quotations" with its bright red cover. Every person was forced to own one and read and memorize its contents. People were warned to always carry it on their person and penalized if found without it. The popular songs at that time included "Socialism is Good" and "Night Soil Collectors Coming Down the Mountain."

On April 4, 1976, a demonstration to mourn the death of Zhou Enlai, the former Premier of China, turned into a poetry movement. People posted their poems all around Tiananmen Square. Many who put up poems were arrested so poems were secreted away in locked places or quickly flushed down toilets when the Red Guards conducted a home search. To speak and write was to risk one's life.

A contemporary Chinese poet called Liu Hongbin started writing poetry when he was a young boy. The school authorities kept a keen eye on what he wrote. In 1983, he was expelled from school for talking to an American professor, charged with disgracing China. In the days leading to the June 1989 crackdown in Beijing, he was one of the writers who posted poems around Tiananmen Square. His first collection of poetry, called "The Dove of the East," was handwritten and secretly circulated in Beijing and his home city, Ch'indao. Somehow one poem called "Sparrow" found its way to Taiwan and was published in the Taiwan China Times. After this happened, Hongbin was questioned. Realizing his life was in danger, he hid and found a way to leave China. He now makes his home in London.

Here is an excerpt from Liu Hongbin's poem titled "Sparrow." It is written without any punctuation:

> I wish I were a sparrow
> in the borderlands' expanse
> freely singing
> with the voice that heaven gave me
> healthy and whole
> with an unaspiring mind
> who then would think of tricking me
> into chains to keep me from so

Our guide could spiel a lengthy dissertation about something, none of which was particularly interesting or understandable, then, turn to us and say, "You understand, yes?" Of course we said "yes" and meant "no." Since what she had just said was usually quite funny, we realized this was her way of being a tour guide. She did attract attention. Wherever we were, she would raise her arm high over her head and yell at us, "Yoo hoo, hello!" No matter how far away we might be, it never occurred to her to approach us quietly. If this drew attention to us, it did not faze her the least bit. Every morning, the moment she stepped inside the large lobby of the hotel (always full of guests at that hour) and spied us sitting in the waiting section on the other side of the lobby, she would raise her arm high up above her head and yell, "Hello, yoo hoo!" Privately we named her "Yu Hu" (pronounced Yoo Hoo) which seemed appropriate.

"Okay, let's go!" says Yu Hu. She sensed we were becoming tired and perhaps a bit bored with this ancestral temple.

The rain had stopped completely, the sun was out, and tourists were arriving en masse. We heard German, Italian and French, but no English, being spoken. We noted we were the only ones with our own guide and van. The rest came in big tour buses.

The next stop was at the blue-tile roofed Sun Yat-sen Memorial Hall, named for the founder of the first Chinese Republic (1912-1949). Although this building looked small from the outside, it had a huge auditorium with a seating capacity designed for comfortably accommodating an audience of 4,000 people. Inside, there were no architectural beams apparent for supporting the ceiling over the entire hall. All the seats were situated around the stage down front. The acoustics were fantastically clear. The entire room was octagonal in shape with side alcoves, each large enough to seat several hundred people. We sat down to look around. The seats were small in size. They were definitely more comfortable for me and the Chinese than they were for Mac.

The interior colors were a soft celadon green with accents of rust. The rust was not a Chinese vermillion red shade, but a rust like the color of weathered iron and a direct contrast to the celadon. Side by side they were most attractive. Mac was particularly attracted to the formation of this entire structure. It caught his engineer's sense of proportion, suggesting how a building could be designed for beauty as well as for utility.

Walking outside, we enjoyed seeing a series of lovely flower beds with cannas in full bloom. Some were a brilliant, deep red. Others were yellow with spots of red scattered through their petals. They all made quite a splash of color on this grey, rainy day. Needless to say, there also was a statue of Sun Yat-sen. How else to keep the memory of his likeness alive. We were told he was born about 62 miles from Guangzhou in the small village of Cuiheng.

We were finding the weather in Guangzhou offensive. Rain was imminent all the time, and the air was steamy and heavily polluted. By noon, we were ready to stop sightseeing because our eyes were stinging. It was very difficult to breathe in the heavy, damp air so we asked to go back to the hotel.

Yu Hu said her agency made a reservation for our lunch at one of the most attractive restaurants in the city. We thanked her and said we preferred to eat at the hotel. She was visibly shocked. How could we possibly want to eat at the hotel when we could have a special meal at this restaurant? And her agency had already paid for it. We suggested she and the driver take advantage of this meal instead of us. She was appalled with this suggestion. "Please," we urged, "enjoy the meal." She thanked us so much. As we approached the entrance of our hotel, we said we would look forward to seeing her the next morning. Nine o'clock would be a good hour. Yu Hu misunderstood our meaning. "We sightsee after lunch, yes, afternoon?" she inquired as we got out of the car. "No, not today," we answered. "Oh!" She was very disappointed with this decision. We thanked her profusely for an interesting morning and again told her to enjoy the lunch. Deliberately, we were being very cautious about eating at a restaurant away from the hotel. Other things were more important to us than sampling the native foods, delicious as they undoubtedly were, and perhaps flirting with upset tummies. We had no time for that.

On the mezzanine of the China Hotel were two coffee shops that were cafeteria-type places, each offering ethnic meals. Another more formal dining room had a long table with a huge buffet. Beside this, in a less crowded space, were tables where one could sit and order a sandwich. This was our preference. We chose a spot where we could rest and enjoy looking around. Suddenly a group of young trekkers wearing heavy hiking boots and carrying bulging knapsacks ambled in. Choosing tables against one side of the room, they dumped their knapsacks on the floor. Some of the young men collapsed in the cushioned chairs while others, mostly the girls, found the buffet table and inspected what was being offered. Cigarettes were lit, and drinks were ordered. Everyone in the group looked weary and unkempt.

Near us were businessmen. We could tell they were salesmen as they were neatly dressed in dark suits with ties and white shirts. Since the Trade Fair Building was directly across the street from the hotel, this was undoubtedly a noon break for them. No one could miss seeing the Trade Fair Building. Flying over its roof were a whole series of enormous colored balloons. They floated back and forth and up and down in the breezes. How I would love to take one of those balloons home.

That evening we went up to the restaurant on the roof for dinner. This was a Western-style, formal dining room. The tables were set with pristine white linen cloths. A bouquet of fresh flowers, glowing candles, cut-glass goblets, elaborate bone china and silverware decorated our table. While we chose our meal, we were entertained by a quartet composed of a piano, two violins and a cello. Observing us as we entered, they swung into "American" music. We heard songs like "Swanee River," "Old Black Joe" and "Downtown Strutters' Ball!" We had not heard any of these classics since we were children. We could not believe Stephen Foster's songs were what these musicians thought was the current American taste in popular music. Perhaps they were subtly tweaking us about civil rights? They might be even more shocked to be told this music was politically incorrect in the United States. Except for the choice of the music, the dinner was delicious, and the atmosphere was very nice.

On our final sightseeing day in Guangzhou, we drove about 12 miles from Guangzhou to a city called Foshan. Foshan literally means "Buddha Mountain" because in the 1600s three bronze Buddha statues were discovered there. Foshan then became an important Buddhist site. During the Sung Dynasty (960-1289) it was known for its porcelain industry. A particular ceramics factory had a kiln that had been in continuous use for over 900 years. We stopped there first specifically to see it.

Since this was a Sunday, there were very few workers. In this government-owned factory, we were permitted to walk through most of its floors. Each floor was a setup for the production of a different part of the ceramic piece that was currently being manufactured by the entire factory. This product was a small figurine of a man (a Buddha?) adorned with a lotus blossom. It was a type of piece often on sale for tourists at curio shops. Today two women, each working at a separate station along a long table, were hand gluing a lotus blossom onto the figure. Once completed, each figurine was placed in a cardboard box. The next procedure would be to glaze the pieces. That work was done on another floor. The whole process seemed like mass production at a snail's pace. The ceramics certainly were not of the quality produced during the Sung Dynasty (960-1289) when this factory formally started, but the production of ceramics in Foshan today was still a major industry.

We were never shown the 900-year old kiln. Maybe during another visit.

The district of Foshan was much more interesting than the ceramics factory. We dismissed the car and proceeded on foot along the sidewalks. Mingling with the people was much fun, and one could see all sorts of interesting sights. With so many people, living space everywhere in China was very limited so the street became a kitchen or a sitting room or, in hot weather, a

bedroom. We passed by a barber shaving a man's whiskers, saw someone pumping up a bicycle tire, watched old men playing cards, and were invited to sit at a table with chairs set up for a noodle meal being made on the spot. People were gossiping and appearing not to notice us pass by, but we suspected every detail of our attire was discussed. Our ambling led us into the Temple of Ancestors dating back to the 11th century. This was in a park where today there were many families strolling with small children. In the temple, Mac joined a group who were throwing coins at a Buddha sitting in a sandy garden below. He threw some too—for good luck. At another place, there was Buddha in an elaborate frame. One could tuck paper bills around the frame for more good luck. Nearby, incense burned in a huge raised bronze urn. This urn's diameter was wide enough to hold dozens of sticks. In this atmosphere, the smoking incense smelled good. There was constant action around the temple, with people engaged in placing money, lighting incense sticks, or simply looking. Children ran freely. Everyone seemed in

a festive mood. Outside the temple were asphalt paths winding throughout the garden. What fun it was to watch toddlers pushing their plastic toys, and the parents laughing at their antics. Chinese children are adorable with their round faces and shiny, black eyes.

Once outside the park, we strolled along the sidewalk, passing merchants who were selling umbrellas, which looked nice, and bric-a-brac, which looked cheap. There was an interesting shop full of pâpier maché dragons. We walked in and craned our necks back to see huge dragons hanging from the ceiling. Painted in brilliant colors of red, purple and yellow, they were fascinating structures of paper. What wonderful fierce expressions on their faces! We walked around to observe them on all sides. Foshan people were known for their skill in the craft of folding and cutting designed patterns from papers. Chinese lanterns made from various materials were produced here too. We wandered in and out of another store that sold bright ceramic dishes we called "Fiesta ware" for using in one's home.

Foshan had a lane on either side of the main street which was used exclusively for bicycles. Today it was full of cyclists. All motorized traffic was excluded from these lanes by concrete barricades. Every city we visited had these traffic barriers, but this was the first time we observed what good safety devices they were. There were many more bicycles than automobiles in every city. It was much easier for a person to ride a bicycle because it could move steadily along through traffic, as compared with the stop and go of maneuvering a car through multitudes of vehicles and people who walked. Bicycles avoided creating traffic jams too. Each rider kept a steady pace of speed. It was neither fast nor slow. Cyclists never dashed around each other like the kamikaze bikers who wheel in and out of New York city traffic, for example. Here no one wore a safety helmet or affected any special cycling apparel. I noted women with full skirts lift up a small edge of the hem onto the handlebar with their left hand. This seemed to keep the skirt from becoming entangled in the spokes of the bicycle's back wheel. It was a very feminine gesture. As both men and women rode their bicycles through the dust and fumes from buses, trucks and taxis, they managed to look neat and fashionable in their office suits and/or dresses. The bicycle was the family's and businessman's principal method of transportation.

Walking through Foshan was fun for us but apparently we wore Yu Hu out. On our return trip to Guangzhou, she put her head down on the seat and fell sound asleep. We did not know this until we asked her a question. Not receiving an answer, we realized she was napping.

A typhoon named "Helen" occurred in the southern part of the Guangdong province while we slept last night. Undoubtedly this was the cause of much of the oppressive weather. No wonder the air had felt so uncomfortably heavy to us.

We missed a sense of history in Guangzhou. Its important twice-a-year exhibitions in the Trade Center drew salesmen, but was not structured for tourists. This city reminded us great deal of Los Angeles, California.

We deliberately bypassed going to Shenzhan. This sprawling city in the southern part of the province was modernized by the Chinese as a showcase of their economic development. Deng Xiaoping went to see it and was especially proud of its appearance.

Supermarkets American-Style

Wal Mart opened its first Chinese store in Guangzhou, and Sams, an American "warehouse" type of store was opening in the outskirts of Shenzhan. This type store was followed by Pricemart in Beijing. Among the various American products offered at Wal Mart are Campbell soups, Bounty paper towels, and Gillette shaving cream, which the Chinese found expensive. Wal Mart also had shelves of dried fish and preserved plums plus various flavors of watermelon seeds. There were racks with soybean milk and congee, a southern Chinese breakfast dish. Other racks had peanuts, dozens and dozens of packages of instant noodles and packets of preserved bamboo shoots. It was easy to guess which of all these items sold best. Wal Mart once brought in a huge supply of paper towels and disposable diapers. People did not know what to do with paper towels and the diapers were too expensive an item for them. However, electronics of any kind, especially television sets and stereos, sold well.

These stores learned the hard way that what worked in Main Street USA did not necessarily do well here. Pricemart designed loading docks for full-size trucks. Then many of their Chinese vendors brought their merchandise in car trunks or three-wheeled pedicabs or even strapped to the back of a bicycle. New docks had to be adjusted for them. All the stores found American-size packaging and items offered by the case did not sell, as these items would not fit into the tiny apartments in which the Chinese lived. Smaller compact-size items were very popular.

Guangxi—The Old Boy Network

Problems were easy to cope with, but the Americans found the worst job was learning how to cope with Chinese business practices. Rules were often made by how the top man interpreted the law that day. Here personal connections, or what is referred to as "guangxi," could mean more than a good business plan. Guangxi is the "Old Boy" network or a linkage of close friends, old comrades, relatives, or co-workers. As part of such a network, special treatment was given, and all problems were smoothed over. This practice certainly kept everyone on his toes.

On our departure day, Yu Hu insisted we should leave the hotel at 5:30 in the morning to go to the airport. We told her we thought her timing was a bit early, but she was convinced we must go then. We breakfasted, had the hotel bill paid and all our luggage sitting beside us in the lobby when she arrived. Yu Hu could not understand how we did all that without her help. "Please, you eat breakfast now. What? You had! When? Oh, in room. Really?"

We stood in a long line waiting to be checked through Customs Control for our flight to Guilin. It was on China Southern Airways. Yu Hu was fidgeting beside us. Mac suggested it was okay for her to leave, as we knew how to get through the check-in procedure. "No, no, Mr. Whitin. I you wait." Our conversation was sparse at this ungodly hour. The very instant the official stamped our forms, Yu Hu waved and skipped off. We bet she went back to her aunt's home to sleep.

We were to board our flight at 7:30. It was then scheduled to take off at 8:30.

How useless standing around while we clock watched! Our seats, middle and window seats, were in row 22, tourist class on China Southern Airways to Guilin. Such tiny seats! Holding my tote bag, I propped one of Mac's briefcases against the seat's edge and lopped my legs over it. Mac did the same with the other briefcase. While not comfortable, we were glad to be aboard—finally. We believed we paid for first-class tickets on all our flights and needed to check this with the travel agent in Guilin or maybe even fax Ugo in San Francisco. Reading a Chinese air ticket, it was difficult to tell whether one was listed first or tourist class. Soon we learned there were no first-class sections on any Chinese airplanes.

This airplane was a Boeing 757, totally filled with young Chinese businessmen in our section. We watched several tour groups of Westerners walk through to the back of the airplane. The two stewardesses were tall, no-nonsense young women. As they walked through our section, they insisted everybody's luggage must be carefully placed on racks overhead. After take-off, a cardboard box with nameless, unrecognizable goodies was served along with a large Coca Cola. A daily newspaper was offered to all the Chinese passengers, but none to we few Westerners.

Something was nudging the side of my ribs. Looking down to my left I saw a toe in a white sock lying on my arm rest. This seemed a little too familiar, I thought, so I coughed gently and the foot was withdrawn. In such tight quarters, one could understand why a leg needed to be stretched. Both of mine did too, but I kept them firmly planted on the floor. Happily, the flight was only 45 minutes long. Flying away from the rain clouds of Guangzhou, I told Mac there was beautiful blue sky ahead. How welcoming that was. The mere fact the sun was shining brightly cheered us immensely.

Interesting reading were articles about the development of entrepreneurial businesses starting in China. Here are a couple stories, both of which I have condensed. They happened around the countryside of Guangzhou. The first written is about an ostrich farm and was printed in Hong Kong's South China Morning Post:

The Ostrich Business

A young couple by the names of Fang Xiaowen and her husband Lin Zhuohui had jobs in Guangzhou. He was a materials' procurator for a sewing machine factory, and she worked in a bicycle factory. When they married, Lin, using money borrowed from relatives to pay for the event as well as for their home, realized there was enough money left over to start his own farming business. Fang decided to help him. They first tried raising pigeons. That business flourished, but they decided the competition would intensify with too many others entering the field so they sold theirs for a profit. They then raised peacocks which also was successful but did not grow as quickly as they wished. One day during a visit to the Guangzhou zoo, Fang spotted some ostriches. From one of the workers, she learned the Beijing Zoo had a surplus of these birds and might be willing to sell some to her. She spent three days in Beijing trying to persuade the zoo officials to sell her birds. She received a negative response when they found out she was a private business person, telling her in no uncertain terms they would not deal with any private business people. On the fourth day, totally discouraged, Fang told her frustrations to an elderly man from the exchange office. He assured her it was against the rules for a zoo to sell its animals to private business people. She challenged him with a quote from Mao Zedong saying "Squandering is as bad as corruption," and the old man told her to wait one more day.

The next day, the zoo sold her 16 ostriches. Soon every zoo in China had heard Fang's story and wanted to sell her their ostriches. The couple found out raising ostriches was not quite the same as raising pigeons. Newly hatched ostriches developed all sorts of illnesses and died. Nobody really knew how to advise them, as there were no other ostrich farm in China. Through experimentation Lin discovered how to mix proper fodder for them.

Contrary to expert opinion, instead of keeping the babies in incubators, Lin sent them out into the sunshine to exercise, thereby developing strong legs. The combination of proper feed and building strong birds worked.

Lin and his wife Fang now have offices in Guangzhou and Hong Kong. They operate two ostrich farms in and around Guangzhou with about 10,000 ostriches. They are projecting a growth to 80,000 birds by 1997. They think ostriches will be a new source of meat, as it is low in fat and cholesterol. Ostrich leather is in demand for many articles like belts, shoes and purses. Such is their success.

The second story concerns a successful entrepreneurial family and was published in *The International Herald Tribune*:

The Pig-Feed Enterprise

The four Liu brothers quit their jobs and sold their bicycles and watches to scrape together $120. With this they established a pig-feed enterprise. In a nation of pork eaters, this is a good business. The brothers' company is called Hope Group Ltd. which now has 10,000 employees and 34 feed mills in 20 Chinese provinces.

The Liu brothers were technical workers in state-owned enterprises. One specialized in electronics, another in mathematics, a third in mechanical engineering and the last in computers. Each earned salaries equivalent to $4.50 per month. So by "jumping into the sea," as the Chinese say, they figured they would not be losing much.

First they tried a joint venture with a state-owned company to make television tubes from oscilloscopes. When this failed, they went to Xinjin County in the Sichuan province where they had been sent as boys during the Cultural Revolution to "learn about peasant life." What they learned was how backward it was. They observed the Chinese farmer used the same pattern of farming he had for almost a thousand years. It took a whole year to fatten a pig for market, for instance. So the brothers returned to the village with some new techniques to improve the work.

They started by building a chicken coop which they would use for an incubator. Friends gave them some used bricks and lent them a truck and even helped by carrying the bricks across the rice fields to start. Using their money to buy fertile eggs, they constructed a makeshift incubator out of an old gas tank. They produced steam by burning coal underneath it. Because they had no place else, they slept in the coop. When the eggs hatched, they sold the chickens, making more than they together had earned in a year. They next raised quails. This business they also sold at a profit. (The village is now a major quail-raising center.) As the Chinese economy was growing richer under the policies of Deng Xiaoping, people were eating more pork. Noting this, the brothers put their earnings into the pig-feed business. This time ten percent of their earnings was used to build a research institute, 30 percent for machinery, 40 percent in building a mixing plant and ten percent in advertising and locating talent from other pig-feed companies to work for them. Two to three pounds of their pig-feed, a mixture of corn, soybeans, fish products, amino acids, vitamins and minerals, fattens pigs faster in four months than twice as much grain did in an entire year. A symbol of the brothers' success is this: One has become a member of the Chinese People's Political Consultative Congress, an organization of various vocations who advise the government at annual meetings in Beijing.

With Success Came Problems

Along with successes, problems could arise too. Some of the lowlands around Guangzhou have become magnets for labor-intensive factories. Migrants from other parts of China come there to work and seek their fortunes. In the midst of this fast growth, there are those who take short cuts, and some schemes take violent turns. A Hong Kong owner of a leather factory was kidnapped. When one of his employees brought the ransom money, both were killed by the gang. A golfing group was snatched in mid-game and whisked away in a helicopter to a remote villa. A Hong Kong electronics company chairman disappeared. These are real incidents that have happened just across the border from Hong Kong. Since the danger level of doing business in Guangdong's factory towns has increased, there is now a demand for body guards. Much of the difficulty happens because of the Chinese legal system. There is no real system for resolving commercial disputes. It is a part of the Chinese mentality to try to settle disputes between the parties.

Corruption grows in all parts of China. Citizens complain about specifics such as paying bribes to get an appointment with a doctor and watching from their bicycles while the military and party members drive around in luxury cars. Officials dine out at expensive restaurants with the taxpayers footing the bill for delicacies and cognac is another complaint. After the Chinese were so restricted under the Communists, perhaps these first abuses of freedom in various directions should be expected.

"A revolution is not a dinner party," said Mao Zedong.

Neither is stability created easily, say I.

Guilin

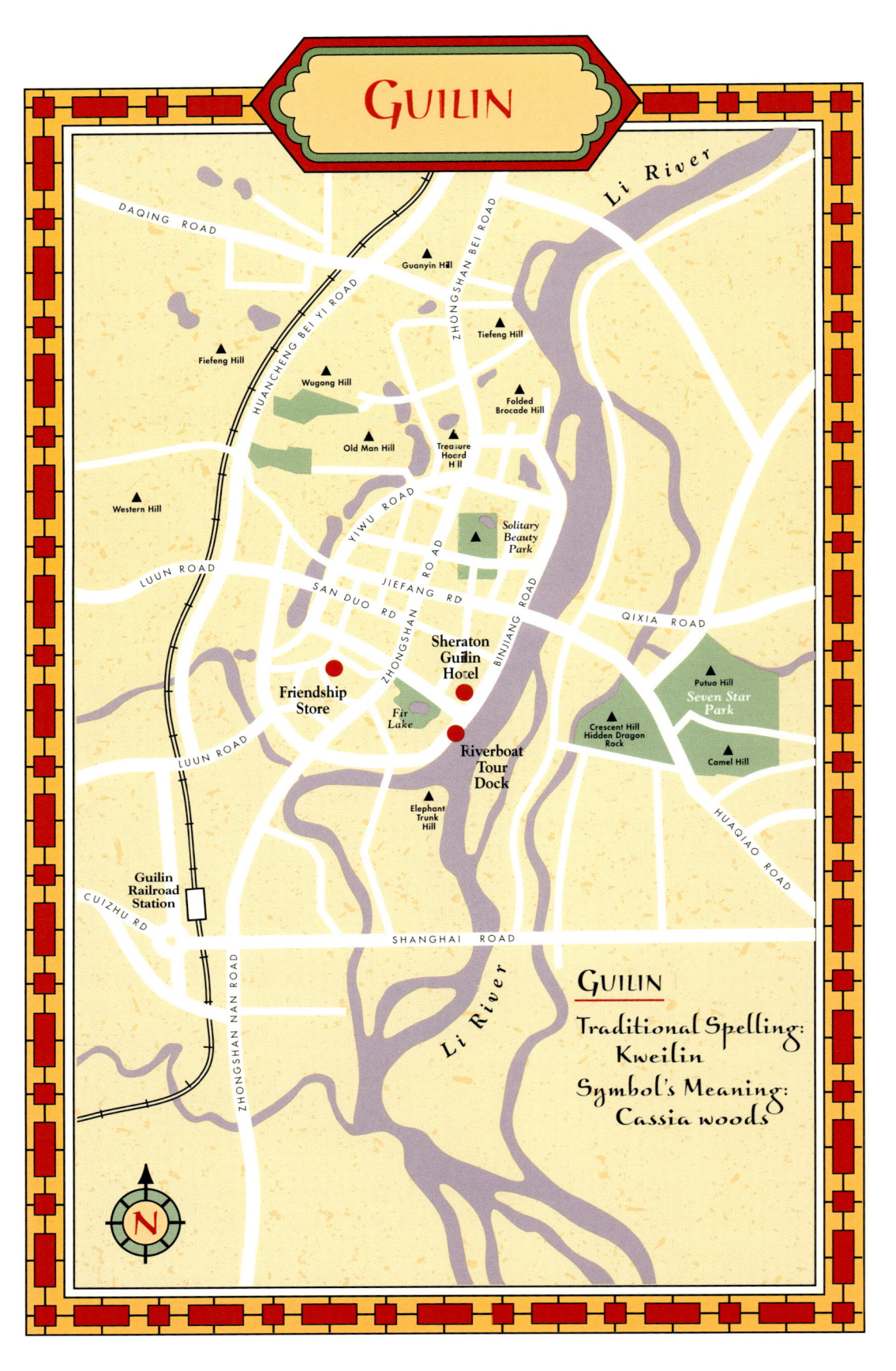

Guilin

Traditional Spelling: Kweilin

Symbol's Meaning: Cassia woods

chapter 5

桂 GUILIN

At Guilin's airport, we walked a short distance from our airplane directly into the baggage terminal. We passengers were like a group of friendly neighbors returning home. Gathering around in small groups, we waited for our bags. For two yuan, we could rent a trolley. That delighted us. Not even the much larger Guangzhou terminal had such a convenience.

With no formalities from any official, we entered the terminal where our guide and his driver warmly greeted us and pushed the luggage to the car. All bags fit into the trunk, although a bit snugly. We were en route to the newly built Sheraton Guilin Hotel where we would reside for two nights. The city of Guilin and its surroundings were renowned for rural charm and scenic beauty. We drove through a countryside entirely devoted to farming. There were fewer automobiles and large building complexes here than in Guangzhou. Everybody rode bicycles. In the early morning sunlight, with everything so fresh and sparkling clean, we savored what we saw. How good to breathe clean, fresh air.

A Capsule of Guilin's Past

Guilin, along the west bank of the Lijiang River (more familiarly called the Li River), is in the Guangxi Zhuang Autonomous Region of southern China. It is a small city, compared with Guangzhou, having a population of only 350,000. Its prominence came about because the Qin Emperor Shihuangdi who reigned from 221 to 210 BC (Ch'in Dynasty 221-206) dug the Lingqu Canal linking the Lijiang and Xiangjiang rivers. This was the main traffic route between south and central China. Guilin was an important center on the canal. It gained further historical importance as the refuge where various governments took up residence when fleeing successor administrations. Principally these were the Mings fleeing from the Manchurians in the mid-17th century. Much later, many people came here during the Sino-Japanese War.

Our guide was a tall, 37-year old man by the Western name of Steve. He did not tell us his Chinese names. Asked why he chose this particular name, he shrugged and said he did not know. We were curious about everything we saw and started asking Steve questions. "Those beautiful tiles on the facade of that building, where were they made?" He replied, "Oh, yes, the farmers are very rich." Puzzled because this was hardly an answer, we tried forming the question in a different way, but he was conversing with the driver and paid no attention to us. We soon learned Steve's answers bore not the faintest relation to what we asked. We noted that as he walked along with us, he quietly hummed a tune. Singing was his way of covering up a lack of comprehending English. (Later in the trip, another guide would do the same thing when puzzled by our questions.) Evidently guides were taught a certain spiel. Outside this set pattern, only a few could carry on additional conversation. It was unthinkable for a tour guide to admit he or she did not understand what their clients said. He might lose face. We took care so none accompanying us would.

As we toured the countryside en route to our hotel, we passed many bicyclers. A few were hauling whole pig carcasses on the bike's back wheel rack. Some of these were tightly wrapped in bamboo sacks. Others were completely bare. Their skin looked pink and shiny. Newly strangled chickens, still with all their feathers, were carried upside down by the feet. Other people had bags of grain or baskets of green vegetables. I was not sure whether all of them had just been to the market and were on their way back home or whether they were carrying merchandise to be sold. We observed no poles with electrical wires nor any TV antenna so we assumed this particular area had no rural electricity. The lack of such amenities might be a good reason why many people preferred to live in or near a large city.

We drove through the entire town of Guilin in reaching our hotel which was situated on the bank of the Li River. Newly opened and sparkling clean, it was modern architecturally and looked very welcoming to us. Our checking in caused some difficulties. Mac reminded the reception clerk our accommodations were to include two bathrooms and one large bed. "Yes, two beds and one bath, we understand," answered the clerk. "No," Mac said. "We want two BATHROOMS and ONE large bed." "Yes, understand." We rode the elevator up three floors with all our luggage to a room which the bellman proudly presented. It had two beds and one bathroom. "No, no!" said Mac, growing impatient. Then we were shown a second room arrangement which was not what we wanted either. Finally, the reception manager appeared, and with a huge smile on his face, led us to another section on the floor, opened the door and bowed us into a suite. These rooms were a combination of a bedroom with a large bed, a living room, a separate dining room and two bathrooms all interconnected by the entrance foyer. Luxurious! Much more space than we needed, but we certainly were not going to complain about that. Apparently registering at a hotel in China will always take time and patience. We recalled our difficulties at The China Hotel in Guangzhou.

We asked Steve to come back in an hour to go sightseeing. We needed to unpack and, particularly to find a good, strong cup of coffee. We felt wan after getting up so early in Guangzhou and eating no snack on the flight to Guilin. He was pleased to accommodate us. As he started back to his car, he pointed out the hotel's coffee shop which was on the mezzanine just above the lobby. We saw waiters moving about. What a find this was! A waiter served us an excellent cup of strong, black coffee along with a basket of delicious donuts. The donuts were covered with big crystals of granulated sugar. Savoring each bite with pleasure, we knew by the time we left Guilin we would be two very spoiled tourists. Such a delightful treat to look forward to each morning!

When Steve and his driver returned, we dismissed the driver in favor of strolling along the river bank. On such a clear, sunny day, it looked like a lovely, cool walk. Beautiful large, green leaf sycamore trees lined the entire bank. How good it felt to stretch the legs!

Many other strollers were equally enjoying themselves. All sorts of people were out this morning. We passed men carrying placards of postcards for sale. There were women gossiping, men smoking, and several aggressive beggars plying this section of Guilin. Tomorrow they undoubtedly will work in another part of the city. Their method of begging was to crowd their victim against the stone wall along the pathway. Thus pinned and unable to move, the victim suddenly found a hand shoved into his face. This intimidation was convincing to some, but not to us. We avoided being so tagged. Several benches were piled with fresh oranges, neatly stacked in tall pyramids. Steve said they were grown in this district. Further along, we saw women sitting on the sidewalk with packages of "junk" spread out before them. The junk was throwaway stuff such as discarded paper wrappers, beads, bits of broken china, thread—a total mishmash which someone else threw away. Lots of kids ran in and out of the crowd, bumping into everybody. Everyone stared at us. My blonde hair and blue eyes and Mac's large frame make us interesting specimens to study.

The river turned around a bend. On the other side was a park. We asked Steve if we could walk over there. "Of course!" he answered, directing us across a bridge onto a narrower road on the other side. It was cooler here. Three boys were rough-housing. They were laughing and having fun teasing and chasing each other. Several young girls played jump rope using two ropes. The object of the game was to keep raising the height of the ropes and jump over them. When the two jumpers stumbled, the girls changed positions and the two holding the ropes became the jumpers. Usually two girls jumped together while two others held the ropes. They were very serious about this game and did not stop while we watched. We reached the park at the end of this road and paid a small fee to enter. Inside were rose bushes in full bloom as well as dahlias, petunias and chrysanthemums growing in well tended beds. It looked like an English garden. Walking out in the open, the sun felt hot so we did not linger. There was a temple on the other side of the park tucked among the trees. It was so picturesque that we headed in its direction.

As we walked along, we noted Chinese people seemed to enjoy spitting. It was in fact a national pastime. There was no hesitation on anyone's part to spit publicly, wherever and whenever the urge struck. Older adults of both sexes seemed particularly adept at this art. It was not at all unusual to see a driver in an automobile roll down his window and send a mighty wad flying through the air as the car moved along. We observed a person walking along the street hesitate a moment, then spit and nonchalantly move along. A nicely dressed woman walked up to a trash bin and spit into it. It was wise to watch where one stepped. Picking one's nose in public was also a custom. No one frowned on this. Neither of these practices was thought to be unsanitary. After a while, we would pay no attention should we observe either taking place, but today we were a bit squeamish. We have not been in China long enough.

We understood the health authorities throughout the country were trying to wage public campaigns for halting public spitting. If caught by police or health workers, the perpetrator was given a fine on the spot. Some health enthusiasts carried microscopes and made the spitter get down on his hands and knees to examine the sputum. So far, being shamed in public has had little effect on stopping the habit. The microscope idea seemed a bit far-fetched to us. Later we noted people sneeze and cough without covering their nose and mouth. They have never been taught this is unsanitary.

Up a few broken stone steps which led into a courtyard, we walked to the entrance of the temple. This place was in need of renovation. It smelled musty and sour. Everything about it was cluttered and disorganized. A boom-box sat on a folding chair, playing loud contemporary jazz in a completely uninhabited room. We did not meet a single other being. Perhaps the music was to liven up the place. It certainly needed something. Circling around the room were a series of alcoves. Each one displayed a Chinese mannequin dressed in a different costume. These appeared to be various court-style Chinese robes from some obscure, ancient period. We really did not know, for there were no identifying signs attached anywhere. There was an even stronger smell of sour decay in the air so we quickly walked through the room to an inner courtyard with a beautiful pebble stone floor. These soft grey pebbles were round, uniform in size and had been laid with care. The edge of every stone stuck up at the same angle and height. On the other side of the courtyard was a tall, gilded throne. We imagined it must seat Buddha. The throne was angled in such a way that we could not see. We walked around the chair to find no Buddha in it. Someone had either taken it away for repairs or stolen it for resale. We were disgusted that we had let ourselves be lured inside this temple. Even our guide was bored, and no other visitors ever appeared.

There was a special garden in Guilin at the bottom of a small, but very steep rocky mountain which was known as Peak of Unique Beauty. If so inclined, one could climb to its top by a series of 306 steps carved out of the rocks. At the top, one could view a beautiful panorama of the countryside. These steps were very steep but attracted many tourists. At their beginning, the climber passed by Whirlpool Hill, where sat a giant iron Pot of a Thousand Men and a cast iron bell weighing two and a half tons. Both dated back to a temple from the Ch'ing Dynasty (1644-1911). At the foot of Mountain of the Gentle Waves was the Pearl Returning Cave. We elected to visit this instead of climbing the steep incline, particularly since the day had turned quite warm. Down a series of steps, we descended into a stony underground passageway. Drops of cold water oozed from the rocky ceiling, falling on our heads, and the big drop in temperature felt delightful. We were inside a large, twisty cave or tunnel with openings at either end. The path wound through rough stone walls and around dark, mysterious corners. Where we would end up was a delightful puzzle.

Steve began to narrate an old fable as we ambled along: It seemed this very cave was home to a dragon. He held a marvelous, huge pearl in his mouth. A fisherman saw the dragon with his pearl and decided he wanted to steal it. So one night he crept up into the cave and, while the dragon was sleeping, took the pearl out of its mouth. When the fisherman got back into his boat with the pearl, a great sense of guilt took hold of him. He was ashamed of what he had done. So, he turned his boat around and took the pearl back to the dragon. He carefully replaced it in the dragon's mouth and went back to his boat. Steve sighed. "And, then?" I asked, "Was that the end of the story? Did they both live happily ever after?" "I don't know the answer to that," Steve answered. "This is how the story was told to me."

Steve pointed out Buddhist

sculptures and inscriptions on the walls from Tang and Sung Dynasties (7th to 13th centuries). There was also a touchstone on which swordsmen tested the strength of their weapons. We reached the end of the cave. There was a landing there, where small boats could anchor. Perhaps this was the place where the fisherman landed when stealing the dragon's pearl. Today a fisherman was demonstrating to two admiring female Westerners how cormorants caught fish. They oohed and aahed as the birds snapped up the fish being thrown to them. When cormorants are taught to catch fish, the fisherman places a slender cane ring over the cormorant's neck, pushing it firmly down to the end of the bird's gullet. This will prevent the cormorant from swallowing its catch. On command, the bird dove down for fish, then swam back to the fisherman's raft or boat. The fisherman took the bird and squeezed its food pouch called an ayus. This caused the bird to disgorge the fish into a wooden bucket. The fisherman then removed the cane ring from the bird's neck and gave it a fish to eat as a reward. After a short rest, the cormorant was readied to fish again. Fishermen liked doing this at night, using the light of a torch that brought the fish to the surface, enabling their cormorants to easily catch a great amount.

The next morning, we boarded a two-deck river

boat at the Zhujiang Wharf, a few miles from Guilin, for a cruise down the Li River. The purpose was to view unique scenery along its banks. The Li River wound through miles and miles of landscape of naturally sculpted pinnacle rocks. These were strange outcrops that jutted up and out from flat ground like triangular spears. Called karst formations, they were formed from limestone beds of seas which covered this region millions of years ago. Being eroded over the centuries by wind and water, they now looked like spears or towers of stone. As we started our cruise early in the morning, a misty, grey fog floated over and around the rocks, while the sun was trying to break through. This spectacular landscape was the one often seen in Chinese paintings.

A Scene From Amy Tan

A wonderful scene in Amy Tan's book "The Hundred Secret Senses" shows the significance these rocks can play in young girls' lives. In it the older, Chinese-raised sister, Kwan, tries to explain them to her younger, skeptical American-raised sister: "See that?" I hear Kwan say, "over there." She's pointing to a cone-shaped peak off in the distance. "Just outside my village stands a sharp-headed mountain, taller than that one even. We call it 'Young Girl's Wish,' after a slave girl who ran away to the top of it, then flew off with a phoenix who was her lover. Later, she turned into a phoenix, and together, she and her lover went to live in an immortal white pine forest."

Kwan looks at me. "It's a story, just superstition." I'm amused that she thinks she has to explain.

Kwan continues: "Yet all the girls in our village believed in that tale, not because they were stupid, but because they wanted to hope for a better life. We thought that if we climbed to the top and made a wish, it might come true. So we raised little hatchlings and put them in cages we had woven ourselves. When the birds were ready to fly, we climbed to the top of Young Girl's Wish and let them go. The birds would then fly to where the phoenixes lived and tell them our wishes.

Kwan sniffs. "Big Ma told me the peak was named Young Girl's Wish because a crazy girl climbed to the top. But when she tried to fly, she fell all the way down and lodged herself so firmly into the earth she became a boulder. Big Ma said that's why you can see so many boulders at the bottom of that peak—they're all the stupid girls who followed her kind of crazy thinking, wishing for hopeless things."

I laugh. Kwan stares at me fiercely, as if I were Big Ma. "You can't stop young girls from wishing. No! Everyone must dream. We dream to give ourselves hope. To stop dreaming—well, that's like saying you can never change your fate. Isn't that true?"

The Rocks

Many Chinese poets and painters were inspired by the unique forms of these peaks and landscapes. Along the river between the peaks are rocks and caves, deep pools, springs and waterfalls. Vegetation grew on some. There was a photograph to be taken at every bend. Some peaks had been given special names. We saw "A Boy Worships Buddha" and "Dragonhead Hill" as well as "Wangfu Rock," so called because it looked like a woman carrying her baby. The poets said she was yearning for her husband's return. We saw another that depicted A Man Turning a Wheel. Dragons Playing Water and Five Tigers Catch a Goat were two others on our route. I liked the ones called An Old Man Pushes a Mill and A Boy Worships Buddha. The Chinese have great imaginations. Each peak had its own mythology to make us pause for thought and contemplation. One had to look hard to see the imagery, but everyone will remember the uniqueness of the landscapes on both banks while admiring this beautiful natural scenery. The Chinese were not content with just a simple name like say, "Flat Rock." Every notable object must be assigned a special role.

These river boats were motorized, two-level affairs carrying 62 passengers. I counted all the seats on the lower deck for something to do. There were six rows on either side of a main aisle. Each pair of seats held six people, three on either side with a table in between. They were Chinese style, wooden seats with a curved padded back rest. The pads were too low down to give our Western backs any comfort or support. Mac could not get his legs under the table at all. I did so only by sliding mine down sideways. The deck was fully enclosed with sliding glass windows. Were the seats a little more comfortable, it would be a great place to be for sightseeing. The upper deck was totally open and had no seating at all. Up there were two small souvenir kiosks with various stone jewelry and some t-shirts for sale. We did most of our sightseeing from up there.

Upon boarding, we were shown to our reserved seats. Immediately a waiter appeared offering us hot green tea. Steve announced two meals would be served during the trip. Obviously this jaunt was designed as a cruise for a group of friends to enjoy the pleasure of being together, while viewing a lovely countryside with bamboo forests and bizarre rock formations, and while being served a freshly cooked breakfast and luncheon. A wonderful combination for a delightfully lazy day.

A family reunion was in progress at the end of the room. One daughter came from Chicago. She explained to us this was the first time in 26 years the entire family had been together. Some members, she said, came all the way from Indonesia for this event. They all were so obviously pleased to see each other and most especially to be with their mother and father. How their cameras clicked!

Our food was cooked at facilities in the stern of the ship. The cook used a huge wok while his two helpers sat nearby cutting up ingredients. We could peek into the room to watch the process, but were not allowed to walk inside. After all the cooking was completed, the leftovers and garbage were dumped overboard into the Li River. Then the cook cleaned up his kitchen by spraying the place with a garden hose. Just in front of the kitchen was an iron ladder with very wide, steep steps to the upper deck. A toilet facility was situated to the left of the kitchen. Its white porcelain model was mounted on the floor, Japanese-style. The facility looked clean. Frankly, we were relieved it was here.

During the entire outing, Steve appeared once to see if we were settled, then vanished. Where he went was a mystery. We explored every section of the boat several times and never bumped into him. Suddenly, he would reappear out of nowhere. He always casually approached us, usually urging us to partake in one of the meals, but not to cue us on the sights. He was unhappy when we refused both meals. Perhaps he was not allowed to eat if we did not, even though we strongly urged him to do so without us. One time he offered us each an orange. We thanked him but said no. He ate both in the car ride back to Guilin. He did not even offer one to the driver. What an enigma he was. We suspected he was not confident enough of his English to talk more. On this trip, he was only concerned that we were not eating.

Sitting at our table on the lower deck was so uncomfortable for both of us that we stood mostly on the upper deck, resting our bodies against the ship's rails because there were no chairs. The wind blew furiously all during the voyage. Luckily it was a soft, warm wind, and it was a misty, not sunny, day. Had the sun been out and the day clear, we would have been very hot and uncomfortable either up or downstairs. The only signs of life we saw during the entire trip were some ducks swimming along the banks and water buffalos submerged in a pool of water. They looked funny completely covered by the water with only their noses sticking out. Somewhere else further along, we saw another large and muddy pond. Looking closer, we saw there were many pairs of big eyes at water level, watching us. Every inch of this pond was completely full of buffalos. Once a big black bird flew over our upper deck. It had bronze colored wings. A friendly butterfly inspected us too.

By the third hour of the trip, even though we were traveling at the brisk rate of 15 miles per hour, we were definitely becoming bored and more than eager to be wherever we were going. The map said we would land at a village called Yangshuo. Its pier was Overlooking Pavilion. Suddenly our captain veered course toward the right river bank where there was a small dock. Deck hands raced outside, walking along the ship's rails. They closed all deck windows. Immediately the cabin felt hot and stuffy. We pulled alongside a barge. Out jumped our captain. He and another workman started working a hand pump. Back and forth they moved the lever. Back and forth. We watched, puzzled. Why were they doing this? Someone said we were taking on fuel. Fuel? We wondered why we did not have enough fuel before we started. No one explained. We sat half an hour watching this slow hand pumping process. Other river boats passed by. We had been the number three boat in a group of over 20. We quickly lost our place. None of the others needed fuel. Finally with this job completed to the crew's satisfaction, the captain jumped back aboard and started the engine. Mac and I breathed a deep sigh of relief. Now we would be heading to our final destination. To our complete astonishment, the boat was moved ahead only slightly and docked at yet another barge. After docking, the reunion group with the friendly lady from Chicago gathered their belongings and disembarked.

As their group disappeared up the wooded river bank, a large group of vendors rushed onto the barge and started shouting at us passengers. What a noisy racket they made. These Chinese merchants were extremely shrill in trying to get our attention for selling the many items they had to offer. They eagerly waved large feathered fans, unrolled a satin tapestry, showed all sorts of knick-knacks, plus fresh fruits and other snacks to eat. If they made eye contact with any of us, they started yelling, trying to force a sale. They were not allowed inside the boat. That was why the crew closed our deck windows. Should one try to jump aboard, there was an officer stationed at the entrance of the ship who would fend him off. The moment the reunion group disappeared, the captain started our motor, and we rejoined the procession of river boats going downstream. What an annoying experience.

When we finally arrived at the village of Yangshuo, the captain gave us a final flourish. He steered the boat beyond our assigned landing dock to a place downstream, almost under a gigantic steel bridge. This impressive structure spanned the entire width of the river. Only after we all had a good look did he turn the boat around. Slowly, ever so slowly, we approached Overlooking Pavilion. Finally the lines were secured, and we passengers were at last free to disembark.

This entire trip, some 50 or so miles long, took four hours. Two hours would have been long and about the right length of time. Three hours was very long, but four hours had seemed interminable and stretched our patience.

Back in the Sheraton after a ride to Guilin from Yangshuo, also longer than we imagined it should be, we elected to eat our dinner at the hotel's Chinese restaurant. A shower had refreshed us immensely, and we were starved, having had nothing to eat since breakfast. Once seated, we studied the menu with great interest. We decided on sweet and sour soup, new green beans with ground meat and pork with fresh ginger. Each of these were favorites of both of ours.

I was particularly interested in how the sweet and sour soup would taste since I like to prepare and serve it in our home. I dipped my porcelain spoon into its rich broth and savored the first taste. As it slid down my throat, tears came to my eyes.

"Mac," I whispered, my voice raspy and almost gone, "do be careful. This soup is really hot!" He realized I did not mean "hot" in temperature when he took his first taste. This sweet and sour soup had been so concocted that it was the most spicy we have ever been served at any Chinese restaurant. One knows better than to cool off the throat with water as this would only enhance the temperature.

"Well, that's why the cucumber strips are in that bowl," I gasped pointing to a little dish sitting across from us. "Let's quickly eat one to cool our throats."

"You know I don't care for cucumbers," replied Mac, "but you go ahead. I hope one will help."

It barely cooled my throat. "Well, let's try the pork." That too was hot and so were the innocent looking little green beans. Suddenly it occurred to us that this was Szechuan-style cooking. We were eating only one star Szechuan, which was considered mild by Chinese gourmets. I love hot, spicy food, but this was way beyond my gratification.

The Chinese food here was not at all like American-style Chinese cooked food. Everything was differently flavored, and it was hot for us when only mild for them. It would be impossible for us to eat Chinese every night and stay well. It was too highly spiced. Before we came, a friend who had recently visited China strongly advised us to eat Western food at every possible opportunity. Since every hotel so far had had a Western restaurant, this very sage advice had not been hard to follow. Apparently it was very sophisticated to have an authentic ethnic restaurant in addition to the Western one in a Chinese-managed hotel. Mostly these were Japanese style ones for attracting that particular trade.

Food in China

Traditionally, Chinese food is classified according to four major geographical regions. These are Canton, Shanghai, Sichuan and Beijing. Each has its distinct characteristics. Cantonese cooking, perhaps the most familiar to Americans, is known for its freshness and lightness. Seafood, vegetables, chicken or pork is bought at the market each day. The cooking is done quickly and simply by steaming or stir-frying. The Cantonese dim sum, snacks consisting of various sorts of delicious little morsels, are particular treats. A dim sum restaurant is always noisy, with everyone having choices from a variety of treats passed to the customers on big trays. In contrast, Shanghainese cooking is apt to be oily and strong tasting. More salt is used, as well as large amounts of sweet rice wine. "Drunken Chicken" is a popular dish cooked in this wine. Eels are a speciality in this region too. Sichuan is the hottest of the four types. Peppery, tangy dishes are made with duck, shrimp or beef. The people of this region believe that eating lots of hot, spicy food cooked with chilies and peppers will rid anyone of bad tempers. Substantial food is made in Beijing since this is one of China's colder regions. This also is the wheat belt, so steamed breads and noodles are eaten instead of steamed rice. Beijing duck served with pancakes and plum sauce is a well known dish. Others include "Beggar's Chicken" which calls for a whole chicken to be wrapped in leaves, covered in mud and baked all day in hot ashes. Mongolian hotpot is another speciality. This is composed of vegetables and assorted meats and is cooked at the dining room table. Of the four cuisines, Westerners rank Shanghainese the least popular, Cantonese the best known and therefore probably the most enjoyed, with the other two falling somewhere in between. Sichuan and Beijing foods have more appeal to the adventurous diner. It is a basic rule that a Chinese meal should include "five flavors." They are sweetness, sourness, hotness, bitterness and saltiness. With these a balance and harmony is achieved. Mincing and thin slicing of meat and fish are essential for releasing their full flavors. All methods of cooking are used, but native to China is stir-frying.

The next morning, as we prepared to fly from Guilin to Shanghai, I needed some rubber bands to hold my papers together. Downstairs at the bellhop's desk, I asked if they had any. One young man produced a ball of twine. Was this what I wished? The other scoured around the desk and finally asked, "Rubber band? What is?" They had no idea what a rubber band was. Neither had ever seen one!

We flew economy class from Guilin to Shanghai. We had aisle seats across from each other in a row of six. It made the flight fun. We could see all the action from this perspective. I was sitting with a very nice, middle aged Chinese couple. We attempted to converse. Somehow, we understood each other. The man explained to me that the landing in Shanghai would be bumpy, and it was. The woman gave me some of her newspaper to cover a sticky spot on my tray table that had not been cleaned up from a prior flight. They were the kind of nice people with whom one wished to converse in depth, but could not because of the language barrier.

The stewardess offered drinks. He chose warm white wine, she wished coffee with milk, and I asked for water. Lunch came in individual cardboard boxes. With some difficulty, I pulled off the top cover and saw many little envelopes inside. Apparently this was not the correct way to approach the box. The couple each opened an end, then pulled out a single envelope. The element of surprise was part of the essence of the meal. My first envelope contained dried shrimp crisps which tasted good. On opening the second envelope, I encountered something I could not recognize. It looked sort of like a dried red bug with legs. I took a bite. It was chewy and not that bad tasting. Mac was watching and laughed at me. He skipped eating his. The last envelope contained a small cake with some sweet paste in its middle. These snacks were fun to taste, including the thing that looked like a red bug. Mac enjoyed a Coca Cola and not much else.

Announcing the length of the flight, the stewardess spoke Chinese. Everyone was very attentive and listened quietly. She repeated the same message in English. Now everyone was talking loudly because no one understood what she was saying. As it turned out, the flight was an hour and forty five minutes. Everyone was very quiet as the plane touched down. Then pandemonium broke loose. Passengers jumped up, and some stood on their seats to collect their belongings in the overhead containers. The stewardesses had a terrible time restoring order before the airplane pulled to a stop at the gate. Everyone was orderly disembarking, however, and obviously happy to be in the metropolitan city of Shanghai.

SHANGHAI

SHANGHAI

Population: 13.1 Million
Traditional Spelling: Shanghai
Symbol's Meaning: Up from the sea

chapter 6

上 SHANGHAI

Everything was modern and well organized at Hong Qiao, the airport serving Shanghai. One deplaned into the large modern terminal through a covered ramp, the very first we encountered in China. There was no difficulty in finding the section for claiming luggage. Plenty of trolleys were available, and the luggage came quickly on a rotating carousel. An official checked claim tickets on our bags. This was all that was required to pass into the passenger area. The simplicity and orderly manner of this arrival gave us a boost.

A Mr. Wang Xiao Wei was our guide and formally presented his card. He was a boyish looking man who wore glasses and conservative businessman's clothing. He looked much younger than his 24 years. Wang was his family name, Xiao Wei his given names, but he introduced himself to us as "Richard," his chosen English name. He helped us push the trolleys across the street into the parking lot where the car was sitting. Richard introduced Feng, a cheery, plump man who would be our driver during this visit. Feng and Richard figured out how to stash all the paraphernalia into the car's somewhat limited luggage trunk. With a minimum of fuss, we were off to the Shangri-La Hotel in the Shanghai Center at 1376 Nanjing Xi Lu.

"Over the Sea"

The word "Shanghai" translated means "over the sea," even though the city is not on the sea at all. It is located at the confluence of the broad Huangpu River and Suzhou Creek. Shanghai is in Jiangsu Province, the eastern part of China, and is the largest port in the country. After the end of the Opium Wars in 1842, the victorious British forced the Manchu authorities to grant them concessions along the Huangpu. An influx of Westerners poured in and made fortunes importing opium and exporting tea and silk. Before this, Shanghai was a backwater with no Westerners and was not as important as the cities of Suzhou and Guangzhou.

People and Districts

The British designated area is bordered on the north by a road called Yangjingbang, on the south by one named Li Chia Zhuang and the west by the Huangpu River. Officially, this was called the British Settlement. When Americans joined them at a later time, the settlement then was renamed the International Settlement. The French Settlement on Huai Hai Zhong road is today in front of the Garden Hotel. This road, with its Western-style, red brick houses and Art Deco decorations, is still a fashionable street. The French buildings are a delicate contrast to those of granite and black marble in the British/American Settlement. In 1900, about 600 French people lived here. By the 1920s, they built the French Club which became famous as a spa for its members.

In the 1900s, there were more than 50,000 people from various countries living in Shanghai. The French and English were responsible for enriching the city with distinctive architecture and their sophisticated ways of living. Shanghai was nicknamed the "Sin City" because of antics that took place. Almost nightly there were dinner and dancing parties attended by the foreigners and occasionally a few invited Chinese ladies. This caused raised eyebrows since Chinese were not welcome in the settlements as guests. Life was stimulating and very much alive. The popular sports were riding, cricket, rowing and tennis.

In the 1920s and 1930s, Shanghai was the commercial, financial, industrial and cultural center of China. When the Communists took power in 1949, one fifth of the entire country's industrial output and two thirds of its foreign trade was passing through this port. During the World War II, the Japanese occupied the city and lived in the foreign settlements which the English and French had vacated. When the Communist Red Army took over in 1949, foreign concessions and private ownership were abolished. Not until Deng Xiaoping reopened Shanghai to foreign investment in 1984, was it again able to assert itself as the industrial, financial, shipping, fashion and fun capital of Asia.

Mac and I were excited to be back in this city that so represents China's future.

No More Communism Here

Shanghai's 12 million inhabitants have firmly turned their backs on the Communist way of life, even though they are still controlled by regulations from Beijing. Now they complain of traffic jams, overcrowded pavements and markets, quite a change in openness of expression from yesterday's subservience under the ever-watchful eyes of the Communist Party officials. From a prosperity originally based on "village crafts"—silk production, embroidery, furniture making and pottery, the local industries moved to textiles, clothes and shoes, and now are assembling radios, cameras, television sets and automobiles. Local computers are for sale here, making the information age available. A sound educational system has been restored, particularly in science and technology. Living standards have risen so dramatically in the last decade that it is unlikely there will be any going back to Communism.

While Feng wove in and out of the speeding traffic, we sat back and savored all the new things to see. When we were here two years ago, everyone rode a black bicycle. Today they were riding the same black bicycles, in spite of the many automobiles on the roads. In our American cities, we are accustomed to traffic being principally motorized vehicles, so it was awesome to see more bicycles in use here. This was true in every Chinese city we visited. Supposedly, there were some seven million here in Shanghai. Richard said he owned two and will never learn to drive a car. "Too dangerous," he told us. The brand of these black bikes was called "Seagull."

A Gift to President Bush

When President George Bush visited Beijing, a Seagull was the gift he was given. It is a fact that the Chinese have a low rate of heart disease. Their regular exercise of pedaling to school, to work and to the market place, added to the healthy diet they eat, has much to do with their living a longlife span.

Although most people still consider the railroad as the chosen mode of transportation, automobiles were in abundance. In 1991 when we were here, there were hardly any private cars. Today, in 1993, many drive their own car and taxicabs are readily available. Of course, this accumulation of traffic produces horrendous traffic jams which were previously unknown. In prior years, only Party officials rode in automobiles, and those were big black limousines. Richard pointed out the blue taxis which seemed to be everywhere. He said they were part of a fleet developed by an entrepreneur. This man required his potential new drivers to have a six-month period of riding as co-pilot with an experienced driver, plus attending special safety training classes. Only then did he allow the new person to drive a taxi alone and/or carry passengers.

We noted policemen were communicating with each other via cellular phones. Shanghai was the fourth city in the world with an eight-digit telephone number system, and people were still waiting to be connected to it. When competed, it will boost available telephone numbers from eight million to 80 million. Thus Shanghai will join Paris, Tokyo and Hong Kong as the only cities to have eight-digit telephone numbers. These were unique acquisitions in a city that was once the very cradle of the Cultural Revolution.

More changes. We were driving on beautifully paved highways and seeing modern high-rise office and apartment buildings, new fashionable stores and many hotels whose companies' logos we recognized. There was a Colonel Sanders restaurant, his smiling face selling take-out chicken dinners, and the Marlboro man in his cowboy hat was advertising cigarettes on a huge billboard. The people bustling along the sidewalks seemed full of energy and purpose. Richard had a slogan that seemed appropriate. He said, "In one year we change little, but in three we change everything." Given a reasonable political environment, one could predict a great future. The contrast of Shanghai with cities in Russia and India was ludicrous. None in those countries were in the same league with what we saw here. Judging all by similar standards of self-esteem, ambition or adaptability, none came up to the same first-class world culture of Shanghai.

The house where Mao Zedong and his cohorts met in secret to plan the Cultural Revolution was pointed out. This was in the former French concession. We recalled the history of that time.

Mao's Cultural Revolution

The Cultural Revolution started in 1949, when Mao Zedong and his generals stood at the Gate of Heavenly Peace overlooking Tiananmen Square in Beijing and proclaiming to the world the birth of the People's Republic of China. It had been a Long March to that day. Its beginnings started back in 1911, when the Chinese people overthrew the Manchus of the Ch'ing Dynasty. The Ch'ing Dynasty had been on the Dragon Throne since 1644. Although various local dictators throughout the country tried to impose a new rule, it was Sun Yat-sen who started to unite the whole country into one nation. He died before accomplishing this. His successor, Generalissimo Chiang Kai-shek, assumed Sun Yat-sen's leadership, bringing hope to the people.

Two groups of reformers developed, the Kuomintang, led by Chiang Kai-shek, and the Communists, headed by a group consisting of Mao Zedong, Zhou Enlai and others. After many disputes, a split developed between the Generalissimo's party and the Communists which ultimately led to civil war. Many skirmishes were engaged, with neither side winning. The Kuomintang remained at their base, while the Communists swept down the length of China, gathering with them local militia in the rural communities plus other bands who had worked underground. This is referred to as the Long March. About the same time, the Japanese invaded Manchuria and continued an invasion into the Mainland. Although he made a token effort, Chiang Kai-shek refused an all-out fight with the Japanese, preferring to destroy the Communists instead. He reasoned that after Pearl Harbor was bombed, the Americans would win the war against the Japanese and then would provide him with the supplies he needed to defeat the Communists. By 1945, when Japan was defeated, the Kuomintang was full of corruption and had lost its mandate with the people. The Communists had captured much of the U.S.-supplied equipment sent to the Kuomintang and had recruited so many Kuomintang troops that, together, they fought and defeated the Generalissimo. On October 1, 1949, Mao Zedong was able to declare the formation of the People's Republic of China while Chiang Kai-shek fled to Taiwan, taking with him the entire gold reserves of China. Some two million refugees and soldiers from the Mainland went with him.

Two primary reforms were immediately decreed by Mao: The first was to redistribute the land to the peasants by dispossessing and sometimes executing the landowners. The second reform was to lift the status of women to being equal with men. They were to work alongside men doing similar tasks, as well as establishing themselves in the hierarchy of the local communes and in all positions of government. Mao emphasized, "Women should hold up half of the sky." Prior to this, many Chinese girls were not even given names. Communal living was established. Children were taken away from their homes and sent to the countryside to learn peasant values. All adults, including husbands and wives, were required to live in segregated dormitories. The commune took precedence over the traditional Chinese family life structure, thus breaking apart the families as a unit.

Revolutionary exhortations boomed over loudspeakers, awakened people in the morning and followed them throughout the day. Between being required to memorize Mao's quotations and hearing Communist propaganda all day long from loudspeakers, there was no time for an individual to think privately. Total thought control was the aim of the Party. It wanted no one to have any ideas put into his or her head by anyone or anything other than those which came from the Party. Mao exerted external discipline as well. Mandatory weekly meetings were held where everybody had to criticize himself for incorrect thoughts and be subject to the criticism of others. "The individual is subordinate to the organization," he preached. The Communist Party determined all things for everybody, starting with the clothes to wear and the style haircut to get, the city in which to live, the job to have, the amount of rice to eat, the clinic to use, whom one may marry and the kind of activities for "volunteering" to do. Eventually, people became almost identical. They all dressed alike in Mao suits, cut their hair in the same style, rode the same black bicycles, and shared a faith in Communism which had them repeating the same lines over and over. Communism became the people's only religion.

Mao was ambitious for China to develop into a great industrial nation. He proclaimed China's industrial output could overtake that of Britain and the United States in 15 years. He ordered the output of steel to be doubled. Instead of depending on the steel industry to accomplish this, he involved the entire population by sponsoring the "Great Leap Forward" movement, which started in 1959 and ended in 1961. A quota for steel per commune was established. The farmers were urged to forge the steel in their communes instead of plowing the land in the fields. Every effort was to go into this endeavor, plus every scrap of wood and metal available. Thus trees were chopped into logs for fueling the foundries and woks and plows were melted down for their steel. As the years passed, the commune system became inefficient, and farming productivity dropped. Crops suffered, and some 30 million persons starved to death during the years of the "Great Leap Forward" initiative.

No one has estimated how many people died overall as a result of Mao's Great Proletarian Cultural Revolution from 1966 to 1976. Certainly it deprived an entire generation of schooling. Scarcely a family in China was untouched. Countless lives were ruined. The former president was beaten to death in prison, and the son of Deng Xiaoping was paralyzed after being shoved from a fifth floor window. Priceless relics were smashed. It was a time when one citizen turned against another, students terrorized teachers, and children defied their parents.

The Cultural Revolution is not in today's textbooks. May 16, 1996 is the 30th anniversary of its beginning. The Communist Party ordered there be no commemorations even though people were taught by Mao that the most glorious thing was to make achievements and sacrifices for the Revolution and Party. The Cultural Revolution shaped the formative lives of millions of people. It is that generation of people who are now reaching the heights of their careers. They run government departments, businesses and academic programs, make films and write novels. Most Chinese can claim to have been a victim at some point during the Cultural Revolution. Few ever admit to being victimizers.

Upon Mao's death on September 9, 1976 at a mere 83 years of age, new leaders came forward. A dream of building a new, modern China was spelled out by Deng Xiaoping. He first started by freeing the farmers from communal living, telling them to work for themselves and to reestablish the traditional family structure. This was all the incentive they needed. Farmers had always done their best work as a family unit. All land had been confiscated during Mao's regime. Deng adopted a free market concept of letting farmers own land, giving each two mus or about a half acre. This inspired the farmers, who went to work with revitalized energy. They readily accepted the responsibility to provide quotas of staple crops for the government. In return, they rented the land from the government for a 15 year lease. Each farmer was allowed to sell his produce for whatever the market would allow. (Prices were probably set by the state.) If, for some reason, a farmer decided not to grow a crop one year, a member of his family was required to do the work. The government stipulated that a crop must be produced if the farmer was to retain the land, to help feed China's population of over a billion people. With Deng's new farming reforms, agricultural production doubled in the country within five years. Instead of using water buffalos for plowing, many farmers were soon able to buy efficient small tractors which could be converted into trucks for taking produce to market. Replacing the buffalo with modern technology increased farm production and helped feed China's huge population. Quite suddenly, farmers had income to buy watches and new bicycles. As electricity slowly began coming to the countryside, they also could have radios and rice cookers. They were the first group to enjoy newly earned freedom and riches beyond their imaginations. Seeing these peasants become rich caused much envy among the city dwellers who were still plodding along at their same government jobs and earning meager salaries.

Life in the country was hard. One needed to be strong and industrious to survive. Farmers worked on the land three days, then marketed in town on the fourth. They repeated this continuously, year after year. The schedule was a bit daunting for the weak-hearted, but this was the way it had been for centuries here in China. Until the Cultural Revolution, farming was the industry of free men working with and for their families on lands they had inherited from their fathers. Their mission in life was to transmit this land, enriched, on to their sons. It never was their aim to amass great wealth. If a family member decided to go out into the larger world to make his living, it was always with the understanding that he might return to the place of his birth to spend his declining years among those persons who were dear to him in childhood. Healthy work, sufficient leisure, open hospitality for one's neighbors, a contentment with habits undisturbed by foolish ambition and a oneness with Nature are the characteristics of the Chinese farmer.

Mao's idea of placing everyone in a commune and telling farmers how to farm had resulted in idleness and a continual drop in food production. Masses of people starved as a result. Even after Deng Xiaoping succeeded Mao and allowed the farmers to work for themselves, there was not enough food being produced. In 1993, China's food prices climbed to new highs, and Beijing sought new reforms to feed its huge population. Sorely needed was modern transportation and refrigeration to get the produce quickly to the cities before it spoiled. Up-to-date methods in the animal feed industry and grain growing techniques must be learned. Irrigation and flood control needed to be modernized. The small, and sometimes inefficient farm continued to exist. Since the mayors of towns controlled the transport of products out of their districts, they expected to be reimbursed for their services, which added to the problem. Most of all, foreign capital and marketing expertise were needed. Much of China's future hangs on the solution. The business of feeding a population of over a billion persons is a major problem yet to be solved.

When Feng turned our car from the four-lane boulevard into the driveway of the Portman Shanghai Center, we ceased reliving past history. He stopped the car at the entrance of the Shangri-La Hotel. Looking around as we got out, we observed the entire compound was a huge multi-level structure under one roof. It contained two tall office building towers on either side of the hotel, with shops and several restaurants on three levels in between them. Apparently, these were reached by stairways and escalators. There was a sizeable indoor parking garage. The complex was one of the most uniquely modern structures we had seen in China. The entire development was a complicated joint venture between the Portman Group, based in Atlanta, Georgia and the City of Shanghai. It was pulled together by Jiang Zemin, then mayor of Shanghai.

At the time of our visit in 1993, Jiang was one of three members from Shanghai on the seven-man council in Beijing, which ruled the country by consensus. He was the leading candidate to take over as Chairman upon Deng Xiaoping's death. (Actually Deng had bowed out of all official duties in 1989, thus ending the lifelong leadership tradition that had been practiced by his predecessors. When we were there, this was a little known fact inside or outside of China.

A Deng Achievement

A great achievement of Deng's, but an underrated one, was ending the vicious cycle of revenge among the leaders and instituting civil rules in the political game. Leaders could no longer be enemies, but must work as rivals who negotiate and compromise. During our stay, it was a popular pastime speculating who would succeed the over 90-year old Deng Xiaoping. Current political guessing centered around three top leaders: Jiang Zemin, who was secretary of the Communist Party as well as Chairman of the Central Military Commission, Prime Minister Li Peng, and economic expert Deputy Minister Zhu Rongji. If they "hang together," they would retain the necessary, vital support of the three million member People's Liberation Army and 100 million men and women in the People's Armed Police. The Liberation Army controlled more than 20,000 commercial enterprises registered in the name of military units, and the central leadership permitted them to spend part of the profits on improving the low standard of living of the troops.

Absolutely nothing was delicate in the architectural composition or engineering of the Shanghai Center. Its sophisticated design was structured entirely in massive amounts of steel-reinforced concrete. Automobiles delivered their passengers directly to the hotel's entrance where a uniformed doorman officiated. Later we learned people queued up for a taxi which was then dispensed by a starter. To go into the hotel, one walked over a wide, curved bridge, with flowing water underneath, to an automatic revolving door entrance. This door had three large partitions. Each could easily hold five or six adults without any of them feeling crowded. As we walked toward it, we noted a huge waterfall splashing down a high wall on our right. On the other side of the entrance was a fountain that sprayed water up as high as the third floor of the hotel. Enormous round, aubergine-colored columns stood alongside untinted gigantic, sandblasted concrete square ones. Large shiny, dark sapphire blue pots of greenery were scattered throughout the garage. By deliberately controlling this building's design in every detail, the architects had achieved a clean, modern look on a heroic scale that was truly handsome and anything but monotonous.

A subtle awareness and respect of ancient Chinese culture was apparent in the interior. One noted this walking through the main lobby. To find the reception desk or the concierge or looking for the elevators or the lounge, one always went around a corner. It is an old Chinese belief that evil spirits move in a straight line. Here there was no need to worry. One could never reach his destination without making many a turn.

There were eye-catching details to notice. The ceilings vary in height, but mostly soar two or three floors high, making the interior seem airy and spacious. Their variances increased interest in the architecture too. Many original art pieces were tastefully displayed throughout the public areas. We found tucked in various alcoves several large ceramic Tang horses and a huge Tang camel, as well as several fierce-looking warrior figures and a large Buddha head. There were sizeable metal pots, displays of highly glazed ceramic pottery, ancient armory, and fascinating weavings hung on walls. This week the lobby was decorated with yellow leaf plants massively grouped in corners. What a feast for one's eyes!

While waiting for our rooms to be ready, we ambled into the Bubbling Well Lounge, ordered an espresso and absorbed this lovely setting. We sat in lounge chairs upholstered in a silvered grey leather placed on a mauve carpet with a low rosewood coffee table between Mac and me. A handsome scroll of a Chinese lady hung to our right above a small sofa upholstered in a soft grey wool fabric with tiny mauve stripes. The colors in the scroll were predominantly celadon green. Celadon green, a rusty mauve and silvered grey were the three shades consistently used throughout the building. The grey blended beautifully with the concrete interior walls. The rust was a color somewhere between mauve and true red. Aubergine, perhaps, was its hue. Some of our friends who are color experts might call it a "lightened" red. These interior furnishings enhanced and complemented the grandness of the architecture.

We lunched at the Tea Garden restaurant beside the waterfall. We sat by an outside window so we could observe the passers-by. There was a young couple with their toddler. They photographed him by the waterfall and again as he sat on his father's lap. We saw the back slit in his trousers was open. He was wearing a "convenience" panty for toddlers which purposely opened easily while the little one was being taught toilet training. Pampers diapers were for sale in both the supermarket and drug store here in the complex, but were considered expensive to use.

Over there, crossing our parking lot, was a handsome elderly Chinese woman walking arm in arm with her daughter. The mother was clothed in the symbolic, navy, quilted Mao-style jacket over loosely fitting, navy trousers. Her hair, cut in a bob, was a soft white grey. It curved in a simple pageboy just below her chin. She was so natural and lovely that I scarcely glanced at her daughter.

As we settled in our room, there was a knock at the door. "Excuse me," said a tiny, uniformed maid. "I haven't *Chinese Daily*. If I have, I send to you. Is okay?" This round-faced, bright-eyed young girl was answering our query as to why today's newspaper had not been delivered. A minute later, another knock. "Here is paper. Is okay?"

Richard needed to coordinate our sightseeing ideas with reservations his bureau had already arranged. They had planned visits to the Modern Art Museum and the CAO Yang residential district as well the Shanghai stock market. In addition, we had requested a tour of the large Volkswagen factory, but apparently that was not a possibility unless we knew people working there. Shanghai Volkswagen was the country's biggest joint venture, with a production capability of 150,000 Santana model cars annually. It was expected to grow to 300,000 soon. Chinese liked automobiles built with soft seats and back cushions, contrary to the hard seats the Germans preferred. This condition had to be corrected before the cars would sell here.

Richard's plans sounded fine with us. In addition, we wanted to walk down The Bund and have Richard point out the buildings built by the English early in the century. They were impressive because they were so massive and stately. We would try to sort out the names of the streets by taking a map of the city on our drives. The major streets seemed to have more than one name, making them confusing to find. For instance, Bubbling Well Road was now called Nanjing Road. Other major streets were Zhongshan Lu and Giefong Lu. Zhongshan was the name of the birthplace of Sun Yat-sen. "Giefong" means liberation while "Lu" means road. If the weather permitted, meandering through a garden was certainly an option we would enjoy. Sadly, dark clouds were gathering overhead and might bring rain.

Suggesting we might visit Suzhou, Richard was interested that we had been there in 1991. He asked our reactions. We started by telling him our Shanghai guide hired a taxicab to take us and arranged for a guide to meet us once there, but he himself was sorry that he could not accompany us. The journey lasted two and a half hours on a two-lane highway full of potholes in a run-down shamble of asphalt. Cars, tractors, horse-drawn carts, trucks, buses and cyclists all took their share "out of the middle of the road," as Mac described the driving conditions. Pouring rain made sightseeing difficult. Our driver smiled a lot and was very competent with his automobile, but was unable to speak a word of English. That made the trip tedious. We missed knowing the various sights we passed.

The Gardens of Suzhou

Suzhou claims the most beautiful gardens in all of China. During the Cultural Revolution, all the garden societies were shut down. Afterwards, the Chinese Garden Society established a branch in 1978 called the Suzhou Garden Society. Through their activities, they exchange ideas with many countries. With their advice, a replica of a Ming Dynasty (1368-1644) garden is in the Metropolitan Museum of Art in New York today. The Suzhou Garden Society's idea in creating a garden is to have as many perspectives as possible within a confined space and to duplicate, in miniature, scenes from nature not found locally. Thus pavilions, temples and rock sculptures are used, as well as trees and flowers.

We walked through two gardens before the rain drove us inside. One, called Surging Wave Pavilion, has a long history. The guide said it originally was built in the 10th century. During the following centuries, it was destroyed and restored several times. We were taken to such lookouts as Fish Watching Pavilion, Pavilion for Viewing Waters and View of the Mountain Pavilion. The idea of these designs was to give the feeling of rambling through thickly forested hills. We appreciated the very green foliage which shone in the misty rain. The rain also enhanced the ponds with drippings making interesting designs in the water. White geese occasionally swam by.

The other garden we ambled through was called Humble Administrator's Garden, originally built in 1513. This one reflected the simplicity of the Ming's artistic style. We walked on bridges that zigzagged at sharp right angles over ponds. Those angles certainly prevented the evil spirits from following anybody. We passed a lovely stand of thick bamboo. There were verandas to sit on that look out onto water. Our guide named various lookouts, like Pavilion of Fragrant Snow and Pavilion of Expecting Frost, but we found it more interesting just to walk along and enjoy the ambiance. As we came back to the entrance, the rain fell in earnest. To the dismay and great disappointment of our guide and ourselves, we chose abandoning any more garden touring and returned to Shanghai. Another time when the weather was more benign would be nicer for garden sightseeing.

A treasured recollection from Suzhou came while driving out of the city. A farmer was riding his bicycle on the way to market. Strapped to its back side was a large basket. This basket was jammed full of live white geese. When we passed, all the geese swung their necks around in unison to look at us. Their group reaction was very funny. We laughed and laughed and so did our driver.

The route back to Shanghai took us along the Grand Canal. It was full of long lines of cargo barges, all loaded with either agricultural products, wood or coal, or packaged boxes and barrels of various shapes and sizes.

These were products being carried downstream to Shanghai for processing or storage in warehouses. Some barges were large enough to have living accommodations for their crew. We saw laundry hanging from clotheslines and witnessed garbage being dumped into the canal. Mostly the crew sat on the railing, smoking and watching other traffic going by.

Interested in our dissertation, Richard asked if we should plan another trip to Suzhou. We thought not. Then Mac suddenly remembered he had an appointment at the Shanghai Institute of Organic Chemistry the next morning. Would Richard enjoy accompanying him? Richard smiled his consent, delighted to be a part of something completely non-tourist. On this note, we parted until tomorrow.

Thanks to our seat-mate on the flight to Hong Kong, the one who coughed and smoked his way across the Pacific, the next morning I knew I had developed his cold. Just enough time had elapsed for these germs to have incubated. A quiet day in the room might get it quickly under control, and what a treat to be inactive after a week of constant traveling. So Mac, with Richard in tow, went on to the laboratory without me. Around eleven o'clock, Mac telephoned to say Professor Huang, Dr. Su and Dr. Cen at the laboratory had planned a small Chinese meal and since it would be a special meal, they would like me to join them. Could he send Feng back to pick me up? I declined with thanks for their thoughtfulness and became engrossed in several projects. Then Mac surprised me by returning earlier than I had expected. Laughingly he related the "small meal" turned out to be such a feast that he thought he might skip dinner this evening. Meantime, Mac added, Richard had arranged for us to visit the Putuo Children's Palace at four o'clock this afternoon, followed by a visit to a retiree's apartment. Would I like to go? Absolutely!

The Children's Palace in the Putuo district was on the other side of Shanghai from our hotel. This was an after-school educational center, specializing in certain extracurricular activities. Although all children from this district were eligible to attend, only exceptional students were accepted. The school's brochure stated its purpose was to "educate children in the rudimentary knowledge of science, culture and art by way of various activities and to develop them morally, intellectually, physically and aesthetically." The brochure continued, "The school began in 1960. A group of 60 teachers and workers offered more than 20 courses which included folk music, chorus singing, dancing, Chinese painting, calligraphy, computer science, ship- and plane-model making. It was attended by six- to fifteen-year old pupils from primary to middle schools." What an exciting place for the very talented child who wanted to learn an extra skill not taught in his or her regular school. We understood ambitious parents aspired to have their offspring accepted here, so there was competition for entrance. On the grounds, were a basketball court, a children's park, an open-air stage, a table tennis room and a reading room, plus an indoor theater with a large auditorium. These facilities were open every afternoon after the regular school day.

We were escorted around by the deputy director, a woman whose name was Chen Jian. She personally ushered the three of us in and out of several classrooms. In each, the children performed for us with great enthusiasm and energy. What a series of entertainments.

First we visited a quiet, very disciplined classroom where eight older boys and girls were being taught how to dissect a crab. Their dissection trays, with the tools needed, were sitting neatly in front of them. After they completed the dissection, the crab's skeleton would be lacquered and mounted on a piece of wood. The best of these will hang on the bulletin board for viewing. These children were serious and attentive to their older male teacher.

The protocol when leaving a classroom was to clap one's hands and bow. This was the way of saying "thank you" to the entire class. The children, replying with big smiles, waved their hands and shouted "goodbye" in English. Leaving was a cheerful, noisy experience.

Next was a room where little boys and girls were working with crayons. Chinese children did very precise art drawing. Some examples were pinned on their bulletin boards. Today these six- and seven-year olds were being taught to draw in perspective. We leaned over their work tables to see more clearly how they were coming along. A plump, little boy, wearing big, round dark-rimmed glasses that gave him the appearance of a wise old owl, caught my eye. He put his thumbs in his ears and wig-wagged his hands back and forth. I smiled and wig-wagged one of my hands back at him. My mistake. He wig-wagged again and stuck out his tongue, smiling broadly at me. Too much! I shook my head ever so gently and looked away, giggling to myself. Honestly, kids were kids, no matter what their nationality or where they were.

We were directed into a music room. There, a dozen five-year olds were perched on little chairs, each holding an accordion. What a big instrument beside those little bodies! A parent sat behind each child. They came to carry the heavy accordion for their son or daughter. As we took chairs in the front of the room facing the class, the teacher started playing the piano. Each child played along. I thought it was a most complicated tune. Their little fingers scaled up and down the keys with great precision, and they had no trouble pumping the instrument in and out. It was amazing. The male teacher then called on one tiny girl to play a solo. She promptly started. Halfway through the piece, the child on her right gasped audibly. Apparently the player had made a mistake, but we did not notice it. This gasp disturbed the concentration of the tiny girl so she made an even bigger blunder. This time she could not finish playing the piece. Ashamed and embarrassed, she put her head down on the accordion. Without pause, the teacher turned and nodded to another small student on the other side of the room. This little person ran through the piece perfectly. On our way out, we made a point of walking by the first little player. I gently patted her head and said thank you, while her mother smiled at me.

In the next class, we were invited to watch older children who were learning to play on a traditional Chinese stringed instrument called a yang chin. It had 21 or 25 strings and resembled a zither. We had never seen an instrument quite like this one. The children played it by tapping its strings with a bamboo beater whose ends were oval in shape and about the size of a teaspoon. They played with precision and made loud music with the resulting sing-songy sound that we would term "Oriental." It takes time to develop a taste and understanding of this type of music.

We were urged to hurry along. A performance was about to be under way at the theater. This place had a full size stage with cushioned pull-down seats similar to the ones in a movie theater. The room had space for as many as a hundred spectators. Maybe more. We watched an adorable musical play in progress. Four girls, each about eight or nine years old, were the actresses. To begin, each girl held a doll and stood beside the doll's bed. With these props and music, a dance was created. As the scenario unfolded, the dolly was fed, the dolly was kissed and rocked in her "mother's" arms, and then the dolly was put to bed. The acting was very stylized pantomime and performed with exaggerated gestures, but at the same time, it seemed very soft and feminine. Our actresses finished and stood together in a straight line. Waving goodbye, they blew kisses to the audience. We waved back and clapped our hands. Each was made up with rosy cheeks and bright red lipstick. They wore pretty flowered dresses with white tights and black patent leather slippers. They reminded me of our granddaughters when dressing up.

Our last visit was to a class back in the main building. A children's chorus was rehearsing. This chorus had members of all ages. We were told they had performed for the public many times. Not only did they sing with enthusiasm, but their renditions were polished, if not professional. All their voices blended well together. They looked happy while singing. We were treated to two songs. When we waved farewell as we exited, they enthusiastically waved and, in a single voice, boisterously yelled, "goodbye." Nothing musical there!

An interesting philosophy was practiced in this school. The belief was that every child was capable of doing and should be encouraged to do "something" he or she could accomplish with pride, because this skill or accomplishment would give the child self esteem. The "something" could be to sing well or learn a dance, speak another language, or draw, whatever, but it was important for each child to know he or she could do that one thing well. Self esteem was a value the school felt was important and very worthwhile to acquire.

After a farewell cup of tea with the deputy director, we returned to the hotel. We were buoyed up by what we had seen and felt very cheerful. Like magic, my cold seemed to have vanished.

The next morning Feng drove us to another school where we had been invited to meet the children. Called the Chao Yang Kindergarten, it was also in Putuo district of Shanghai. This place was a large People's Government development which housed some 60,000 persons. About 12,000 of these were retirees. We suspected it was a model neighborhood to impress visitors. Later on, we would stop at one of the apartments where a retired couple lived. Unlike our visit yesterday to the Children's Palace, these events today were undoubtedly "staged" for visitors like us. Richard did not tell us this beforehand nor did we question him whether this was true after our visits. Chao Yang, the Kindergarten's school deputy, was a woman in her mid-forties who warmly greeted us when we arrived. She personally escorted us around.

The Kindergarten sat in a wooded garden and had many separate low buildings. The garden was full of shade trees and paved walkways. There was a big jungle gym and a delightful playhouse for the children. As we entered the first classroom, a tiny child, along with several others, ran up to the door to greet us. One reached for our hands to lead us into the room.

We were encouraged by the deputy to mingle with the children, so we let ourselves be pulled to teeny chairs. I was settled on one side of the room with Mac on the other side. Now we were ready to "play." Several little girls brought their dolls over to me. I made each dolly "talk." They giggled and thought this was so funny "because dolls can't talk!" Then I was led to the other side of the room. Here I was "going to the store." Two serious shopkeepers sold me a small, pretend-bottle of milk. One child handed me the bottle, while the other took the money. All these little people were four years old. They were adorable looking and well disciplined. Very alert and knowing exactly what they wanted to do, they radiated a childlike dignity.

We entered an older classroom. These were six-year olds. Boys were making airplanes and tanks of Lego blocks. Girls were creating a large village with small blocks of little houses at a work table. Some wheeled tiny buggies with minuscule baby dolls in them. Girls at another table were drawing pictures of people. "Here, Granny, for you!" two of them said, thrusting their drawings into my hands. Thanking them, I was suddenly "Granny" to them all. "Granny, come! No-no, Granny here." Grabbing my hand, they led me to the window sill to see their growing plants. These were various beans, undoubtedly brought from home. Sitting in small bowls of water, all had sprouted. The children noted the differences between the sprouts. Above them, pasted on the wall, were squares of cardboard with the elementary Chinese characters clearly written. This was a first lesson in learning to read simple characters. We admired all these exhibits. Our guide said we must go so the class could continue its regular schedule. We waved goodbye and received back the now expected goodbye shout.

Outside, under the shade of the leafy trees, groups of boys and girls were playing. Using a child-size soccer ball, the object of the game was to tap one foot on the top of the ball, then jump changing feet and tap the other foot on the top of the ball. The child must bounce back and forth constantly to keep the ball moving. It looked difficult, but these six- and seven-year olds were good balancers. Maybe we were watching budding soccer players. I asked if I might take pictures. That was met with great enthusiasm. Everyone wanted to be photographed. Lining up in all sorts of comical poses, they laughed while I snapped their pictures. They loved being silly.

Several of these children had one or two black teeth. The blackness was a sign of tooth decay. How strange a dental problem should exist when every child we saw was extremely healthy and obviously well cared for. Could it be, knowing these baby teeth would fall out when the secondary ones came in, the dentists chose to ignore them? I wondered if good flossing and brushing habits were being taught.

Each classroom had its own teacher. These women stayed in the background while we visited, and permitted their pupils to be our hosts. We felt welcome to walk around as much as we chose. What a happy way to greet guests from another country!

The ever-courteous cup of tea must be shared with the school's deputy before we departed. This is polite Chinese etiquette. One is supposed to drink tea piping hot. This means putting the cover back on the cup after taking a sip. Otherwise the tea cools off too quickly. Following this custom, we really did not burn our tongues, although we both thought we surely would.

This trip to Shanghai shall always remind us of children. It was a joy to see how loved they were. Everywhere, we saw mothers and fathers alike openly cuddle and fondle them. Since China had a policy of one child for each family to try to stem an ever-growing population, that one child was very precious. (Farmers were the exception and were allowed two children. Should a farm family give birth to a handicapped child, they may have a third offspring.) Grandparents were very much a part of the child's life too. We saw many grandparents, male and female, walking hand in hand with their grandchildren. Smiling at each other and totally absorbed in each other's company, they were oblivious to any one else. We learned a grandparent often picked the child up after school. With both mothers and fathers working, this was an enormous help for the family. We never saw a child wandering around alone. Only once or twice did we ever see any crying. Children are wanted. They are loved, and most of all, they are respected.

Many three- and four-year olds wore straw hats to shield them from the sun. The hat made their faces seem even rounder and their eyes smaller and darker. When perched in a bamboo child's seat on the back of a parent's bicycle, they seemed like little mummies, looking around at the scenery with an absolutely dead-pan expression. Nary a smile did they crack. As the parent pedaled through all the traffic, the child sat calmly, looking side to side, showing no emotion at all. When we happened by and waved, the little one saw us, but never waved back. All these children were dressed in brightly colored Western clothing. We even saw a few little girls wearing fancy organdy dresses with ruffles. Perhaps they were going to a party.

Back in our car, Feng drove to the apartment building where a retired couple lived. It was on the third floor of a large complex of similar buildings. After we climbed three flights of undecorated concrete stairways, there stood the wife, waiting for her guests by the front door. Smiling and nodding, she invited us to come in. She ushered us through the neat, somewhat dark kitchen (no windows, but complete with a gas stove, electric refrigerator, sink, several cupboards, a broom closet plus a small bathroom) into a spacious, sunny room that was a combination bed and living room. The end wall was completely windows with a door opening onto a nice size balcony porch. Here the laundry was hung and belongings were stored. As we entered the living room, her husband stood to greet Richard, Mac and me with handshakes and a big smile. In anticipation of our visit, several folding chairs had been added to the furniture in the room. They were arranged in a small circle. A large upholstered sofa, a double bed with a shiny pink satin bedspread and a table with two chairs furnished the room. We noticed two calendars hanging on opposite walls. One had a picture of Audrey Hepburn and the other showed a young Judy Garland in a dancing costume. They were "very nice" gifts from his former employer, the man told us, with Richard's translation. No family pictures were anywhere. A radio sat on a table near the bed.

We glimpsed another woman as we passed through the kitchen. Apparently, she was a neighbor to help our hostess serve coffee to us. The wife was offering coffee because, Richard translated, "Americans did not like tea," adding, "but she and her husband preferred tea." She excused herself uttering several "ha haws" and "ho ha, ho haws." We realized she was excited and a bit flustered entertaining foreigners, particularly Americans.

Mac and I sat on the sofa, and he initiated a conversation with the husband. He asked the husband about their family. Did they have children? Yes, they had four, and several grandchildren. Mac said we had lots of children too, a total of six, but not so many grandchildren. Mac inquired how old our host was. That is the same age I am, laughed Mac, and the man smiled broadly. They felt an age bond. The man volunteered that he was retired. His company was a tire manufacturer. Mac answered he was retired too, and his company made chemicals.

Usual Questions Chinese Ask Westerners

These were not the kinds of questions we had expected. Usually the Chinese bluntly ask a Westerner about his financial affairs: How much do you earn? How much did your watch cost? Your camera? Does your wife work? How much does she get? How much does your home cost? These would be disconcerting questions to us. In contrast, the Chinese were happy to answer such questions. When they compared their costs to ours, we reminded them that Americans themselves were expected to pay taxes, medical bills, rent/mortgage fees, and school tuition, plus many other expenses. In China, those are services provided by the government.

We were not introduced by name to the couple, nor told his company's title. Neither was our identity revealed. The wife came back with tall glasses of steaming hot coffee laced with milk. I placed mine on the dining room table beside me. Dropping this glass on the floor was the last thing I wanted to happen and it was too hot to hold. They nodded and "ha ha-ed" to let me know this was a fine thing to do, but they were probably wondering why I was not drinking the coffee when it was piping hot.

All of a sudden, the front door burst open and in dashed a sturdy young boy. He was their grandson, the eight-year old son of the couple's daughter. Every noon, he came here to his grandparents for his lunch. This day, he ran through the living room past us to the outside porch. We said "hello" as he raced by. He knew we were the American guests his grandparents were expecting, but he would not speak English with us if he could possibly avoid it. His arrival was a signal for us to depart. We picked up our coffee and drank about half of it. It was too hot for finishing. We nodded to the wife and told her the coffee was delicious and a treat for us. After a sip or two more, we stood. Profusely thanking both husband and wife and her neighbor, we turned, saying goodbye to the grandson who came into the room. He replied in very proper English, "goodbye," then blushed. His pronunciation sounded like he was studying our language. "Very good!" we both told him. He smiled, proud of himself for "talking" to us. Our hostess "ha hawed" us to her front door. Her husband waved, everyone smiled at each other, and we walked out. It was a pleasant visit and just long enough, before we all ran out of conversation.

The Elderly Chinese

The Chinese grant the elderly much reverence due to their deep experience in life, and to the wisdom they have garnered over a lifetime. It is believed old age brings forth wisdom. In the past, the concept of parents being sent away to an institution or an old folks' home to spend their last days profoundly shocked most Chinese. The term "family" in China means an extended one, to include aunts, uncles and cousins as well as sons and daughters. The elderly are to be treasured and housed with their sons and sons' family who care for them until they die.

It is the duty of the sons of the family to be responsible for elderly parents. Bachelorhood is almost unknown because children are considered essential for continuing the family line. That is one reason why a family always hoped for many sons. (Farmers needed them to help with the work.)

Traditionally, much of the wealth of the peasants was measured in the number of children they had. There were reasons for this. Two major ones were the necessity of a son to carry on the proud family name and to worship the ancestors. The second reason was to ensure that in old age an infirm peasant would have ample number of sons to support him.

The Sixtieth Birthday

When a man or woman reached a 60th birthday, it was time for a special celebration. A banquet was held at which every family member made enormous sacrifices to be present because the man or woman being honored had reached such a special plateau. From then on, with every passing year, they acquire even more dignity and status.

In olden days, a man of 60 could carry a staff which was a symbol of longevity within his village. A proverb of the Tang Dynasty (618-907): A man of 70 is a rarity. By the age of 70 he could walk with the aid of his staff, and by the age of 80 he could carry it before the Dragon Throne and not have to kneel before the emperor. Any person reaching 90 was regarded as being sufficiently venerable for the emperor to heed his advice.

Mao said...

When Mao was in power, he had urged families to have many children because he believed this made China strong. Four or five children in a family was not unusual. By the 1970s, however, people were counseled to use birth control to slow down the population growth. By 1980, people were urged to have only one child. Today, anyone who violates this guideline faces heavy fines and sometimes sterilization. This "one child policy" has upset the family structure. Instead of many children helping support elderly parents, now it may be the responsibility of only one child. When that child marries, he has essentially two sets of elderly parents to support. This is a heavy burden. Many elders have worked their entire life for no wages and expect upon retirement that their company or rural collective will care for them with pensions. Sometimes these are not granted. There is no welfare fund from the state since the state has not budgeted for this. Thus they become dependent on the kindness of family and friends for their livelihood. It is a growing and sad situation.

The Cultural Revolution deprived an entire generation of its education and youth. Now these people are the parents who are raising a one-child family. That child is being indulged with every sort of toy, book, educational material and food that the parents were denied. The child is raised without either the traditional Confucian values emphasizing reverence for elders which were always the foundation of China's extended families or the Communist values imposed for three decades under Mao. Those values have no credibility today. Parents worry whether they are raising their child correctly. How a lack of values will affect the children remains to be seen. They may turn out to be a generation of spoiled, self-absorbed tyrants or they may turn out to be very nationalistic, assertive Chinese. It will be interesting to see the results.

We thoroughly enjoyed talking with Richard. His English was excellent in pronunciation and American in style. Not only did he have a large vocabulary which included using our slang and idioms, more important to us was his ability to reason in our language. He loved American history and had developed an interest in our culture as well. He read extensively to increase his knowledge.

Teasing us, Richard quoted what a Chinese man thinks is an ideal life. With a twinkle in his eye, he said, "It was when the man ate Chinese food, lived in an American house, and had a Japanese wife." Knowing we had visited Guangzhou, he informed us the Cantonese would eat anything on four legs except a table. That included snake meat and monkey brains. We asked him what cities he would like to visit in the United States. Without hesitation he said, "New York, Miami and Los Angeles." "Well," said Mac, "you certainly picked the three most dangerous ones in the United States." Richard thought Shanghai was similar to New York whereas Beijing resembled Washington, D.C. He was not sure which Chinese city was like Los Angeles.

We suspected some of the young men and women assigned to us as guides were preparing themselves for jobs with international companies. Guiding was a good way to associate with foreigners and learn how to converse more fluently in English, or perhaps in Japanese or Russian. They became at ease with the foreigners too, which was most important. All were good candidates for any company. All of them had grown up during the Mao years. Whether any were Red Guards we did not know nor did we presume to ask. (Of all of our guides, only one seemed a possibility.) Richard hoped to go to the University of California to study for a MBA degree. Then he would return to Shanghai and work for a company that could use his knowledge of Chinese and English while utilizing his business degree.

Discussing Politics

The average Chinese was leery of discussing political matters with a foreigner and indeed it would be rude of any foreigner to initiate such a discussion. Any outright criticism of this sort could be intensely embarrassing for him. While he may or may not agree with what was being said, he cannot comment. Just to be present with someone sounding off on the Party leaders and/or the government could put a Chinese person in the position to undergo criticism by the Party and/or a re-education session imposed by the government. We took care in what we talked about with our guides. One never knew whether the driver had an understanding of English. We assumed some did and pretended they did not. We noted after each conversation we had with Richard (and this occurred with our other guides too), that he spent time talking with his driver. We tended to think they were analyzing what we had just discussed.

Richard took us to the stock market. Any participation in it was strictly for the Chinese person who must be properly registered before he could buy a share of stock on the exchange. He must show papers stating he was a citizen. We signed in as guests and were invited upstairs where there was an observation room to watch their big board. We expected a scene often described in America as a "Chinese fire drill." Just the opposite was true. The brokerage room below was quiet and well organized, quite unlike the scenes of the New York or Japanese stock exchanges. In fact, it was one of the quieter rooms we ever saw. Both men and women worked there. Each donned a red coat when entering the floor and quietly, without any conversation with co-workers, went to his or her desk to sit in front of a computer. The big board looked different with Chinese characters. We watched those change as stocks were bought or sold. Everything was so orderly.

We asked Richard if we could briefly stop at the Friendship Store. This is a large department store where a bit of everything was sold. Since many foreign items could be purchased there, it was a tourist attraction. Around the courtyard framing its entrance, and on either side of this big store, were a number of little kiosks. One sold paintings. Mac suggested we look in before we went inside the big store. I was skeptical of finding anything interesting. As we walked through the small kiosk, there were so many pictures hanging on the walls and piled in stacks on the floor that it was hard to see anything. Mostly the themes seemed to be Chinese landscapes or various poses of the Household God or scrolls of calligraphy. The sameness of the themes being created over and over by different artists dulled our appreciation of any particular one.

I shook my head and started walking toward the door. Mac followed. Suddenly he stopped. He stooped down and pulled out a painting slightly hidden in another pile. Its theme was entirely unlike the rest we had been seeing. This picture was very modern and stylish. It showed a young girl, probably a prostitute, dressed in pale blue with a perky chartreuse green ornament pinned in her hair. She was staring out of her bedroom window. She had slender hands with bright red nails and lovely etched eyebrows and slanted eyes. A bamboo curtain was rolled up above her head. A crowing rooster fluttered his wings on her right side. The artist had created perspective with interesting angles suggesting depth in the room and putting a balcony in front of the girl to suggest she was looking out on a street below. We studied this picture for a long time. It interested both of us, and we decided to buy it. Richard asked the owner of the shop if it was for sale and at what price. Mac, with Richard's assistance, bargained a bit. Agreeing with the amount, the store owner assured us there was no problem exporting it from China. Since it was not an antique, it was not a national treasure that could not be exported. He removed the painting from its frame, rolled it up and slipped it into a round plastic tube which he twisted to close. (The tube turned out to be as interesting as the picture. Our framer in the United States never saw one like it. It could be twisted to any number of lengths for closing.) Everyone bowed and smiled as we left.

The Little Art Kiosk and the Friendship Store

Three years later we returned here when revisiting Shanghai. Immediately we looked for the little art kiosk. The property had become an office, and no one knew where the art dealer had gone. This was very disappointing. We were looking forward to seeing if we could find another picture to buy from him.

Friendship Store was very much still there. Like one of our large city department stores, it was well organized with efficient, well trained sales persons and is very much an established business in Shanghai. Every sort of product was available, from foreign cosmetics and clothing, to household china and children's toys. Various foreign cameras, video equipment and cutlery attracted attention. We were able to buy Kodak and Fuji camera film in whatever speed and number of frames we desired. That was not possible every place in Shanghai. There were escalators up and down all the floors. It was possible to find household furniture, antique statues, masks, fans, jade jewelry, watercolor paintings, toys for children, chinaware and Western and Chinese clothing. We noted the floors with the Western products attracted mostly American and European tourists.

Before going back to the hotel, we took a walk along The Bund. Its name means an embankment or quay. It was a wide walking street, winding beside the Huangpu River for several blocks. Today there were crowds strolling, chatting or scolding their children in an atmosphere of relaxed normality. Wearing rain gear and carrying umbrellas, we too walked along slowly, meandering among the people and admiring the neoclassic European architecture of the bank and commerce buildings across the avenue and the docks with a variety of ships berthed on the river side. Richard pointed out the commerce houses of Jardine, Matheson & Company and Butterfield Swire Company, both which had long ago established their Chinese headquarters there. There was the Park Hotel, which was constructed in 1934. Then it was Shanghai's tallest building at 24 stories high. Now one had to look around skyscrapers to see it.

We ended our stroll by walking into the Peace Hotel. It was once called the Cathay or Sasson House and was one of the first built in Shanghai by Victor Sasson, a native-born man from an old established family. Most of the interior of the Peace Hotel had been kept in its original form. The Victorian-style wooden dado, Art Deco mirrors, sculptured woodwork and light fixtures by Lyric were all Sasson's original choices. The hotel advertised its suites of Nine Nations, which we did not see. These are Chinese, British, American, French, Russian, Japanese, Italian, German and Indian. Each portrayed the ambiance of their countries in furniture and decor. All faced The Bund and Huangpu River. A famous band called the Old Jazz Band was a sextet of men in their late '60s who played old favorites nightly in the hotel's bar. They were crowd pleasers, especially for Westerners.

Other Buildings Along The Bund

Other prominent structures along The Bund were bank buildings like the Hong Kong and Shanghai Bank Building, as well as the Shanghai Customs House and the Bank of China. They were all built in the early part of this century. Their British architects adopted Neoclassic and Victorian-Gothic styles for these financial and commercial buildings. We were told these will be preserved because foreign tourists like us expect to see them. They were all that was left of what was the International Settlement. During the Mao years most of these buildings along The Bund were taken over by the Communists. A return of these buildings to their original foreign owners was under way. Banque Indosuez, formally the Bank of Indochina, signed an intent with the city government to buy back its old property. Currently, it housed the headquarters of the city police. Wah Kwong Shipping Agency of Hong Kong and Bangkok Bank of Thailand have both signed similar agreements. Two Chinese banks, Bank of China and Changjiang Shipping Corporation, also signed papers to recover their buildings. A total of 37 properties along the Huangpu River, mostly those built in the 1920s and 1930s, were currently for sale. Some of the neoclassic ones that had been closed since the Communist Revolution were in poor condition from misuse after Shanghai fell to the Communist forces.

Richard pointed to the red flag flying from the roof of a huge building. This was the headquarters of the Shanghai Municipal Party Committee.

Headquarters of the Shanghai Municipal Party Committee

The building originally belonged to Hong Kong and Shanghai Bank, until it was confiscated in 1949. Late in 1994, the directors of Hong Kong and Shanghai Banking Corporation met at its former palatial headquarters on The Bund. Shanghai's deputy mayor, Xu Kuangdi, showed them around the imposing building. They found it in very good condition. Rumors were the bank was negotiating to buy it back. There was another rumor that the Shanghai Stock Exchange will bid against Hong Kong & Shanghai Banking Corporation to buy the headquarters since the facilities of the stock exchange were inadequate for the rapidly growing securities market. We would agree the stock market building seemed very small. The two brass lions which once guarded the Hong Kong & Shanghai Bank have suddenly reappeared from wherever they had been hidden. Their names are Stephen and Stitt after two former bank executives who were there when the building was first opened. The lions were originally cast in Britain and were last seen in 1955. (Mac and I laughed when we heard their names. We named two Korean sheep we bought in Japan "Mike and Jerry" after two banker friends of ours.)

West from the Peace Hotel, we strolled down part of a three-mile shopping street on Nanjing Lu which aspired to be Shanghai's Fifth Avenue. More than 350 shops and sidewalk stalls were here. It was a popular place to buy shoes, clothing, gifts and the like. When Nike products were introduced in a store in early 1993, people bought $6,000 worth of shoes by lunchtime. As we strolled along, we noted Ray-Ban sunglasses on various adults, as well as copies of Louis Vuitton handbags being toted by many women. We were told that one warm Sunday evening last August no fewer than a million and a half people strolled down this street to enjoy window shopping. We (particularly me) could appreciate what fun that must have been. There was enough merchandise there to dazzle everyone.

Richard took us for a stroll through the Yu Yuan Garden. Built during the 16th century by a high Ming official, it was a garden and residence for his mother. It was made up of rock formations, pavilions, towers and lotus ponds. The zigzag Bridge of Nine Turnings was one of Shanghai's best known sights. Walking on it, one crossed a man-made lake to Huxingtang, a beautiful little pavilion that was a classic Chinese-style tea house—a lovely sight. This garden looked like what one visualized traditional China surroundings might have been in the past. Its style was very Oriental. Today, it lost much of its tranquility because there were so many people visiting. Everywhere someone was walking or watching colorful carp swimming in the pool or mediating or in some corner performing stylized exercises of assumed poses in very definite positions. We pushed our way past everybody and walked over the bridge to peek inside the tea house. Then we left. One should come here early in the morning to appreciate its beauty, before crowds gather.

On our way back to the hotel, Richard suddenly turned and asked if we might like to stop at the antique street called Dongtai Lu, located off Xizang Nanlu. He said the entire street had stalls lining both sides. Local merchants offered a variety of items. Maybe we might find a valuable antique. It sounded like fun. Feng made a few quick turns, and we got out on a narrow walking street. Indeed, there were dozens of stalls crammed with bits of everything one could imagine. We saw porcelain teapots in many colors and sizes, wood carvings, brassware, badges with Mao's smiling face, small statues of animals, gods, women, some smiling statues of a fat Mao, jade, bracelets and rings as well as bead necklaces and hair ornaments, various single buttons (what did one do with an odd button?), old Chinese coins that had holes in their center, blue and white ceramic pieces (definitely not Ming), opium pipes, enough of Mao's Little Red Book to supply several classrooms, baskets in many shapes and sizes, plus all sorts of old clothes. What a mass of stuff. I suppose if anyone desired something not seen, it could be found in some nook or cranny.

An old man walking with a staff followed us down the street. When we turned around to retrace our steps, he continued following. I stopped at one booth to inspect some Mao icons, and he approached me. "I speak good English-English," he said proudly. Then, "I lived all my life here in Shanghai." He was a slight, almost skinny person, perhaps five foot eight, using a wooden staff to assist his walking. As he smiled at me in a friendly way, I could see he was almost toothless. A small crowd gathered around us, interested in this conversation between one of theirs and the foreign lady with yellow hair. "How did you learn to speak such good English?" I asked. His pronunciation was very British. "I lived with the English," he replied. "Yes, I can hear that you did," I answered. He chuckled and repeated our conversation to our audience in Chinese. They all nodded and smiled at me. I started walking from the kiosk toward the direction where our car was parked. "Goodbye!" the old man shouted. "'Bye!" I shouted back. The even larger crowd smiled as I departed.

In 1995, on a new visit to Shanghai, we stayed at the Garden Hotel at 58 Maoming Nan-Qu. The original structure was built by French architects in 1926, to be used as a spa. When the present Garden Hotel was designed, it incorporated as a part of its architecture much of the original French building. Today it is a handsome five-star hotel managed by the Okura chain of Tokyo. In the 1920s, there were more than twenty grass tennis courts in the garden. Today the garden was lovely, but strictly used for strolling and walking around a large pool where Mao swam on warm mornings.

History of the Garden Hotel

Originally known as "The Club," it was used by the U.S. Army for a time. In 1939, at their request, an indoor swimming pool was installed. When Mao Zedong came to power in 1949, The Club was renamed "The People's Cultural Palace" and the gardens became a sports field. Mao had trees planted and created a garden where he could go for leisurely strolls. He also had balconies built on both wings with a roof over them so he could enjoy walking even on rainy days. These were damaged over time and finally removed. They were rebuilt into verandas.

Madame Mao

During the Cultural Revolution, the People's Cultural Palace became the residence of Jiang Ch'in, Madame Mao Zedong. Born in Shandong Province to a violent-tempered merchant father and a mother who combined domestic service with prostitution, she studied music and drama, later becoming an actress. She moved to Shanghai in 1933 and began a stage and screen career. Through these media, she met Mao and became his fourth wife in 1938 after he was divorced. The Party agreed to this marriage on the condition that she never appear publicly as Mao's wife and that she refrain from politics.

She, however, had other ideas and came to political prominence during the Cultural Revolution. Eventually rising to the highest ranks within the party hierarchy, she formed a Shanghai faction of four with Zhang Chunqiao, Wang Hongwen and Yao Wenyuan. They would become known later as the "Gang of Four." Mao lashed out at Jiang for this and politically separated himself from her.

In 1966, to revive his deteriorating Cause, Mao called upon the youth of the country to rise and rebel. All schools and universities were closed as Mao tried to restart China anew. A firm advocate of radical ideologies, Madame Mao enthusiastically endorsed Mao's Cause by fomenting revolt. Turning to the country's youth, whom she found to be pure idealists, she told the young people to rebel and become Red Guards. The pressure to do as one's forefathers had done was very much a part of Chinese culture, but it strangled young people with ideas. When Madame Mao encouraged these juveniles to rise up and strike down all remembrances of the past, there was a constituency ready to do as she asked.

Guided by the fervent enthusiasm of Madame Mao, the students were instructed to roam the land and wipe out the "Old Fours," that is, Old Ideas, Old Culture, Old Customs and Old Habits. The students, called Red Guards, set about cleansing the nation with fiery revolutionary enthusiasm. They denounced their parents and relatives, an unheard of act against the family. They lopped heads off of ancient statues, destroyed temples, burned books and schools alike. Businessmen and teachers, especially university professors, were in disgrace. They attacked their teachers, sometimes forcing them to kneel on broken glass to confess their errors or other times making the victim assume the "jet airplane" position for hours at a time. This latter punishment was frequently used at the denunciation meetings held weekly all over the country. Two students would grip the arms of a victim, twist them around behind his back, pushing up so fiercely that often the arms were dislocated. The person was made to remain like that for hours at a time or until he fainted.

It is ironic that while urging the Red Guards on to even more excesses, Madame Mao was living in a sumptuous private apartment at the People's Cultural Palace. Contrary to her left-wing remarks and denunciations of the arts, she indulged herself in luxuries. She liked to wear smart clothes and watch films forbidden to others. She had delicacies flown in from various parts of China for her dinner parties. Although a lover of the performing arts, it is a fact that she brought about the death of hundreds of artists.

Trying to understand the contradictions of Jiang Ch'in is to comprehend the philosophy of the Cultural Revolution. After Mao's death, Deng Xiaoping had her expelled from the party. In 1981, as the leader of the Gang of Four, she was condemned to death for "counter-revolutionary crimes" of attempting armed rebellion and torturing politicians during the Cultural Revolution. The death sentence was later reduced to life imprisonment in 1983. She committed suicide in 1991.

As we entered the Garden Hotel's lobby, we noted the understated Art Deco of the building. The design details around the windows with exquisite woodworking was especially beautiful. There were interesting chandeliers hanging from the ceilings. Specimen plants in huge black-glazed pots were assembled around various alcoves in the lobby. The ambiance was one of quiet elegance. Apparently much frustration went into the renovation, but perseverance was rewarded, for the occupancy rate was now well over 90 percent. Visiting dignitaries often resided here when coming to Shanghai. We understood German Chancellor Helmut Kohl and the French Minister Edouard Balladur had been guests.

Rebuilding the Garden Hotel

Michio Kurihara, a director of the Japanese Nomura China Investment Company, was responsible for completing the building project. When the hotel agreement was signed in 1984 by the Jin Jiang Group and a subsidiary of Japan's Nomura

Securities, the document required 45 chops to make it official. Mr. Kurihara was quoted as saying, "Myself, I did not know the system or how strict the bureaucracy was. Every day, I took stomach medicine."

This was understandable, for the early years were troubled ones. The local branch of the construction bureau suggested that Ohbayashi, a Japanese company, be hired to build the hotel, using foreign wage scales for its crews. When local laborers were being paid around $20 U.S. a month, the Japanese offered to pay $18 U.S. per hour. They negotiated to reduce this to $12 or $15 U.S. per day, which was still costly. The municipality urged them to hire a local Chinese company rather than a Japanese contractor to reduce costs. They used both.

To fill their work force and use local labor, the Japanese recruited some 2,000 inexperienced workers from the countryside to do the construction work. Those directing them were also new to their tasks. The troubles began. Walls would go up, but since the electric and water pipes had not been laid, the walls would have to be torn down. Theft was so rampant that 300 security guards had to be employed, but they stole too. The project took five years to finish. It was three years and $28 million U.S. over budget.

Difficulties did not end with the construction. The hotel opened in 1989 under the management of the Tokyo-based Okura Group. The Shanghai government allocated several hundred Chinese mid-school graduates as employees. These recruits slept through training sessions until the hotel began paying 10 RMB (the native coinage which is known as "People's Money" and is denominated into yuan and fen) for each phrase learned in English or Japanese. Half remained unemployable, mostly because of theft, and were dismissed. For being let go, they and their families threatened to harm the hotel and its staff. The hotel had to ask the government to provide protection for its staff. Eventually, the then-mayor Zhu Rongji was able to ease the situation.

There were Cultural Revolution problems evident among the staff when the hotel finally opened. Manager Kurihara said nobody smiled, and nobody greeted guests. Kurihara told them, "Your smile brings guests who pay your salary, so you should smile." The Chinese cooks had to be replaced by Hong Kong chefs because the locals were reluctant to train apprentices. In China's fiercely competitive environment, information is an advantage, so why share it? This was the Chinese chefs' mindset.

The hardest task of all was to train the local staff to treat their Chinese guests well. They thought, "Who are they to be here?" If the Chinese was married to a Westerner or a Japanese, they were treated one way when with their spouse and another when they were alone. "If there was a problem with someone, it was you against one billion Chinese," said Manager Kurihara. When the hotel's pool was not opened to all of Shanghai's 14 million residents, headlines in the newspaper implied this decision was racist and exploitative.

We were pleased these problems finally settled down so the hotel could open for guests and operate.

Our one evening in their handsome Chinese dining room was memorable. We were escorted to a quiet corner which was intimate and comfortable. Reading the handcrafted menu, we chose a simple dinner with three dishes including Cashew-nut (their spelling) Chicken, Sautéed Vegetable, and Black Mushroom Soup. We also requested steamed rice. Our waitress did not serve us the usual complimentary tea, but offered instead a wine list. On the table were two small serving dishes, one filled with sugared walnuts and the other holding tiny pickled onions. The formal place setting was arranged on a starched white damask tablecloth in precise composition. A small gold-rimmed octagonal service plate held a smaller, white, delicate porcelain plate, while a small round dish sat beside them. Chopsticks were placed next to a large serving spoon laid on a silver holder. We ordered wine and were brought delicate stemmed goblets for sipping it.

As we waited for dinner to be served, we nibbled on the sugared walnuts and gazed around. The room was large, with enough space between the tables to give each party privacy. We were in a non-smoking section. Chinese men who smoked tended to do so excessively. We never saw Chinese women smoking in a public room such as this.

The food came all at once. There was a small oval platter of Cashew-nut Chicken. The pieces were cut very small and easy to handle. The Sautéed Vegetable was pieces of green iceberg lettuce carefully folded in a bundle and gently cooked to keep their color. The soup was a clear broth with large whole black mushrooms floating in it. Steamed rice was presented in a porcelain bowl. We were expected to serve ourselves. We began by sampling the chicken. Savoring this morsel, we tasted a bit of the sauteed lettuce. Both were delicious. The lettuce was particularly delicate in flavor. Its lovely green color was refreshing to the eye. We sipped the soup with porcelain spoons from small bowls. A mushroom floated in each bowl. The flavor of the broth was rich and delicious, but the mushroom was slippery and difficult to hold with chopsticks. Patience always was a virtue when using them. One needed to be relaxed and never in a hurry. When we completed our first serving, the waitress removed the service plate and our soiled dishes. She placed a clean plate in front of each of us. We might proceed with a second helping if we wished. This was leisurely dining at its best.

We decided to order a small dessert. Mac's favorite was on the menu. It is called Sago, a tapioca pudding served with coconut milk. I chose a bland almond pudding garnished with tiny pieces of various fresh fruits. Both desserts were perfect endings to a lovely meal.

Mid-Autumn Festival

A nice Chinese custom under way was The Mid-Autumn Festival. It is celebrated during September which is the eighth Lunar Month in the Chinese calendar. At this time, special wishes are granted by the Moon Lady, Chang E, who long ago flew up to the moon after drinking her husband's magic potion. She is symbolized by a rabbit which gave her everlasting life. Families and friends gather together from far and wide to enjoy festivities and to share mooncakes made in many designs and flavors. Mac observed the boxes of mooncakes we saw for sale on various bakery shelves and said they did not look appetizing to him, but he would be glad to buy one for me. I answered, "Maybe next Mid-Autumn Festival."

In 1995, a new Shanghai was under development in Pudong. We were eager to go there and see what was happening. On our way, we passed over a perfectly beautiful expansion bridge called Nan Pu (South River Bridge). It was designed by a Chinese engineer who had an eye for a simple but dramatic structure to span the river. Built with a slender, gently rising span of concrete, it was held up by a series of unadorned metal rods on either side. These extended in a graceful pattern up to the center and ran down the opposite side. There were two huge, austere concrete, rectangular towers on each side of the bridge's center. Three lanes of traffic could pass on either side. When driving across, one had the feeling of lightly rising on a cloud instead of plodding along on another piece of concrete highway. I thought I would go back to Shanghai just to see it again.

Pudong is a new community being built on what was once farmland. Its boundary starts after coming off Nu Pu bridge. It is a mammoth development. As a matter of fact, one fifth of the world's construction equipment was now being used to work there, as well as in the city of Shanghai. Pudong was challenging Hong Kong to be the future's most modern Chinese city. We immediately saw giant skyscrapers under construction. Richard said they would house offices of banks and newspapers, many of them joint ventures with foreigners. Warehouses and factories in nearby industrial areas were also being erected. Shopping streets, modern docks and large residential districts were already planned. All this supported jobs for thousands of workers. The farmers who were on this land producing crops gave it up after negotiating good contracts for themselves. While the local authorities were concerned about shortages of items like electrical power, foreign residents watched what was happening and believed now was the time to "put a toe" in China.

The most imposing structure in all of Pudong was called the Shanghai Oriental Pearl TV and Radio Tower. It dominated the entire area. Built with shiny red glass and grey concrete, it was constructed of three cylinders, each nine meters in size. These were supported by three tilted standings, seven meters in diameter, each positioned at an angle of 60 degrees. All these soared straight up-wards. There were eleven steel spheres in various sizes inscribed in the body of the Tower. It was one enormous edifice.

Tower Data

Four hundred sixty eight meters high, the Tower was the highest one in Asia. It made the Eiffel Tower in Paris look short. The construction of the Oriental Pearl TV and Radio Tower in Shanghai started in 1991 and was completed in 1993. In May 1994, the 118-meter high antenna pole was successfully connected with the tower body in the first attempt. This was no small trick of engineering. The antenna had multiple uses and accommodated ten radio frequencies and nine TV stations which serviced the whole area of Shanghai. This was quite a boon for Shanghai's current 13 million population.

Future Plans

Future plans call for the spheres to be developed into hotel suites, with the top sphere serving as a special meeting room which could be rented out for company conferences of 25 to 30 people. Since only one elevator was utilized to go up that high, it would be easy to monitor who went in and out. The Tower management thought the hotel idea was a good one. For a few hundred dollars a night, visitors would be able to rent a room with a magnificent view of Shanghai looking out over the Huangpu River.

Tallest Towers

Tallest towers are a source of national pride and fascination for tourists. First to be built was the Eiffel Tower in Paris, standing at 320 meters. This was followed by the Chrysler Building in New York. Then came the Empire State Building and the World Trade Center, also in New York. Later came the Sears Building in Chicago, higher than all these, but outdistanced by the Trade Building in Kuala Lumpur at 1,084 feet. None of these are as tall as the Canadian National Tower in Toronto which stands at 1,822 feet.

Ladies must deposit their purses and parcels with a woman in a security booth before being admitted inside the tower. Gentlemen must leave their briefcases and cameras. Not wanting to deposit my billfold, passport and camera there, I stuffed these into various pockets, then handed my depleted purse to the attendant. We stood in line with many others, waiting our turn to enter one of the six high-speed elevators for a ride to the outdoor deck on the largest sphere. We and 27 others were literally counted on board by a young woman guide, smartly dressed in a severely tailored navy blue suit. Exactly 30 persons, not 29 or 31, were allowed on each elevator at a time. Our elevator ran upward at the speed of seven meters per second and covered the distance from the bottom of the tower to the sphere in 40 seconds. There was an even faster high-speed elevator, a double decker accommodating 50 people which ran at a speed of four meters per second. It was the only one of its kind in the country. This information we learned from Richard when we got out on the deck. It had been broadcast via loud speaker in Chinese inside the elevator during our fast ride. Viewing Shanghai while walking around a full 360 degrees on the platform was an awesome experience. Richard pointed out The Bund and various buildings we had driven past, plus the many bridges crossing the rivers. The harbor was full of ships. Many were being reloaded at docks; others were navigating up- or downstream. Shanghai looked impressively modern.

Back downstairs in the huge entrance lobby, we enjoyed walking around its circle. There were kiosks for snacks and souvenirs as well as a few small sitting rooms for resting. Huge black and white photographs of world cities lined the back walls. We recognized Niagara Falls, the cities of New York, Moscow, Sydney, Venice, Hong Kong and Guilin, and The Great Wall of China.

We were intrigued with the impressive engineering that went into designing and creating Shanghai's impressive tower. As we retrieved our things from security and walked toward our car, we kept turning back for another look at it. A truly magnificent sight.

As we drove further on into Pudong, we passed a group of large billboards on either side of the road. Each one advertised some product a manufacturer produced that was being used in the construction of buildings in Pudong. We recognized many familiar company names, but nearly jumped out of the car when we saw a billboard with the name Dow Corning on it. This company was a joint venture of the parent one, The Dow Chemical Company, where Mac worked for many years. We knew it well. We were so excited that we both yelled for Feng to stop the car so we could photograph the billboard. Richard calmly told us no one was allowed to stop on this road, but Feng would go around the block and return here. "Please have camera ready," he said, adding, "Remember Feng cannot stop the car here." So we went around what seemed like an agonizingly long block. Mac was poised with our camera by an open window. As we approached the sign, Feng slowed down only slightly, and Mac snapped a couple of pictures. How welcoming it was for us to see Dow Corning's billboard with its advertising written in English and Chinese characters among many other foreign manufacturers.

This sightseeing day in Pudong was a nice ending for our stay in Shanghai.

We promised Richard and Feng a return visit one day in the not too distant future. Who knows what wonders the people in Shanghai will have wrought by then.

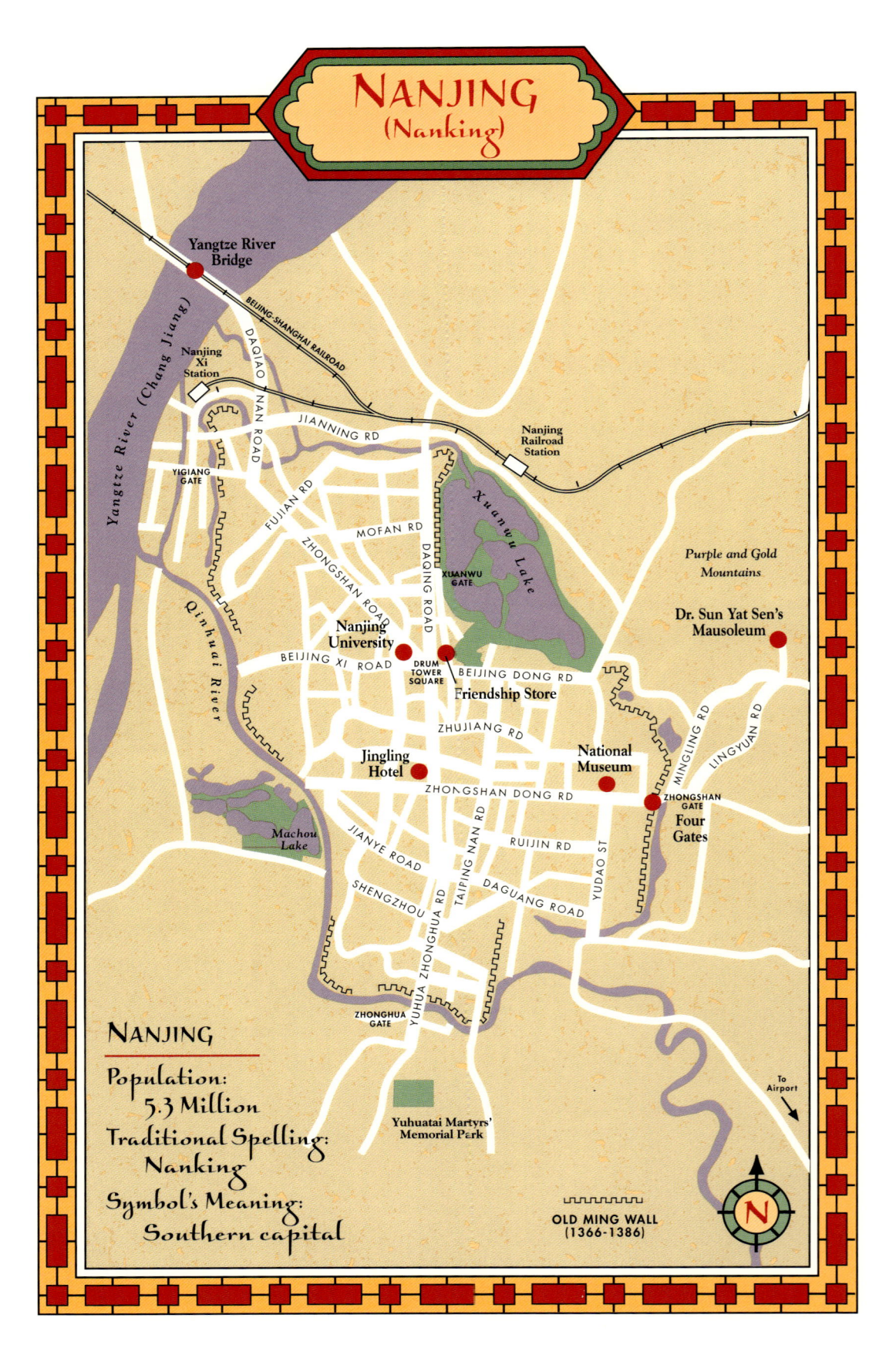

NANJING (Nanking)

NANJING
Population: 5.3 Million
Traditional Spelling: Nanking
Symbol's Meaning: Southern capital

chapter 7

南 NANJING (Nanking)

In a fax from Nanjing, China dated May 31, 1993 and sent to our son, Mike Whiting, in the United States, Mac wrote the following:

"I am sitting in our room on the 24th floor of the Jingling Hotel in Nanjing looking out over the sometime capital of China. It is now the capital of Jiangsu Province. It is graced by sycamore trees which keep the clean and busy streets very pleasant. This morning, we visited the Yangtze River Bridge. Each day, 25,000 vehicles and 180 trains cross over the one mile wide by 35 foot deep river. Three days from now, we will start a four day boat trip from Wuhan to Chongqing on the same river.

"Nanjing is not one of the largest Chinese cities, only seven million people, mostly on bicycles. It is booming. Hundreds of shiny new buildings are going up. The people are active and aggressive and smart. Forty eight universities reside here, mostly vocational like Northwood University. They badly need some pollution controls."

"In the country, they still farm mostly by manual methods. Each farmer owns half an acre, more or less. Every plot is irrigated by a centuries-old water system of water management that seems to serve every acre of arable land.

"Needless to say, we are learning like crazy and loving every minute of it. Today we also visited the 1912 offices of Sun Yat-sen, founder of the Republic of China; and the National Museum, which displays the progress of civilization here over the last 5,000 years by tracing the development of ceramics, metallurgy, weapons, fabrics and other artifacts." End of fax.

We rode "soft-seat" in the upper section of the train from Shanghai to Nanjing, a four and a half hour trip.

"Soft-Seat," "Hard-Seat"

"Soft-seat" literally meant a "cushioned" seat. They were only found in the first-class section of the train. People who rode soft-seat were generally foreigners, and no one who rode in this section conversed with strangers. Only backpacking youngsters went "hard-seat" which was the way all the common people traveled. Should a foreigner elect to ride hard-seat, people will make room for him with amusement. Then, perhaps, someone with a little knowledge of English will come forward. Questions begin: "Where are you from? Where are you going? What do you think of China? Why is a rich foreigner like you in hard-seat?" All this would be done in a most friendly way. The Chinese are curious about the foreigner and are genuinely interested in what he has to say.

The National Railway Administration

With more than 55,000 kilometers of railroad track in China, every province in the nation is reachable. The National Railway Administration is a vital cornerstone of the Chinese economy. It is one of the most efficient organizations in the country, but wise counseling says dining cars should be avoided as the food served may be contaminated. Bringing one's own food is customary and safer.

The only stop on our trip was at a small place called Wuan for a total of eight minutes. Our fellow seatmates, who sat directly across from us, got off to smoke as there was no smoking allowed in our section of the train. After reboarding, the man opposite me, who had been talking non-stop to his seatmate, pulled out several neatly wrapped plastic bags from a canvas tote. He handed one parcel to his friend and then proceeded to open his own. I was fascinated as to what this might contain. From several paper wrappings came something done up in a banana leaf and tied with raffia string. As he untied the string and peeled away the leaf, I saw a moist, seed-like meatloaf concoction. He took a big bite. "Hmmm," he said, satisfied and chewing loudly. It did look good. His friend ate quietly and finished his without comment. I looked out the window, pretending not to watch, while Mac read a newspaper. The woman across the aisle had her shoes off. She was curled up in her seat with one leg crisscrossed over the other. She wiggled her bare toes as she paged through a fashion magazine similar to *Vogue*.

Once we reached Nanjing, we waited for the other passengers to get out. An empty car gave us more space for coping with all the suitcases. We had developed a system for taking luggage off trains. First, we both carried the smaller pieces out onto the platform. Mac stationed me there while he went back to lug the two bigger cases off. This worked very satisfactorily. The only problem arose when someone or somebodies wanted to help. The "helping hand" upset Mac's balance, making it hard to carry either bag. He had tried a number of times to diplomatically ask for no assistance. However, Chinese men were very intent on being of service. More than once Mac lost his temper saying, "No, thank you, but NO!" The reverse side of this was when we left a city. Then our guide fended off the unnecessary helpful advances, and we encountered no problems.

The suitcases sat on the platform, while we looked around to see if anybody was meeting us. A tall, skinny young man wandered about. Hesitantly, he approached. Asking if we might be looking for him, he presented an identification card to Mac which said he was from the China Travel Agency. He never finished the sentence. Mac was annoyed. He thought the agency forgot to send someone. He asked the young man none too pleasantly where he had been. Would he please help with the bags? Then, everything happened at once. We were whisked out of the terminal and into the car, while all the luggage was stuffed into its trunk. Without further ado, we headed in the direction of the Jingling Hotel.

His name was Stretch, and he was over six feet tall. American friends dubbed him "Stretch" because he was unusually tall for a Chinese man. He used the name with obvious pride. Stretch was really Chen Keneng. Since the Chinese write their family name before their given name, we were happy he wanted us to call him "Stretch" and not "Keneng." Pronouncing "Keneng" was not easy. He would not like us to call him Mr. Chen. That was too formal.

As we began the drive, Stretch talked about Nanjing. He told us the city had a population of seven million, its longitude was 118° E and latitude 32° N, and today's current temperature was 60 degrees. With these basics out of the way, he launched into the geography of Nanjing, telling us it lay on the southern bank of the Yangtze River, nestled to the east around a curve of the foothills of the Purple and Gold Mountains. This was too much to cope with right now. We were groggy from the train trip and could not concentrate on a long dissertation. We asked to postpone further discussions until tomorrow. "Fine, okay," he said, "I just want you to understand where you are."

The Jingling Hotel was large and extremely busy. There were businessmen and groups of tourists standing, sitting and lounging all around the lobby. Stretch led us to a desk which had a placard reading "Special Services." Here, the manager discussed our preference in accommodations and assured us he had these rooms available. When we actually saw the layout, our eyes drank in a panoramic view of the entire city and surrounding countryside. We were on the 24th floor and could see clearly for miles. What a huge amount of construction! There was scaffolding on almost every building. Nanjing was growing by leaps and bounds. We noted the scaffolding abutting a nearby skyscraper. It was bamboo, not the steel we use for framing. Although those poles looked flimsy and unstable to our eye, construction workers were walking inside this framework. Obviously it held their weight securely. Still, it made us nervous to watch.

The Jingling Hotel had three restaurants—all on the second floor and adjacent to each other. One called the Dynasty Grill, a Western-style place, was where we ate our first evening meal in Nanjing. The food tasted minimally good. The main chef was busy entertaining a group of Italian businessmen. They were enjoying a delicious spaghetti dinner which was not offered on the menu. That food made us hungry. Next door the Bamboo Villa restaurant served Chinese fast food. It was plainly decorated and had many long tables with white tablecloths. When we ate here, we sat near the back of the room with many other Chinese families to enjoy a dinner of sautéed beef, a vegetable dish with bean curd and mushrooms, shredded chicken soup and steamed rice. Sugared walnuts were the hors d'oeuvres. They were delicious and so was this entire dinner. The Plum Garden was the hotel's speciality dining room, serving Huaiyang and Cantonese food. We saved it for our last night in Nanjing. There were many individual tables and the decor was very Chinese, with lanterns and bamboo plants everywhere. That night we enjoyed shredded pork with green pepper, fresh green beans with fresh garlic, duck soup with spinach, steamed rice, and, after a long protracted discussion, some sugared walnuts. None of the waitresses here, who were a different crew from the Bamboo Villa restaurant next door, grasped what we were ordering when we asked for "sugared walnuts." Eventually one smart girl guessed we meant "walnuts"—"sugared walnuts?" "That's it!" we exclaimed. "Oh," she answered, "the Chinese word for walnut is 'yao guo'." When the dish of nuts was served, every waitress in the entire dining room came to our table for its presentation. The girls were elated that they had interpreted our request correctly. Thanking them profusely, we proceeded to eat every nut in the dish. They were very good.

The next morning, at our stated meeting time, Stretch was nowhere to be seen in the packed lobby. Easy as he should be to spot in a crowd because he was so tall, he simply was not present. There was a lot of traffic jammed around the front entrance. We suspected his car was caught up in this so we stood outside watching for him. Soon, sticking up above the roof of a car, we saw a black umbrella being waved wildly back and forth. That was Stretch, signaling us to come down to the car. We greeted him happily and said hello to our driver who was a young woman.

As we left the driveway, he began a dissertation. First, he announced the day and its date. Second, he told us the month, and third, he revealed the temperature in both Centigrade and Fahrenheit. Then he reported other current world news happenings he thought pertinent and of interest. We looked at each other and almost giggled out loud. It did not matter whether we were interested in hearing any of this or not. It was his way of taking care of the trivial details he deemed we should know when we first met.

He freely volunteered information about himself. He was 37 years old. He had traveled extensively throughout California. He knew Los Angeles, San Mateo, San Francisco, Sacramento and once visited Las Vegas. He had one daughter who was 11 years old by the Chinese calendar. She loved to read, as he did. We assumed he had a wife, but he never mentioned her in his dissertation. He believed he would be sent to the United States to work for his company. Asked where, he said, "probably New York." He and Mac drifted into a discussion about the telephone system in Nanjing. It cost $5,000 to put telephone service in a private home. The portable cellular phones, which were popular to own, cost a small fortune. Mac suggested one day the service would be run by fiber optics. That technology interested Stretch, as China had not developed this system.

Stretch suggested we drive out to the Yangtze River Bridge first, then to the old Ming wall and finally to the Fort of Nanjing. If there was still time, we would visit the National Museum. We thought this was an ambitious itinerary for one day, but did want to see all of these places during our visit. The bridge was the first logical stop, since its distance was the furthest away from the wall and the museum. It would take time to reach it, with the amount of traffic on the road.

The bridge was a gigantic structure of steel girders, rising majestically over the Yangtze River. We parked in a space under it and walked up to an observation platform. Here we could watch the trains and automobiles driving across, as well as river boats and barges steaming down river under it. Standing there, one had the feeling of the enormous strength of this structure. It was so huge that it seemed out of scale with the surrounding land and the river. We asked if we might drive over it. Stretch said we could go part way. Why not the entire way he did not explain. There was a gradual grade going up onto the bridge which made a lovely approach to the main crossing road. That grade also provided the space for the railroads on the deck below. A monument which was a composition of three male laborers marked the entrance onto the bridge. These towering figures represented the workers who built the bridge. We wondered if they were copied from a Russian design, as they closely resembled ones we saw in Budapest, Hungary which were designed by a Russian sculptor. Stretch said the bridge was under construction between 1960 and 1968, and finally completed in 1969. It was designed and built without any foreign aid, a source of local pride.

Commercially, this was an important bridge, as it was currently the nearest one to the mouth of the Yangtze River. Formerly, commerce hauled by land from north to south had to go inland at Nanjing and then followed the coastline to continue on. Before this bridge was completed, the other bridge crossing the Yangtze River was at Wuhan, west of here. That was the only river crossing for products to get from the north to the south. Coal in Manchuria heading to Guangzhou or Shanghai or any other coastal town was carried entirely by inland rail from Wuhan. Now it could be delivered here, be carried by rail across this bridge, then sent down to Guangzhou and Shanghai, making the delivery much quicker.

When we returned to our automobile, serious lecturing began. Stretch talked about the Nanjing wall and the fort where we now headed. "Two hundred thousand people worked 20 years building Nanjing, or Southern Capital, as it also was known," he said. "Included in the construction was a beautiful palace and the massive city wall, you know. That work used almost every building material and involved all the construction workers in southeastern China, right down to our border with Vietnam. All other construction was stopped. Every brick in the wall was handmade, with an inscription of the chop of its maker, plus the date of its manufacture. If a brick was defective, the identified maker lost his head. It was that simple and that important." He added, "The wall is 34 kilometers in length." Stretch paused, looking at us to see whether we were concentrating on what he was saying, then, "The wall has 13 gates. It is 21 meters high and in some places 40 meters high. It is almost seven meters thick."

He continued as we drove along. "The wall was built from 1366 to 1386, the first years of the Ming Dynasty. It provided workers jobs for over 20 years. As I said, all other ceramic production ceased while it was being built. There are 21 vaulted halls within its walls. In those halls 3,000 soldiers were housed. Their method of defense was to trap the enemy between the walls and stone them to death!" I gasped. "That wasn't very nice, Stretch. Did it work?" "Oh, yes," he replied, then paused. "It was in 1937 that the very first hostile penetration of this wall occurred. The Japanese came with gunboats, aircraft and tanks, and they completely destroyed the Forbidden City of Nanjing."

"Rape of Nanjing"

It was a fact that the Japanese troops massacred an estimated 300,000 people. It has been called the "Rape of Nanjing" and was considered the single worst atrocity committed during the Japanese occupation of China, which lasted from 1931 to 1945. The massacre occurred over a six-week period in November and December 1937, after the Japanese military captured Nanjing, then the national capital.

Stretch continued. "Their object was to colonize China for Japan by taking the coal and iron ore to Japan for manufacturing there. This was known as the Sino-Japanese War. Chiang Kai-shek had made Nanjing his capital, but moved it to Chongqing when threatened by this Japanese invasion. The city was finally liberated from political struggles by the Communists in April of 1949. We are proud of how modernized Nanjing has become. You know we hold international trade fairs and technical conferences here." Stretch concluded his capsule of history.

Stretch loved to quote statistics. When we strayed from the subject at hand, he reminded us that unlike the United States, whose population is 250 million people, China's population is 1.4 billion persons. "That's billion, not million." he said with a sigh. We drove on, quietly absorbing this fact.

"Here we are," said Stretch, as we came to a stop. "We are at the old fort which is a part of the city wall of Nanjing. Now we're going to see the four gates. Let's get out of the car." We saw the fort was a handsome, thick-walled stone structure. One could picture soldiers standing above, guarding its walls, probably dressed in some kind of metal armor. Stretch pointed. "This entrance is important because it has gates. See them? There they are. Count them: One, two, three, four. Now we need to see them from above." We started climbing the steps, which were slippery because it was misting. There was no guard rail on either side. Each tread was high and built from a single slab of stone. Their wetness, plus no protective rails, made the climbing difficult. The steps went up and up and up in a steep ascent. They looked formal and austere in appearance, which was appropriate in a fort. But so many steps! The two men with their long legs reached the top much before I did. "There they are. Four gates," exclaimed Stretch. "Count them: one, two, three, four. This is an important entrance because there are four gates." A pause. "Now we have seen the four gates, we'll go down. Let's go."

We shall never forget Stretch's emphasis of "four gates." What an interesting panoramic view of Nanjing we had from the top of the fort. Before following him down, we walked to each side and looked out at the range of views. They framed beautiful vistas of the city. We were glad we came.

Arriving at the National Museum, we exclaimed to Stretch that it looked like an exact duplicate of one we had visited in Taipei, Taiwan. In fact, this was correct. When Chiang Kai-shek left Nanjing, he took the plans of this museum with him, as well as many of the Nanjing museum's treasures. Then Chiang Kai-shek proceeded to construct an identical one in Taipei. After admiring its handsome facade, we walked up a wide flight of stairs to the entrance. One entered a huge lobby with a high ceiling where an enormous bust of Chairman Mao dominated the room. Past him, we walked into a hallway full of small kiosks offering for sale various Chinese products like teapots, paintings, painted vases and lacquered bric-a-brac. Each merchant tried to entice us to buy something. We smiled, but headed for the main exhibition, whose title was "The Five Thousand Year History of China."

All the exhibits were rich displays and each had full documentation explaining what it was. Pleasing to us were the placards written in both

Chinese and English. We began in the jade room, which had wonderful pieces of jade in various colors. Many were carved with intricate figures, flowers, birds, vines and scrolls. Most were very large. There was a lengthy written explanation of the importance of jade in the spiritual life of the Chinese that was a bit daunting to absorb, much less comprehend. We shook our heads and simply enjoyed the beauty of the various pieces. From this room, one walked into a metallurgy exhibition with big pots and interesting tools, all manufactured and used during various eras. Then we came to the transportation exhibit. Here were interesting vehicles such as ancient sedan chairs, old carriages and many models of river boats. The next room contained pottery and cooking utensils. There was a placard with a collection of culinary equipment that amused us: "The Western Szechuan diet is as a hot woman; the South China diet is as a village girl; the Beijing diet is as a lady, while South of the Yangtze River the diet is as a maiden of a humble family." Following this was a larger sign reading, "The King's life depends on the People and the People's on Food." As we continued into more rooms, a tight-lipped museum guard approached and asked us to leave. She indicated the entire museum was being closed, as it was the lunch break for all the employees. This severe woman guard, with her hand on the exit door handle, was quite persuasive in hastening our departure.

When we came out, Stretch was sitting on a bench reading a book. He was surprised to see us so soon. We explained what happened, then insisted on returning tomorrow because we found the entire exhibition fascinating. This pleased Stretch.

The next day when we entered the exhibition, Mac headed directly to the metallurgy room, and I went to the weaving room with the fabric displays. There was an old loom suspended from the ceiling but inclined downward so it was possible to view it on all sides. It was amazing how similar it was to the Cranbrook-style loom I used when learning how to weave. Basically, looms were unchanged from their ancient beginnings. The specialities in this exhibit were the beautiful silk fabrics produced from the looms. These materials had been woven with silk threads in gorgeous shades of blues, plums and true oranges. One lovely piece was a cream colored background with small colored butterflies scattered throughout the entire design. What a complicated job of weaving! There were some woven in the jacquard pattern which the Chinese were proud of having developed. There was a bolt of very fine gauze in a heavenly azure blue. A tall exhibition case displayed garments made from the brocade fabrics that were actually worn at an emperor's court. They were cut in a kimono style, full length to the floor, with deep pocketed sleeves. (Court ladies were said to carry their tiny Pekingese dogs in those pockets.) Matching silk shoes with very pointed toes were displayed alongside each garment. One voluminous robe had hand embroidery around the neck and on the sleeves. Just imagine the time consumed weaving the fabric, then fashioning the robe—all entirely by hand.

I noted beads were the accessory worn with this clothing for men and women alike. Their stringing was fascinating. They were long necklaces that hung all the way to the wearer's knees in front and to the waist in back. The beads themselves might be made of carved bone or bright ochre-colored amber or a black opaque glass. Often, some place along the length of the necklace, there was a larger bead quite unlike the rest in size and color. Perhaps with the black beads this might be an opaque colored pink one or a clear sapphire blue sphere or a lovely piece of carved coral. The pink and blue ones were Peking glass. These necklaces had back interest too, as they cascaded down to the wearer's waist. Of course, these necklaces were Chinese court style and were worn only by those important personages.

Both of us ambled into the next exhibit, which discussed food. This was of great interest because included were the actual ceramic dishes used to process them. There was a discussion of the various grains which were grown. I made notes of the ceramic implements on display because their names and shapes interested me: A gui is a three-leg pitcher; bo-an, an earthen bowl; dou, a stemmed bowl; he, a small three-leg pitcher; gu-a, a vase with the top curving outward; pei-low, a bowl with cover; li, used to boil grain; hu-a, a pitcher with a tiny pouring spout; ewer, another type pitcher; qui tu xu, a rice cooker; zu, for roasting cow or sheep; and finally, bi chu, for cooking vegetables. I noted the Chinese cooking techniques seemed similar to food preparation today.

There was an impressive religious section in the museum, full of various poses of Buddha. Some were busts, but others were large models of Buddha sitting or standing. All were handsome. Each was a perfect specimen with no broken or missing parts.

The museum's final exhibition concerned construction. We immediately thought of Bob Anderson and his Loomis Construction Company workers in Idaho. How they would study these materials and techniques. (And probably shake their heads in wonderment that this type of construction worked.) Here were many examples of building materials, from ceramics to bamboo. We were particularly fascinated with the development of bricks and ceramic tiles which were particularly Chinese in size, style and design.

Since we happened to be the first tourists in the museum that morning, we leisurely strolled about and had a quiet time to study without any interruption. It was fun to read a placard and exclaim to each other over something of interest. Abruptly, this ambiance was broken. A large group of raucous tourists arrived and immediately scattered throughout the entire place. We felt assaulted. It was difficult to escape them, as they were everywhere. Later we asked Stretch who they were. "Oh," he answered, "tourists from Taiwan and Hong Kong." "How do you know that?" we inquired. "Oh, I can tell by their voices."

There was nothing in this museum depicting the horrors of the Rape of Nanjing. We understood that near the Nanjing University campus was a museum constructed in memory of the victims of the Rape of Nanjing by the Japanese 10th Army after World War II. Busloads of Chinese school children arrived each day for a tour. The purpose was to instill a sense of patriotism in the children and, particularly, to not let them forget this history. We did not choose to go there. Stretch had told us a bit about the atrocities from this massacre. It was a tragedy that was not forgotten in Nanjing. We did not question him closely, feeling it too sensitive a subject.

We felt satiated by all we had seen and absorbed at the National Museum. How good it felt to sink back in the seat of the car and reflect on the splendidness of the carefully assembled exhibits. We needed a few moments of calm to digest such a feast. No wonder the Chinese are proud of their 5,000-year old history.

Stretch had been resting while waiting for us. Now he wanted to talk as we gathered in the car. He began by apologizing for what he was about to say. He must discuss the current items available to buy in Nanjing because his agency insisted he do this with every client. "Please," he said, "do not think you must buy anything, that is, unless you wish to do so." He firmly asserted that he got no commission from what we might purchase, but he did know which shops were the best for buying merchandise in Nanjing, if we would like his help. "We should realize," he continued, "Nanjing offers many interesting things. There are such items as silk fabrics of the finest quality, jade and water stones, crystal, lacquer pieces, ivory carvings and Chinese paintings. Would we like to see any of these?"

When he paused to take a breath, I answered that everything he mentioned sounded very interesting, but what I really would enjoy purchasing was a Chinese raincoat. "I mean, Stretch, the kind we see everybody wearing while they are bicycling in the rain." Designed as a poncho and cut in a single rounded piece of heavy plastic, they were practical for both men and women. When worn, the poncho covered the head, leaving only an opening for the face. It ballooned out over the back of the bicycle and was large enough to cover the person who might be a passenger on the back of the bicycle. It totally covered the front handlebars too. Mac spoke up and said he wanted to buy an umbrella. Well, an ordinary raincoat and a simple umbrella were the last two items Stretch expected us to want. He was visibly disappointed not to be able to show off something he felt was more appropriate, like a special piece of jade or a lovely Chinese drawing. With some disdain, he said the articles we wanted were found in a department store. He would keep his eye open for such a place. Maybe one was around the corner. Should we go and see? "Okay, let's go." Our idea of a department store was perhaps something similar to a Macy's or a Nordstrom's although we had seen no evidence of such places while driving around Nanjing. Probably we had not been in the right area.

We left our lady driver parked at the museum and proceeded on foot to the department store. Now it was raining hard. Stretch opened his umbrella to share with Mac, while I pulled the hood of my bright yellow Michael Kors raincoat over my head. I tucked my camera inside one of the large zippered pockets. I stayed drier than either of the men with their umbrella.

Stretch casually remarked while walking down the street that there was part of the old Ming wall at the end of this particular block. Did we wish to see it even though the rain was coming down very hard? We certainly did. We sloshed through the puddles on the sidewalk toward the wall. We stopped within inches of it, close enough to touch and smell the bricks. Noting they were three to four times larger in size than any standard brick made in the United States, we observed they were a kind called a "hard-burn" brick. On each one, we could clearly identify the chop of its maker and the date it was finished. We remembered Stretch had told us in his history of their manufacture that the man's logo must be on each one. We checked many bricks on the wall and saw every brick was so identified. I traced my finger along an imprint of one chop and thought about its history. Once, so long ago, an actual human being hand-crafted this particular brick which was incorporated in this wall. In the poignancy of this thought, I reflected on the skill of the man who had created something so lasting that I could see and feel it today. His brick was now well over 600 years old. Any of these bricks were older in age than the United States was as a nation. Didn't that bring history alive? Shivers went down my spine just realizing that fact.

There really was a department store on this street. We passed it while walking to the Ming wall. Its appearance did not in the least resemble what we know as a department store, so we had walked by it. Down some wide steps from the sidewalk, Stretch guided us through an opening on the ground level into an unimposing, dark room. Inside was not what we expected. It seemed a bit like an old-fashioned country general store, or a depository for a little bit of everything, but not a lot of anything. No sign outside advertised this place as a business, indicating it expected customers, nor did we find anything enticing to buy after looking around inside. It had quite a different ambiance from what we expected of department stores in the United States, which work diligently to entice their customers into buying the minute they cross their thresholds.

No wonder Stretch was not enthused about shopping in one and preferred hunting for lovely silks or jade in other stores. Looking about the room, I saw a variety of dresses and coats in sizes from a child to an adult, hanging on a clothes rack. There was a glass case containing boxes of medicines. Some were labeled; others were not. There was a case filled with foods, mostly dried things like noodles, rice and spices. There were household utensils and dishes on shelves and newspapers for sale near the main counter. We saw no umbrellas or raincoats for sale even though, with all the rain, this was a perfect day for selling both. There were no signs identifying any product, nor were price tags on any item. A customer poked through merchandise to find whatever he wanted. No smiling salespeople waited to help customers.

Stretch asked the young clerk behind the main counter if she had umbrellas and raincoats. From somewhere behind her, she pulled out a heavy, yellow rubberized raincoat. "Oh, no," I said. "That material is too heavy." It was not a typical Chinese poncho either. She folded the coat and placed it under the counter. Then she brought out a pale blue, very thin plastic one. "This is not good quality," I remarked to Stretch, "and not a poncho." I was discouraged and baffled. How strange. Everybody we saw pedaling their bicycles down streets in the pouring rain was wearing ponchos, but those ponchos seemed particularly difficult to find. Yet no rider was without one.

Stretch felt impatient. He asked if she had an umbrella. "Yes, have one," she said and produced a black number in a plastic case. "Ah," said Stretch. He pulled it out of its case and pushed it open. He turned and twisted the thing, eyeing it for flaws. "Was this what you wanted?" he asked Mac after it passed his inspection. "Fine, that's just fine," answered Mac, not even looking at it. Stretch still examined it carefully. "Okay, how much?" he asked the girl. She answered it was ten yuan. "Hmmm," he murmured. The girl reached behind her. From a back shelf, she pulled off two packaged ponchos, one in yellow and the other in a pinky red. "My goodness," I exclaimed, "that is exactly what I want. Where did she locate them, Stretch?" "From behind the counter, I guess," he answered with no enthusiasm. "You want?" "Yes, that's exactly what I do want. How much?" "She said 20 yuan," he answered skeptically. He felt this was too much, and we should bargain for a better price. Twenty yuan amounted to $4 in our money and was a very good price by our standards. Not only was the plastic of excellent quality, but it came packaged in its own zippered carrying case. If one could be found like it in the United States, it would cost a great deal more. "Okay, I buy," I told Stretch, deciding not to bargain. Mac handed the clerk a 50 yuan note. "Is that best you have?" asked Stretch. Mac checked his money and said it was. The girl opened her cash register. She did not have 20 yuan change for our 30 yuan purchase with Mac's 50 yuan note. Luckily Stretch had small bills and paid for us. We reimbursed him when we reached the hotel. He found us uninteresting shoppers. A poncho and an umbrella? We, however, were very happy with our purchases.

Later in the car, Mac commented to Stretch that the amount of stock/merchandise in that store was one tenth of what it would be in a similar store in the United States. Stretch was flabbergasted.

This day ended our sightseeing in Nanjing. Being with Stretch made our visit here such fun that we cannot wait for another time when we can return to this interesting city. There was still so much to see and much more history to absorb. However, in keeping with our itinerary, tomorrow we must fly on to Wuhan.

WUHAN

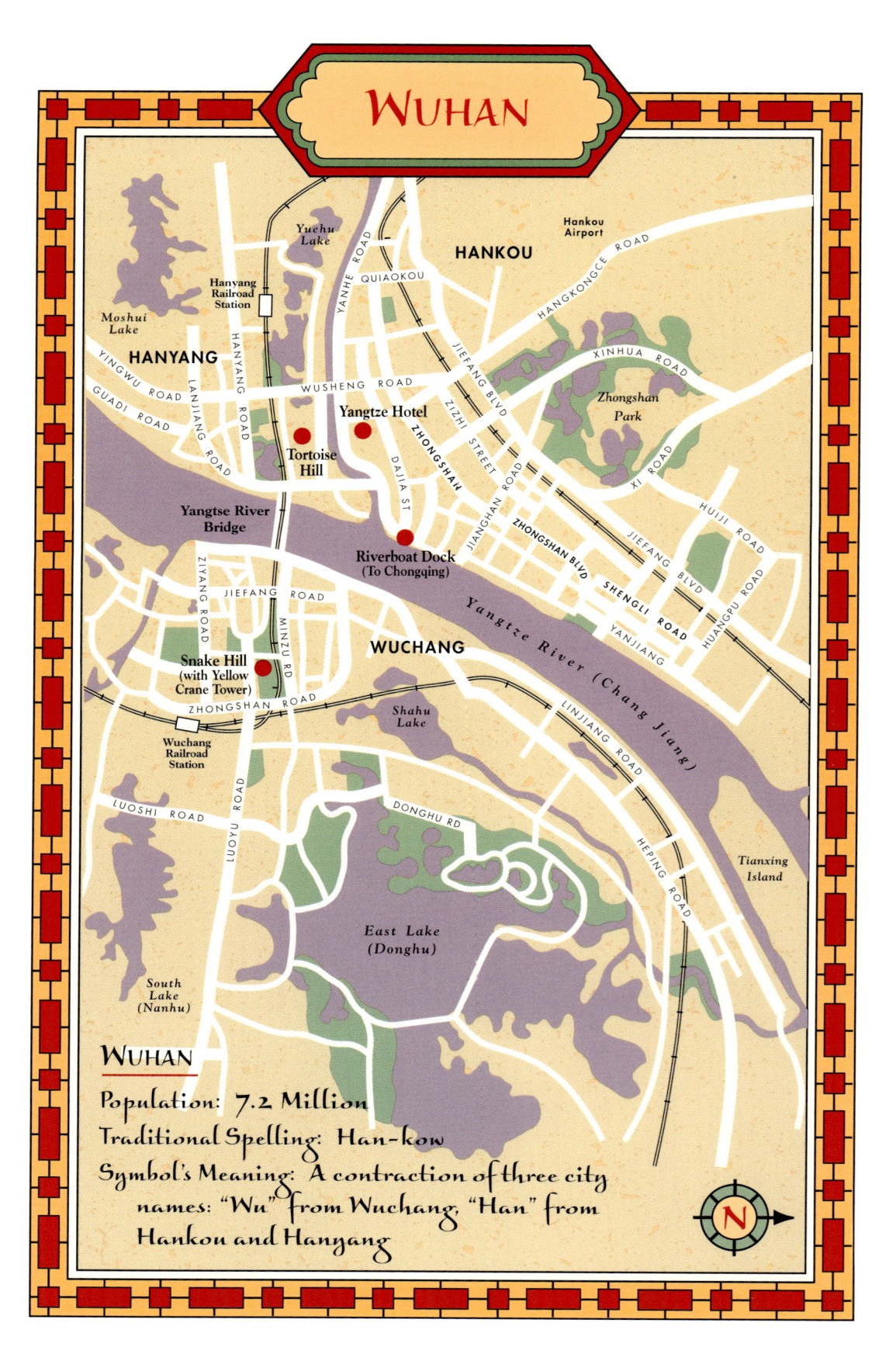

WUHAN

Population: 7.2 Million

Traditional Spelling: Han-kow

Symbol's Meaning: A contraction of three city names: "Wu" from Wuchang, "Han" from Hankou and Hanyang

chapter 8

WUHAN

We were ticketed on flight #5307 of China Eastern Airlines, bound for Wuhan. Concerned that our baggage was overweight, and that perhaps the airline would refuse our pieces, Stretch asked another boarding passenger, apparently a businessman as he only had a carry-on briefcase, if we might use his weight allowance. The man nodded his approval. We were asked to weigh our own luggage at a special counter. With Mac's help, Stretch accomplished this. The bags were accepted at the check-in counter without any questions. Stretch walked with us to Passport Control. There we bid him farewell and said we hoped to meet him again in Nanjing. He said he would look forward to our next visit. We proceeded through the various control booths, showing our passports as well as airline tickets, seat assignments, and proof of airport tax payment.

All these documents for a domestic flight to Wuhan.

The waiting room where we were directed lay beyond these booths. It was the size of a huge airplane hanger. With the understanding that our flight left from gate three, we walked across the entire place before we found it. We passed by rows and rows of empty seats, each fastened together in long metal frames. They were molded Herman Miller style chairs in a bright orange plastic, certainly adding some warmth to this cold, barn-like space. We chose a row, piled the carry-ons in seats beside us and sat down to wait for the flight to be called. As we glanced around, we saw a large group assembling nearby. Many carried their own jugs of tea. Each was contained in a quart Mason jar, a third of the bottom holding green tea leaves while the other two thirds of the jar was filled with liquid. It was somewhat ghastly seeing those spreading green leaves. Not only did they turn odd shapes, but they made the water a sickly brown/green. Outside on the tarmac, a noisy trolley piled high with white boxes was pushed toward gate three. A man wheeled it inside and to the back of our section, turning it sideways. Without further ado, he left the building. A few passengers from our section got up and went over to it. Apparently these boxes were lunches for all of us traveling on flight #5307.

As the others ate with their chopsticks, noisily slurping the food, we watched the take-offs and landings of an old, slow military jet. Its landing was very flat and low since the airplane had no flaps. Then a group of men in uniforms walked out from the far side of the terminal toward another military airplane. While they stood on either side of the plane, its right motor was started. The engine was feathered, revved up, feathered again and then turned off. A ladder was brought up to its side. One man opened the engine cowling and studied the motor inside. Apparently everything worked to everyone's satisfaction because the cowling was closed. All the men walked off the field. A commercial jet landed. It taxied toward the two military airplanes to park. We watched people disembark and believed this might be our craft. No such luck. Where ours was, we had not a clue. It certainly was not on schedule.

Another hour passed before our Wuhan flight was finally announced. At least this was what we think the loudspeaker broadcast. The announcement was in Chinese with no translation. Others who had been sitting as long as we started to form a line at gate three. We assumed that was where we belonged. Only when the attendant at the gate accepted our passes did we know for certain this assumption was correct. As we passengers walked out onto the open tarmac, a sound like "rat-a-tat-tat" hit our ears. And again, "rat-a-tat-tat." "Tell me those weren't real bullets, Mac, were they?" I said hopefully. Chugging along beside him, trying to keep my tote bag over my left shoulder while holding the round plastic tube containing our Shanghai painting in my left hand, and still clutching Mac's second briefcase in my right hand, this was no way to duck bullets. "I hope they were not real, but that certainly sounded like them, didn't it?" Mac answered. He continued philosophically, "Well, either he hit the backstop or he missed, but I think we're okay." Neither of us was comforted by those rat-a-tat-tat sounds, but none of our fellow passengers seemed the least concerned. It turned out to be a military pilot practicing shooting at a dummy target very near our runway.

We boarded the airplane up a shaky metal ladder. With two stewardesses standing at the top watching, we struggled to get aboard. They made no effort to help anyone. Looking at our seat assignment ticket, one nodded and pointed to row 11 on the right hand side of the cabin. When Mac sat down, I started to giggle. His shoulders reached far above the top of the seat, and his knees touched the one directly in front. Could a person be more cramped?

Every spare inch of this airplane's design was concentrated on seating as many passengers as possible. It was the smallest commercial aircraft we had flown in China. Typed a Y-7 and manufactured in China, it was a high-wing turbo-prop very similar to a Fairchild F-27. The flight was scheduled to last one hour and twenty minutes. Mac was curious whether flaps would be lowered for landing. Since I could see out of the window and he could not, I would check. I reported no flaps were used because this airplane had none. This meant we would not have their help in slowing down the airplane for landing. Undoubtedly, it would coast a long way before coming to a stop. Arriving in Wuhan, we hit the ground going a mighty speed. Happily, this runway was very long.

The young man who greeted us, Tom, was not our guide at all. Our real guide was meeting her father, who was returning that day from an overseas trip to Indonesia. Tomorrow, she would meet us to look around Wuhan.

Tom offered his services to guide us today as we drove to the hotel, although he reminded us it was Sunday. We politely refused. Wuhan is a business city and not really a sightseeing one. For us, it was an overnight stopover until we boarded the ship for the Yangtze River boat cruise which was scheduled to start tomorrow afternoon.

Wuhan, A Major Transportation Hub

Wuhan, in the Hebei province, is the name given to three closely linked municipalities called Wuchang, Hankou and Hanyang. They are located at the junction of the Changjiang and Han rivers, which link up with the Yangtze, flowing east to Shanghai or west to Chongqing. The cities were interconnected when the Changjiang Bridge was completed in 1957. Designed like the Yangtze River bridge in Nanjing, it is built on two levels, the lower one for trains and the top one for all other traffic. This was the first huge bridge constructed to span the Yangtze River between Chongqing and Nanjing-Shanghai.

Wuhan is a major transportation hub, situated at the furthest point inland that sea-going ships can navigate. This includes ships up to and including 8,000 tons. Its railroad center makes connections with cities all over China. Particularly important is its north-south rail line from Beijing to Guangzhou, which continues on to Hong Kong. All these excellent transportation facilities make Wuhan a base for opening China's inland markets and gaining access to natural resources like coal and iron ore. Perhaps Wuhan might be thought of as equivalent to St. Louis, Missouri which sits at the confluence of the Ohio and Mississippi rivers flowing down to New Orleans, Louisiana. Beijing has named Wuhan an "open city" with tax and investment incentives. Last year, the city signed contracts worth $2.5 billion for manufacturing and real estate deals. Suddenly, it is China's most popular inland city for foreign investments.

Historic Wuhan

Wuhan is of some historical interest. The three best known events for which it was the theater were the army revolt leading to the downfall of the Ch'ing Dynasty in 1911; the workers', strike when building the Wuhan-Beijing railway in 1923; and the Kuomintang government retreat from Nanjing in 1937 when the Japanese invaded. Today, Wuhan is noted for its dense population of seven million, for its heavy industry and, above all, as a workers' city. Some of China's most important foundries are located here. With the recent assistance of Germans and Japanese, the Wuhan Iron and Steel Complex was expanded to include a three million metric ton steel rolling mill. Taiye Iron Mine, an open pit, provides the iron ore and limestone. Here also is China's largest heavy machine tool plant. There are other companies manufacturing chemicals, fertilizers, construction materials and cotton fabrics.

The Yangtze Hotel, recommended to us as the best in Wuhan, turned out to be a dismal businessman's lodging. With a business class rating, its literature pointed with pride to air-conditioned rooms with refrigerators, TVs, in-house movies, and fax and overseas telephone services. Downstairs, there were several restaurants, a disco, bar, beauty salon and pool room. When we entered the lobby, it was primarily filled with businessmen waiting for their room assignments. We asked Tom to come upstairs to the rooms we were assigned to be sure these accommodations were passable. Opening the door of our suite, we bumped into an electric sweeper sitting dead center in a windowless living room, and when we discovered where the light switch was, we saw a pile of dirt shoved into a corner. The suite was unattractive, but since we would be here only one night, we decided to keep it. It did have a TV, refrigerator and telephone, just as its literature advertised. A pretty bedspread brought a bit of cheer. It was a yellowish damask with a bit of rose color in an abstract design which kept it from being a complete monotone. The view from the bedroom window was blocked by a newly built extension of an automobile round-about directly in front of the main entrance of the hotel.

Without exception, this hotel was the poorest kept of the many we stayed in on our entire trip through China. The hotel personified what many Americans thought all hotels in China were like, and nothing could be farther from the truth. This place, from the lobby, hallways, and dining rooms to our accommodations, was dirty. We found the personnel inefficient and indifferent to its guests' well-being. A particular annoyance for us was the bathroom of our suite. Its sink barely ran enough water to brush one's teeth, and the bathtub had trouble filling with water. We would never recommend this place, nor would we ever return ourselves.

Before saying goodbye, Tom warned us to be careful about walking outside. "Why?" we naively asked. "You might be robbed," he answered with a big smile, adding, "Nice to meet you." Was he kidding? This was a welcome to Wuhan?

We rode the elevator down to the mezzanine, where a Western restaurant was located. That entire floor was under construction, with noisy hammering and sawdust particles floating in the air. Flimsy plywood partitions somewhat blocked the workers from view. The restaurant was in the back of the floor. To get to a table, we must walk across a temporary bridge built so one did not step on the electrical cables strung under the bridge. Not seeing much of interest on the menu, we ordered toasted cheese sandwiches and a Diet Coke. We were tired and hungry, so we were inclined to eat anything the waitress brought.

There was an intriguing spiral stairway made of marble behind other temporary partitions on this floor. Not knowing where it might lead, we walked down and ended up in the main lobby. We asked for a newspaper. None had arrived that day. We asked at the business office if there were any faxes for us. There were none. (Talk about efficiency! Later we learned five were sitting in that office. Eventually, they were delivered to our room. One fax was an offer to buy a property we had for sale in Idaho. Sent two days previously, it requested an immediate response. We hoped our reply was not too late for confirming our agreement.)

Strolling down the annex of the hotel, also under construction, we saw a sign pointing to a cake shop. Cake! A piece would taste delicious. We headed in that direction. We passed an empty beauty salon, a barber shop busy with customers, and a dozen or more cubbyhole to-be-shops that were either totally empty or under construction. At the very end of the annex was the cake shop. We peered through the glass door and saw two showcases, each filled with lovely, frosted cakes. A piece of the chocolate one appealed to our mood. (It reminded us of the delicious ones Mac's mother used to make of devil's food, iced with a boiled white frosting and bitter chocolate dribbled down the sides.) As we went inside the shop, a male customer approached Mac. "I change money," he announced, flourishing a small calculator in his right hand. Mac ignored him and said to the women behind the counter, "Tell this man to go away." The clerks laughed. Mac turned to the man, who hovered close to him. In a stern voice, he said, "Go away." The man turned to me with a questionable look in his eye. I ignored him. We studied the cakes. The man hung around. "I don't think we want any of these cakes, do you?" said Mac. He pointed to the especially tempting chocolate layer. "No, I don't think we do," I replied. We turned toward the door leading back into the hallway of the hotel. I went first. A woman blocked my path. She held out her hand, which was full of paper notes. "Change money?" she asked. "No, absolutely no." I answered, disgusted, and pushed past her. She laughed. As we walked back into the hotel, we could hear her laugh and repeat over and over, "No, absolutely, no."

Apparently these two had entered the pastry shop by the public entrance from the sidewalk. We believed they had been watching for someone to hassle and when we walked into the cake shop, decided we were good prey. It interested us that the store employees found our predicament so comical. That they lost business did not faze them in the least. This must be the sort of scam Tom was warning us might happen.

The next morning, we met Brenda, who was our guide. When asked, she said she chose the name "Brenda" because she liked its sound. We told her in detail about the episode with the money changers. She found this a funny tale. She told us money changing was a custom in Wuhan, but she failed to realize we were very uncomfortable being hassled in such a manner. Finally, we cautioned her not to expect many happy American tourists here if this was the kind of handling they would receive. Surprisingly, she could not have cared less how we had been treated. She gave us the impression it was of no significance to her whether tourists came to Wuhan or not. Her haughty and uncaring attitude seemed a strange one for a professional guide.

Brenda took us to a park called the Tower of the Yellow Crane, at the top of Snake Mountain. The original building was built in 1223 in memory of an immortal being who was said to have flown here on the back of a yellow crane. It had been built and rebuilt after the place had the misfortune of burning down several times. The last rebuilding started in 1984 was finished to receive visitors by 1985.

The park, designed around a small mountain, was created for the citizens to enjoy relaxing in pleasant surroundings. Among a series of ornate Chinese buildings, it was landscaped with many leafy green trees, sparkling lakes and small flowering gardens. Benches were scattered here and there for resting or perhaps for a romantic rendezvous. There were cozy alcoves with picnic tables throughout. Many asphalt walkways curved around the mountain, creating interesting scenic views. Around one corner were three or four huge, comical cardboard figures positioned for a person to stand behind to be photographed. This was the only touristy gimmick in the entire park. In many places, one could wander along the twisting walkway and take pictures from any number of pleasing vistas. Everything in the park was a delight for the photographer. The ambiance was quite charming.

Today, we could hardly walk without bumping into some camera enthusiast photographing his relatives. Opposite this park in the distance, across the Changjang and Han rivers, lay Turtle Mountain. Turtle Mountain boasted a huge communication tower with a large billboard advertising Kent cigarettes sitting on its peak.

In the center of the park was the striking five-story Yellow Crane Tower. It was built with a series of lovely curved roofs. The roof tiles of the entire building were a shiny ceramic in a burnt orange color with black flecks. We walked inside the tower to view the beautiful panoramic scene of the countryside and rivers. The ceiling was painted in an interesting manner that emphasized its various angles. Another smaller pagoda building housed a large stone scroll. Carefully positioned in the room's center, the scroll had a poem attributed as a writing of Chairman Mao. We did not ask for a translation. Because we soon were tired of dodging so many amateur photographers and video camera fiends posing their relatives and friends, we left this central section of the park. Walking through its lovely landscaping back to our car was much more satisfying than viewing pagodas and observing the antics of the local citizens. No one harassed us for money changing.

We chose to eat our dinner that evening in the hotel's Chinese restaurant. It was packed with families who had young children. We asked to sit in a quiet corner and were given a large table with a clean white tablecloth set for six people. Dinner was a nice blend of Cantonese food. The food was better here than at our luncheon spot. Slightly behind us in one corner sat a broom with a pile of rubble beside it. Perhaps someone forgot to remove it before the room opened for dinner.

The next morning, we journeyed to the pier for boarding our river boat. It was an eventful ride, and we got a good look at the city of Wuhan. Our route passed directly through its business section. The traffic was thick with all sorts of vehicles pressing to get to their destinations, as well as people crowding each other along the sidewalks. Some workmen had wooden braces strapped across their shoulders with pails of water dangling on either side. Others were hand-carrying large bundles of merchandise. One man, pushing a wheelbarrow filled high with sheets of Styrofoam boards, tried hard not to hit or block anyone. No matter which way he turned, he had difficulty dodging so many pedestrians. Businessmen, alone or in pairs, clutched black briefcases and strode briskly through the crowd. Some women loitered around the entrances of hotels. Others hastened children across the busy streets. There were cars, trucks, buses, pushcarts and bicycles, all trying to move two ways on this narrow street. How the traffic jammed at the intersections! Our driver made some well-calculated, but hair-raising, left turns to keep us en route. Fortunately, we had plenty of time before our ship sailed. When the harbor finally came into view, we thought we were miles from the Yangtze Hotel, whereas we had only traveled a few blocks. Around one more frightening left turn, we reached the pier.

There she was, the Yangtze Princess. To our eyes, she was a huge ship and much larger than we had expected. How glad we were to see her. As the driver stacked our luggage on the pier for the ship's porters, Brenda curtly bid us goodbye. It was obviously a huge relief for her to finish this tour guiding job and be on to something more to her liking.

Wuhan was not a stimulating interim.

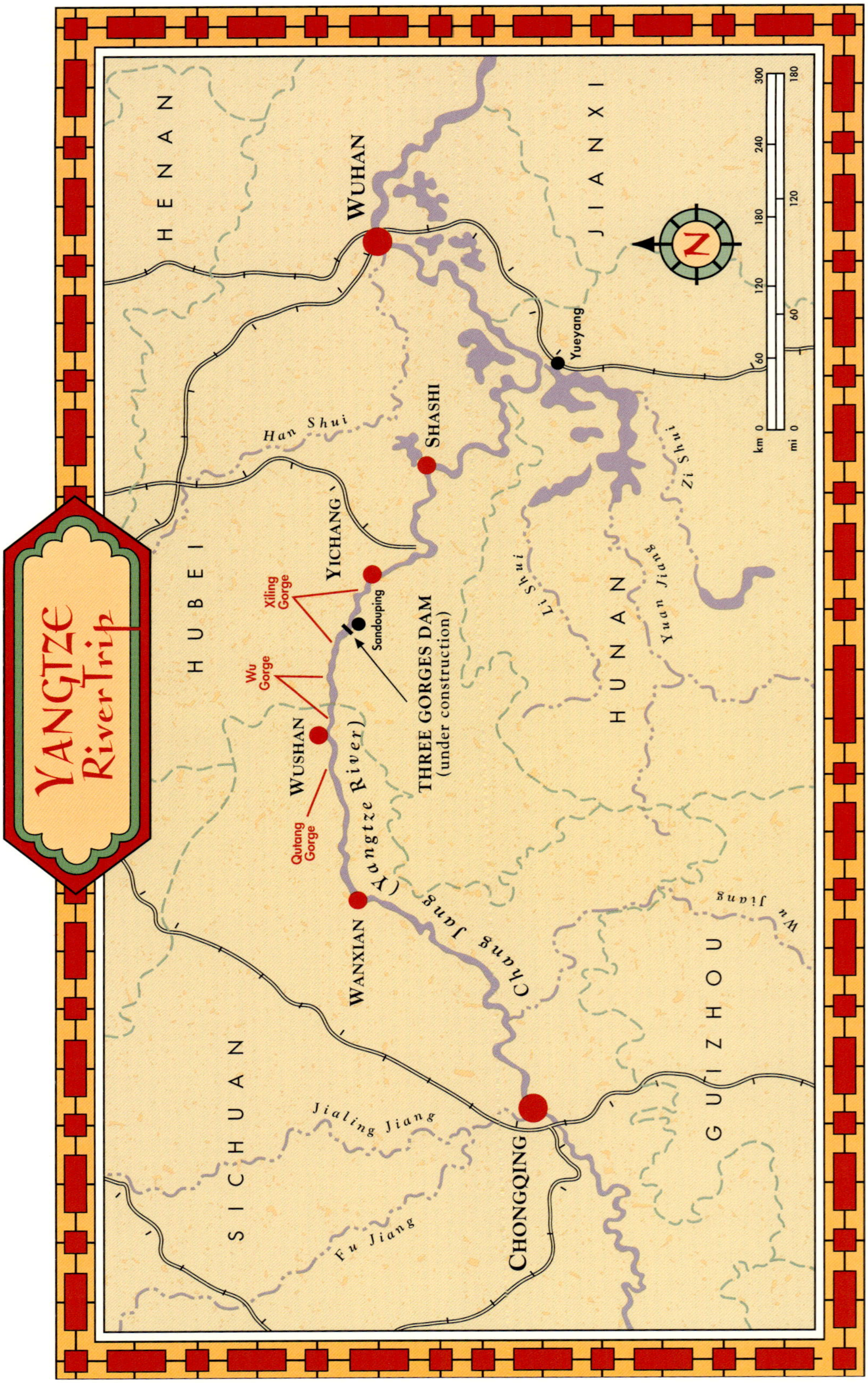
YANGTZE
River Trip
HENAN
HUBEI
SICHUAN
HUNAN
JIANXI
GUIZHOU
WUHAN
SHASHI
Yueyang
YICHANG
Han Shui
Xiling Gorge
Sandouping
THREE GORGES DAM
(under construction)
Wu Gorge
WUSHAN
Qutang Gorge
(Yangtze River)
Chang Jiang
WANXIAN
CHONGQING
Jialing Jiang
Fu Jiang
Li Shui
Yuan Jiang
Zi Shui
Wu Jiang
N
km 0 60 120 180 240 300
mi 0 60 120 180

chapter 9

楊子江之旅
The Yangtze River Trip

A group of smiling young people, part of the crew, cheerfully greeted us as we approached the Yangtze Princess. They grabbed the bags and led the way to our cabin. Passing by the boiler room and crews' quarters, we climbed up several flights of steel steps onto the main deck of the ship. We were greeted there by the purser, Simon, and were told our cabin was on the second deck, room #22A. When all the luggage arrived, we were left alone to look around.

We estimated the room was about nine by twelve feet with a ceiling seven feet high—not much over Mac's head. Counting the additional space of the narrow entryway, hanging closet and bathroom, it probably was a total of nine by twenty feet. The outside wall had two large windows that slid open for good viewing and lots of fresh air. Two single beds were built against each side wall, with their headboards next to the windows. We could lounge on either bed and comfortably watch the scenery pass. Between the two was a table/cabinet, complete with a lacy crocheted doily sitting on top. Underneath were knobs for controlling the air conditioning, radio, calling an attendant or turning on the mirror lights over the desk (only one worked) or the room's ceiling light. There was a small bookcase too. At the end of one bed was a built-in desk arrangement. On its top sat

a tray with two Thermoses. The larger one contained hot water, apparently for tea, as there sat two mugs with covers and two bags of green tea. A smaller Thermos held ice water. A small, low lamp with a shade shaped like a Chinese pagoda was next to it. The shade was green glass decorated with colorful butterflies. A Conic color TV was at the shelf's end. Since all programs would be in some Chinese dialect, unless we wanted to stretch our imaginations and guess what was being said, this piece of equipment was useless for us and took up valuable space. There were some drawers on either side of the desk's knee hole. None were large enough to hold one of Mac's shirts. At the end of the other bed were two large wooden armchairs with soft cushions. The table between these sported a fancy white, state-of-the-art telephone. Directions said one might call overseas. What fun to

call one of our kids! Later, we learned its use was possible only under certain conditions. The hanging closet space was limited, but had some drawers underneath that would hold a shirt.

Suddenly the room felt stuffy. We pushed the air conditioning button and discovered it was not working. Sliding the windows open as far as they would go did not bring in enough air to cool the room, so Mac picked up the telephone and called for help. Three persons appeared, two girls and one man. They wrung their hands, not sure what to do. Mac insisted the air conditioner must be fixed. They agreed. Suddenly, a man with a toolbox turned up. He knew exactly what to do. Soon there was a breeze blowing above our heads. We, the two girls and one man all thanked him enthusiastically. This room would be unbearable without any air circulating.

There was a door opposite the closet that we had assumed was another closet. On second thought, perhaps it was the bathroom. Thank goodness for that. This space had all the usual facilities and a large mirror over the entire sink area, making the room look a great deal larger than it was. I looked for some sort of bathing arrangement and suddenly realized there was none. Did we go down the hall to shower? Hopefully not. Searching a little further I saw "an arrangement" in the corner. A spray nozzle attached to a long metal coil, hung from a hook. There was no curtain to pull, making an enclosure. Apparently one stood in that corner, held the spray nozzle and aimed the flow of water at one's body. If one stood with the back against the wall facing the sink, most of the water should fall behind into a tiny floor drain. If, however, one turned the other way around, with back to the sink, the water would disperse over the entire bathroom. An interesting proposition. The first position kept the bathroom drier, although the floor, I found, usually was a bit damp. But that was much better than mopping up the entire bathroom. The small gully around the edges of the floor to catch the excess bath water looked inadequate, but we would see.

During my initial use of this "convenience," the water ran cold, the floor got wet, my feet never got dry, and I truly questioned whether it was worth the effort. That was until I thought of the alternative of going down the hall. By the time our journey ended, we both had learned how to get hot water and keep the floor properly dry while using the sprayer. This was a very real accomplishment. I never did conquer clearing the brown from the water which flowed into the sink. Besides being a dark cocoa brown in color, each time the faucet was turned on, it ran cold water, always, no matter how long beforehand it was turned on. The brown eventually lightened enough to brush one's teeth. The toilet flusher worked with some difficulty too, but we learned our way around this problem. It was pointless to let strange little inconveniences like these spoil the trip.

The ship left the dock promptly at four in the afternoon. We were disappointed there was no special fanfare or advice to sit down and fasten seatbelts for a takeoff. We were busily unpacking and figuring out where to stow belongings in the various cubicles. Hanging space was at such a premium that we unpacked only the essentials for the cruise. It was exciting to be en route.

Since neither of us was enthusiastic boat people, it was only with Ugo's strongest recommendations that this cruise was an experience not to missed, that we scheduled it in our itinerary. The cruise would last four full days and two half days, and we would be sleeping aboard four nights in total, since we were going upstream. Had we gone downstream, it would only be three days total with two overnights. How we would survive shipboard life remained to be seen. We reminded ourselves of a friend whose business made him a frequent flier between Europe and the United States. Once, his colleagues persuaded him to go with them on a ocean liner instead of another airplane. Very dubious about whether this was a good idea, he was assured it would be fun. Once aboard, with the ship moving smartly along, he started pacing up and down the deck. Up and down, up and down. His friends told him to stop pacing and relax. "Relax? relax?" he shouted. "How can I relax when there's nothing to do!" This precisely matched our feelings as this adventure began.

Simon was the guest service representative on the Yangtze Princess. An attractive young man, he was physically small boned and stood about five feet six. Simon had a nice smile and was trying hard to put everyone at ease. He took a personal interest in us. Soon after our departure, he telephoned to see if we were settled and comfortable. He announced the time dinner would be served in the dining room. This was a very nice gesture, as there was no dining schedule in our room. Later, we learned a calendar was posted daily outside the dining room with the schedule of events. It was entirely written in Chinese. (Later, during the trip, an attempt was made to include some English in the calendar. A very nice gesture for us.) Simon often rescued us with an interpretation. Although he was slightly difficult to comprehend, he understood English reasonably well. He liked to talk with us, saying it improved his English. For a Chinese person, he was a good listener. We found some Chinese were apt to be better speakers than they were listeners.

At the specified hour, we walked into a brightly lighted dining room. Simon motioned us to a table set for ten people. All of them except us were Chinese. This evening Simon joined us. He was the only one at the table who spoke any English. We were delighted to have someone talk with us. The cuisine was a variety of Cantonese-style dishes, served from many platters on a large revolving disk we call a lazy Susan in the center of the table. The food was delicious. We were told there were 80 passengers aboard; 78 of them were Chinese and two were Westerners. There was a crew of around 30 young men and women, all Chinese. What a surprise to find we were the only two Westerners.

That first night out, the ship cruised all night without incident. We slept soundly.

The purpose of the Yangtze river boat cruise was to navigate through the famous Three Gorges. A huge construction project had already started on the world's largest hydroelectric dam, which would submerge these Gorges. If we ever wanted to see them, the time to go was now. Leaving Wuhan, our destination upstream would be the city of Chongqing. It was estimated this trip took about 98 hours.

The Three Gorges are China's equivalent to our Grand Canyon in Arizona. They attract thousands of tourists each year. They are situated in one of those cradles of civilization, where generations of artists and poets have drawn and written on scrolls about the scenes of the peasant farmers' simple life. With fields covered with yellow flowers and cloud-shrouded peaks of sheer barren gorges above, we were told this was the most picturesque topography one could ever experience. These gorges were mammoth in size as compared with the pinnacle rock formations looking like triangular spears that we had observed on the river boat cruise down the Li River, during our visit to Guilin.

The Gorges were known as the Xiling, the Wu and the Qutang. Each had its own historical and mystical story. After viewing the many rock formations along the Li River, we were a little skeptical about being able to visualize all this. We were told the last gorge, the Qutang, was so narrow we would have to wait our turn to navigate carefully through it. Perhaps we might even require a pilot boat to help.

The Gorges

The Xiling Gorge is the first and longest gorge of the three. It was once considered the most dangerous, for it is full of hidden rocks and shoals. The gorge is made up of four smaller gorges with fancy Chinese names: the Gorge of the Sword and the Book on the Arts of War; Horse-Lung and Ox-Liver Gorges; the Kong Ling Gorge; and the Gorge of Shadow Play. Without an interpreter, we never spotted any of these. A temple called the Huangling Temple, which was first built during the Three Kingdoms period (220-280) and reconstructed during the Tang Dynasty

(618-907), is supposed to lie between the Kong Ling and Shadow Play gorges. One needs to have binoculars and more imagination than we do to actually see these.

The second Gorge, the Wu, has the Goddess Peak which, we are told, is the most important site of the entire trip for the Chinese tourists. This is a twelve meter high stone pillar which stands on the highest mountain peak along the Yangtze. From a distance it resembles a young girl. She is supposed to be the youngest of 12 fairies who help guide ships along the river. She brings good luck to everyone who glimpses her. We are sure we saw her.

The Qutang Gorge is the shortest of the three, but the most spectacular. With its steep perpendicular cliff walls, its chief point of interest is the Meng Liang Staircase. The story is this was carved by a bodyguard of a murdered Sung Dynasty official who was attempting to recover his master's body from the cliff.

We did observe Bellows Gorge where coffins buried over 2,000 years ago can be seen hanging from the cliffs. What an eerie sight. All of the passengers are intrigued. What keeps them there without disintegrating? No one has a suitable explanation.

The Three Gorges Dam

Building the Three Gorges Dam near Yichang on the Yangtze is a dream come true for the central planners of China. This will be the largest hydroelectric dam in the world. It encompasses a one mile stretch of concrete, creating a narrow inland reservoir 370 miles long. It will displace some one million people from the neighborhoods and cost more than any other single construction project in history. Very few countries could or would build a dam of this size. Estimated costs place it at nearly two percent of China's gross national product and may soar to $77 billion. Completion is expected in 2009. It is China's biggest engineering feat since The Great Wall and the Grand Canal were built. Ground was broken December of 1994 by Prime Minister Li Peng who has an electrical engineering degree.

This dam's reservoir will stretch from Sandouping, a village in Hubei province to the city of Chongqing in the Sichuan province. That is about as long as Lake Superior in the Upper Peninsula of Michigan in the United States. The reservoir will flood a hundred towns requiring the resettlement of over a million people, that is, one person for every thousand Chinese. It will also submerge over 30,000 acres of prime farmland. The early construction, which cleared away some hills and villages, began in 1993. We could already note the bare hills. In a nation where many factories cannot work long shifts because of energy shortages, the dam's turbines are expected to generate 18 million kilowatts of electricity, the equivalent of ten average-size nuclear power plants. The dam should protect the densely populated downstream reaches of the Yangtze from the yearly heavy flooding they now experience. The United States has voiced skepticism about this project and has withdrawn its financial and technical support. It is felt large dams are tremendously more expensive than ever estimated. The current trend in the United States is to build smaller dams, with more environmentally friendly flood control. The Three Gorges Dam project is exactly the kind of huge dam building the United States is trying to move away from, in favor of smaller and more efficient ones.

The environmentalists worldwide are fully against the Three Gorges Dam. They say it will ruin several thousand years of history, as well as destroy the ecosystem of the Yangtze, threatening farmers and a number of endangered animal species such as the river dolphin and the Siberian white crane.

Technical problems are many. River-borne silt may prove troublesome and more costly than the planners expect. The Yangtze looks very murky to us as a result of this silt. Simon told us some days the water is so clear one can see the rocks on the bottom. This seems only a pipe dream. It is too brown to ever turn blue. It is hard to imagine any fish are alive in it, although we occasionally spot small boats with a fisherman or two throwing nets. The resettling of a huge and poor population is proving politically damaging. The dam is scheduled to begin generating electricity in 2003. All 26 power generating units will be in operation by 2009.

The next morning began our first full day aboard. We eagerly opened our windows' curtains and noted with disappointment that it was raining. Most of the day was spent sitting in the lounge on the deck above ours, watching the sights on the riverbanks from comfortable armchairs. It was interesting watching the activities inside too. Most of the men found the mahjong tables and spent a large portion of the day playing that game. Other people read. Many women gathered to gossip. Some wandered outside on the decks to smoke.

The ship was to dock at a city called Shashi. The plan was to sightsee, have lunch, then shop during the afternoon. Historically, Shashi was important as an outpost on the Yangtze. In its center was the Sun Yat-sen Park with the Spring and Autumn Pavilion. On the south of the city, on a riverbank, was the Pagoda of Longevity which had a lovely view of the city from its top floor. We understood Changkiang Thermos bottles, Mandarin Duck bed sheets and down comforters were produced here. Around five o'clock, we saw many passengers struggle aboard loaded down with packages of these items. The puffy feather quilts were a particularly good buy in Shashi.

Going ashore was of no particular interest, so we inquired if we might have lunch aboard. This request was very difficult for Simon to understand. How could we prefer staying on shipboard when there was excellent food and sightseeing on shore? Finally he agreed to ask the dining room manager if she could arrange this special meal. We assured him the food might be as simple as rice, toast and a cup of tea. The manager suggested noodles and toast. Would this be satisfactory? We were delighted. She and Simon were very puzzled why we preferred such a meager meal.

That noon when we went to the dining room for our "small meal," we were flabbergasted by what greeted us. There was a huge bowl of noodles sitting on the lazy Susan along with a plate piled high with toast. The bowl of noodles was steaming hot. Fresh pieces of tomato and egg were combined with them, making a soupy mixture with a wonderful flavor. The slices of toast were piping hot and tasted delicious spread with butter and jam. We ate far more than planned. Managing hot noodles with chopsticks was not easy. They were slippery and kept dropping back into the soup bowl. Another couple shared this meal with us. He talked a little with Mac, but she kept her eyes down and was silent. Probably, like many of the other women, she did not speak English. Hopefully this was the reason and not that she was uncomfortable sitting with Westerners.

At dinner, we were placed at the same table assigned to us the evening before. The identical group of people, with the exception of Simon, were waiting for us this second evening. After taking our same places, we realized no one was eating. Everyone was looking at me. As a special honor, they wished me to take the first helping of food.

There were many dishes on the lazy Susan. Feeling very shy with nine pairs of eyes watching, I picked up my chopsticks and carefully, ever so carefully, chose a piece of chicken. It seemed the easiest piece of food for me to manage with the chopsticks. As I raised them to my mouth, I silently prayed this bite would not fall. "Thank you, Lord!" I murmured to myself as I succeeded and smiled back at our fellow diners. They all nodded and smiled, then everyone helped themselves from the platters. They were very polite and seemed friendly, but there was no serious conversation among us. No one introduced himself. We did learn our table partners were mostly from Taiwan, with the exception of two men from Beijing and a young woman from Guangzhou. Most were travel agents with the China Travel Service. During the meal, they chatted among themselves, as did Mac and I. It was not an unfriendly situation, just a non-communicative one. Using hand gestures, they were curious to know how we learned to use chopsticks. Both of us ate the entire meal with them. They were amazed at our agility. Asians always seem to be surprised when Westerners use them with ease. I suppose they expected us to ask for forks.

Later, we found out most everybody at our table spoke a little English, but they were shy about saying anything, not wanting to lose face with incorrect English. Each evening, we gently encouraged a bit of conversation from each person, apologizing that neither of us could speak any Chinese at all.

One did not sit around the table after the meal. When the last course was served, one ate, drank up and went. Finish your fruit, raise your glass in a final toast, shake hands all around, repeat your thanks for a marvelous meal, and then depart.

We ended our first full day by choosing an early bedtime and fell asleep the minute our heads hit the pillow. Around midnight, Mac awakened me to watch as we passed under the second huge bridge crossing over the Yangtze. Remembering the first one was at Wuhan and the third was in Nanjing, this one was a similar construction of immense steel structure. Then, we easily fell back to sleep. At two o'clock, he awakened me again to look outside. There were flares shining through a white vapor cloud. This cloud was caused by a large blast furnace. This was our first glimpse of heavy industry along the banks of the river. This furnace was fully ignited with a roaring blaze of fire.

Coal

The main source of fuel here is unwashed soft coal. It provides 70% of China's energy needs and hundreds of tons are burned every year. It pollutes the air. Sulphur dioxide is a problem. It comes back to earth as acid rain and has turned the Guangdong-Guangxi-Sichuan basin into one of the world's worst polluted areas.

We were to go through the lock on the Gezhou Dam around 4:30. The new dam being constructed would have five locks which would speed up traffic moving on the Yangtze. This dam will be 130 feet high, 8,400 feet long and have 21 power generators producing a total capacity of 2,700 million kilowatts per hour. Now I dozed sitting up in bed so I would not fall asleep and miss this experience. I planned to watch from our windows. Mac put on his bathrobe and went up on the deck to see better.

What a strange feeling it was to be in a lock. It was something like being encased in the bottom of a box, only this box was made of concrete and was so huge one could not see all the way up to its top. There were shadows of people standing on the lounge deck clearly reflected on its concrete wall. Suddenly, there was the sound of rushing water. It was pouring into the lock, the concrete box. Slowly, eerily the ship started rising. Up, up, up so high it rose that I thought the ship was going to fall over the top. Then the flowing water stopped. The boat settled. We were in the waters of a huge lake. Totally freed from the lock, we continued on with our journey.

Mac returned to our cabin. We were keyed up from this excitement, the most by far on the trip. We soon fell asleep, exhausted. The ship silently cruised on through the night.

The next morning, our second full day, we were to dock at Yichang. A rafting trip was planned. After boarding buses, we would ride two hours or so to an inland pier called Shennon Creek. There we would board rafts. These will be poled down the creek, which was said to be filled with rapids and lush scenery, ultimately to meet up with the Yangtze Princess. This sounded like fun.

Mac and I were included in the group for the first bus.

An English-speaking guide named Neil was assigned to be with us to describe the special sights along the way. A Chinese girl guide worked with the other passengers on the bus. Mac shook his head when he saw the ancient bus we were to ride in. It was the first in a line of several newer ones. "My gosh," he said, "wouldn't you know ours is the oldest one going?" We climbed aboard and took the very back seats on purpose. Here we had more leg room and more breeze from the open windows. This worked out well because Neil's English translations did not interfere with the loud spiel of the Chinese guide for the others who sat up front. Neil was one of those hard-to-understand guides. He spoke very softly and mumbled, which made him hard to hear as well as difficult to understand.

Our young driver inserted the key in the ignition to start the engine. He put his foot down on the accelerator, and we were off in a cloud of dust. From then on, he never varied the speed, no matter whether we were on the straight or rounding blind curves, and there were many of those. It was a body-punishing ride for a solid two and a half hours. We led all the other buses and did not slow down until someone up front requested a rest stop. How surprising no one asked sooner. The girl guide spoke to the driver. Out of nowhere in this vast countryside, he careened the bus to a full stop. Dust surrounded us and poured in the open windows. "We stop five minutes. Only five minutes," the girl guide decreed, sternly pointing to her wrist watch as each passenger got off. With this unsubtle suggestion for using the restrooms, we quickly understood if there was a need, the time to go was now.

To reach the facility, one hiked down a steep dirt pathway to a concrete block building. All its windows were open since they had no glass. I could see there were very few partitions between the gentlemen's and ladies' sides. Several of our passengers headed toward the building. One group of women supported an older lady who was hobbling. She seemed very stiff in the hips. We elected to walk on the road away from the bus to stretch our bruised bodies. It felt so good to be upright and move the legs.

What a ride! Never had there been such a rough road, nor had there been such a creaky vehicle allowed to be driven on it. We bumped and swayed over a raw unfinished roadbed full of sharp-edged rocks, not smooth pebbles. The bus seemed to have no springs to help cushion the blows. The base of the road was firm enough, but its surface was so very rough. It had been prepared for spreading asphalt, but this had yet to be accomplished. The road was very narrow in width and had no safety guards on either side. We looked down many steep inclines.

All during this bouncy ride, I hung onto my arm rest. As I was literally being tossed up in the air, with my body leaving the seat like a rubber ball, I clutched onto that arm. Coming back down, I hit bottom with a thud. There were no springs in the seat to cushion the blow. Thank goodness for something to hang onto, I thought. Otherwise I might easily have been thrown onto the floor. Much the same was happening to Mac. Although he was much heavier than I, he too was feeling the effect of no seat springs. The longer we sat, the harder those seats became. We started to laugh. This was the wildest automobile ride either of us could ever remember taking. Someone requested music. A loud blast of discordant jazz came from the loudspeaker in front. Maybe this soothed one's inner soul, but it added more chaos to an already unruly situation. Both of us thought our family would believe we were exaggerating our tale of this ride. They would have a hard time visualizing how body-punishing it was. Probably, it was more dangerous than we were allowing ourselves to think. What if we had met traffic on any blind corners of these narrow roads? Luckily, we never did.

In spite of the bumps and humps, there was marvelous scenery along either side of the road. Its lovely serenity did soothe one's soul. This was the picturesque landscape one visualized as classically Chinese, the kind we came here expecting to see. We were winding through the mountain passes of a rural countryside. We passed multi-tiered rice paddies high up one misty mountain plateau. If our ride had been smoother, we would have taken many photographs. As it was, neither of us was still long enough to hold the camera steady. The hazy panorama of the mountains and far off farmlands would make beautiful pictures. This was prime farmland. Every available space was planted. Corn grew side by side, two stalks in parallel rows. They rose straight uphill, which made it convenient for farmers to begin hoeing at the top and work down. The space between the rows was planted with a grain crop. Every inch of land produced some kind of food. We spied young melon and squash plants peeking out from strips of plastic, a modern technology for growing crops. There were orange groves here too.

Around a hairpin turn was our final destination. We believed this was Shennon Creek. Neil forgot to tell us when the bus stopped. We gladly got off, even if we could not see anything resembling water, much less a creek. Both of us felt shaky after all the jiggling. As I stood up, my armrest came with me. Would you believe it was broken? Apparently, it had been the entire trip and never had given me the support I thought it did. Glad I did not know that around some of those curves.

Looking about, we wondered what we were supposed to do. There was a semi-circle of sedan chairs with husky male carriers directly in front. What a tourist ploy, we thought. Who would ever use one of those? (Only my saucy little grandmother when she visited Japan in the early 1920s. She not only rode in one, but told her children "not to be such snobs and get in.") Neil caught up to us, announcing there were 400 steps to walk down to the pier. He said we might be carried in a sedan chair. Did we wish him to hire two? Well, going downhill in one did not seem safe, as far as we were concerned, so we told him, "No, thank you." Electing to navigate those stairs under our own power seemed a better way. Looking down at the steepness of the slope, I thought even my spunky little grandmother would have expressed some qualms about being carried in a sedan chair here.

We began to walk down the 400 steps to reach Shennon Creek. The path was extremely steep, with its stone steps uneven in height as well as narrow in width. Glistening with the fresh morning dew made them slippery. There was no safety railing on either side of the path. Mac led, with me progressing slowly behind him. One was a bit light-headed with the feeling it would be very easy to fall. We descended downward maybe three dozen steps when behind us we heard the chanting of men's voices. Together their low voices flowed in cadence in a sing-song, "he ha-ha, he he." They might have been chanting a ditty they made up like: "Who told you to be poor? Buck up and bear it. Buck up and bear it!" Then, "Here we turn a corner. Watch your step and don't crack your head." Turning around to see what this noise was, we saw eight men carrying four sedan chairs, heading directly toward us. They were walking fast, and it was obvious they were not going to stop. Quickly we jumped to the side of the walk, out of their way. We straddled some mounds of dirt as we tried to balance ourselves on the grassy, precipitous slope. There was hardly enough space for the carriers and sedan chairs to pass without bumping into any of us. We walkers realized they were hauling heavy loads and could not stop easily. Four sedan chairs, each carrying an adult, went past us. The person sitting inside looked exactly like a hen sitting on her nest. I recognized the older woman who had to be assisted down the slope to the restroom. Each chair was manned by two carriers. Each carrier, the one in the front, the other in the rear, placed the shafts over his shoulders and held its poles with his hands. The chair looked heavy by itself. Undoubtedly, it was much more so when carrying an adult.

At the first stair landing, the chairs were set down so the carriers could rest. The person in the chair sloped downward in an awkward position, but he could not fall out because the sides were too high. We walkers passed them. Then we heard "he ha-ha, he he" and knew they were coming toward us again. This time, we quickly stood aside so they could pass. We kept progressing downward. My knees were wobbly when we finally sighted the creek at the end. Hooray, there really was a creek. The treads of the last few steps were higher, as we reached the bottom. Using Mac's arm for support, I needed to concentrate on each one not to fall. Walking constantly downward without a letup put much pressure on the leg muscles and weakened them. Thank goodness, we would not have to climb up this path.

Shennons Creek was a swift-flowing tributary of the Yangtze River. Alongside a simple wooden pier were parked a large group of rafts. Shaped like canoes, they had many rows of seats. Each seat would hold four adults. Now gently floating side by side, they awaited crews and passengers. Beside the pier were some souvenir shops, whose many vendors yelled at us to see and buy their wares. Our guides quickly herded passengers into the large reception room of a pagoda-style building. No vendor was allowed inside. We saw rows of chairs around low tables. Beside a wall was a buffet table set with snacks, soft drinks, bottles of water and hot tea. Everyone was invited to partake. We were urged to eat and rest before boarding a raft. We were told there would be a lunch stop during the trip, but none other. Around a corner were the restroom facilities. We ladies found clean sinks and three enclosed toilet stalls. The porcelain facility inside the stall was mounted on the floor, Japanese-style, and it was a flusher.

Since there were so many people, Mac and I decided to leave the group early to go outside and inspect the rafts. It was a good idea to choose which one we wanted, rather than being piled into one by the tour guides. We pushed through the crowd of noisy vendors. Each had something to sell, from large embroidered tablecloths to silly trinkets. We managed to reach the pier without anyone following. Looking over the rafts, Mac chose one that looked the most sturdy and comfortable. We picked the seat in the front row. After our back seat bus ride on our ancient bus, we had no qualms about seating ourselves in the best seats we could find.

These rafts were constructed of thick wooden planks and shaped like wide canoes. The seats were wooden slats, much like those found on a park bench. They were comfortable. We sat under a white canopy that was rigged to poles spaced along the sides of the boat. Since the weather had turned quite warm, this canopy protected us from sunburn. We were smart to situate ourselves early, for soon the entire group appeared. Such a commotion getting everyone settled! It was a wonder no raft tipped over.

Each raft was pushed away from the pier, and we were off. Three men worked in the bow. There was the helmsman who manned the tiller. He was the captain and navigated us in the direction of the river's current. The second person was the poler. He held a long bamboo, brass-tipped pole. His job was to keep us off the rocks. The third was the bailer who, using a wooden scoop, removed the water that collected in the bottom of the boat, thus keeping us from capsizing. It was amazing how much water collected in the bottom of this boat. In the stern, another man worked a tiller in concert with the captain in front. He was helping with the steering. The current was swift. In many places, there were churning, bubbly rapids. Gliding over them was fast and fun. In other spots, there was deep water that would be over our heads should we capsize. When the boat coasted in the slower currents, the poler moved us along. When we bottomed out on rocks at one point, and the boat was stuck, it was the poler who headed us into deeper water. Mac told me later that when this happened, he picked a spot on shore where he would swim if we sank. I shuddered, wondering what I would have done. Probably the same thing. The thought of being in the middle of the river, stuck on rocks and swimming in deep water with all these people was not a good one.

The river boatmen were strong. Muscles stood out on their arms and legs. Soon we started to giggle. Each time our poler pushed his pole, he let out a ferocious yowl. Maybe this gave added energy to the push. A good bit of spitting went along with maneuvering the boat. When a big push job came, the poler noisily cleared his throat, a lot of spittle flew over the side, and the pole was thrust deeply into the water. He pressed vigorously against the pole with all his might. For this effort, we slipped along very smoothly. The bailer wore a pair of bright red cotton shorts. What made these shorts unusual was a zipper sewn from the waist all the way down the back crease of the pants. All the crew wore straw sandals on bare feet.

It was a cool, pleasant ride. The rapids added zest to the journey. The scenery was lovely. We progressed through gorges, past bends in the river, seeing handsome rock formations and interesting green vegetation. Always there was a cooling breeze on our faces. Thanks to the canopy, we were never in the direct sun. Suddenly, in the distance, we heard a familiar chant, "he ha-ha, he he." We were heading toward it. There was a raft being pulled upstream. Three men with straps across their chests like harnesses used on carriage horses were pulling it. Pulling against the current was hard work. Two men stood in the boat directing its course. All five seemed good-natured. They waved and smiled as we passed.

Luncheon was prearranged at a restaurant located on a hillside about half way through our journey. Since there was no dock, the rafts were pulled onto the rocky bank. People jumped ashore or were helped off. After the meal, there was to be a performance of native dancing. We were not interested in watching native dancers. Events of this sort seemed "staged" to us and not authentic, so if possible, we chose to avoid them. Mac and I shocked Neil by electing not to go ashore. We will stay on the raft. He could not believe we meant this. Don't we want to enjoy some delicious food and see a beautiful exhibition of native dancing? Obviously Neil wanted to go, but he was uncertain what to do with us. We urged him to enjoy himself, assuring him we would be fine. Shaking his head, he obviously was wondering what kind of tourists we were anyhow. Soon, after everyone was on their way to the restaurant, several women appeared on the opposite bank to deliver lunch buckets to the crew. Our raft was poled across the river to receive the lunch. The raft was tied to a stake while the men ate. One offered us some of his lunch which we refused, with thanks for his thoughtfulness. We stood up and stretched. We loved the peacefulness of this river bank while everyone was off eating. We were too warm to be hungry.

Almost exactly an hour later, we saw everyone winding down the hill toward the rafts for reboarding. To reboard our raft, each passenger must be carried by a member of the crew. All our boatmen lined up and took turns lifting a man or a woman onto their backs, piggy-back style. Wading thigh-deep in the river, they carried each person to the side of the raft.

Then the person was positioned with his or her hips on the boat's railing, where they somehow maneuvered their legs over the side and stepped down into the raft. It was an awkward procedure at best and certainly not a graceful sight. The same elderly woman, carried in the sedan chair as well as helped downhill to the restroom, was one of those so boarded. By a great stroke of good luck, no one fell in the river. The bottom of this creek was rocky and uneven for the crewmen to stand in or wade through when carrying a person to the raft. After a while, everyone was once again aboard. We noted all the crewmen enjoyed carrying everybody piggy-back, especially the women. Other rafts had pulled closer on shore than ours so no piggy-backing was necessary for their passengers.

The rest of the trip was a little uninteresting. The river ran slower. There were fewer unique sights, and we were getting tired and thirsty. After a few more miles downstream, we reached a steep stony bank, and the raft was beached. Climbing out of our raft up onto the rocky bed was not easy. We staggered to the top and were guided into yet another boat. This one was substantial in size and motorized, a typical ferry carrier which taxied us to the Yangtze Princess. Neil's farewell was soliciting us to buy his tape of our trip. When we refused his offer, he went away sulking. We never saw him again. We thought his explanation of the "sights" left a great deal to be desired. While we had been poled downstream, the Yangtze Princess had been working its way toward us via the main stream of the Yangtze. We were happy to be back "home," but agreed the trip was the highlight of the entire cruise. Hot and sticky, we headed for the shower. The entire trip from beginning to end took around five and a half hours.

Later that evening, we tied up to the dock at Wanxian. Every boat stopped here. It is an old river town and an industrial and port facility. Textiles are an important industry. Its fresh oranges, tangerines and peaches are known nationwide.

We would stay here all night, awaiting our turn to go through the Qutang Gorge. Everyone was invited to attend a Chinese opera. It was performed in a hall on the floating dock beside the Yangtze Princess. Since we had seen Chinese opera previously, we were content to sit in armchairs on the outside deck of the lounge, enjoying the night air and watching the action on shore.

What a good idea this was. There were all sorts of fascinating activities going on. The first we noted were the various processes for transferring bulk goods. Much of it was done by human labor, without any use of a conveyor belt. Men carried large sacks on their backs, balancing themselves carefully as they walked across a narrow wooden plank and dumped their sacks into the back of a truck.

At another spot, coal was raked into small scoops by a man standing in the back of a truck. A group of men, each with scoops, waited in line to carry the pieces to the back of a second truck, where it was dumped. At yet another spot, a man spread lumps of coal evenly with his rake in the back of a trailer. Then the trailer was pulled away by a small tractor. It was a very slow process assembling coal, but no one seemed that rushed.

Adjacent to the coal operations, in a small inlet made by the Yangtze, a woman was giving her son a bath. We guessed he was around eight years old. She soaped his body, then rinsed him with the nice brown Yangtze River water. She dried him off by flicking his body with a towel. She knew the warm night air would dry him completely.

Carrying his clothes under his arm, he was sent walking up the hill toward town, totally bare. She stayed to do the family's washing. She scrubbed each garment on a rock. When she deemed it clean, she wrung out the excess water and tossed the garment into a large porcelain bowl. She carried her wet, washed clothing home in this bowl.

Many of the town's people perched on rocks along the bank to watch the activities too. We saw several young women, each dressed in their finery, chatting together as they strolled along. At another spot, a young man and woman shared a drink. Further on, there was a collection of sacks. Someone had lighted a fire nearby. We could only guess, but perhaps this fire was for the guard who would spend the night watching that the sacks were not stolen.

On the river, small sampans with a single driver or a single passenger maneuvered in and around the anchored bigger boats. These larger boats were docked in a haphazard fashion. Some lay side by side or back to back. Most were two or three rows deep. We could discern no order whatsoever.

Above all this activity was the town. One could reach it by a series of wide stair steps. Chinese loved wide, very long staircases. Every city had one. They were daunting to climb because the steps were so narrow in depth, short in height and had no guard rails on either side or down the middle. One had to take many tiny steps to go up or down.

There were several trucks carrying dumpsters speeding up toward the town or down to the docks. People walked on these roads too. Everybody avoided using the stairs. We watched a ferry boat unload, then reload and back into the river. A long line of buses, trucks and cars had been driven onto it. As one ferry left, another one was waiting to take its place. Such a variety of activities during these early evening hours! During future evenings, we decided to spend more time outside the lounge, sitting on the boat's rickety, folding armchairs, doing just this. It was an excellent way to observe how the citizens worked and played.

Every sort of article was dumped into the Yangtze River (and all Chinese rivers for that matter).

There were no sanitary dumps anywhere in China. There was apt to be much garbage lying along the road, especially country roads. At the end of the welcoming party our first night aboard, we watched as the cocktail waitresses collected all the empty bottles and threw them overboard. As the trip progressed, we often saw raw garbage indiscriminately tossed in the river, plus every sort of container one could imagine. From one hillside, a bright blue-colored chemical flowed into it. No one thought in terms of pollution. Environmentalists were attracting attention, but much more educational work needed to be done. Huge bursts of yellow/grey smoke belched out from many chimneys, both from factories and homes. No effort was made to avoid this. Sometimes the air was so foggy and heavy it hurt one's eyes. We wore dark glasses almost all the time to alleviate this. The country was trying so hard to catch up economically by making every sort of goods for bettering its people's lives. No one had taken the time to realize what the pollution would cost the people by way of health problems, its land for growing food, and its future animal and fish growth.

All along this trip, we had noted certain places on the riverbank where piles of materials were grouped. These piles were probably loading points for transfers downstream. We often saw coal-bearing rock beds. Occasionally, these beds were connected to a crude conveyor belt. The coal was collected into bags at its bottom and carried by a laborer wherever it was needed. One never saw a man standing idle in China, unlike those we have seen in India, parts of Africa and South America. Here there was much work to be done and energy needed to do it. We observed ship building along the banks. Boats were assembled in many different places. They were huge structures, and we were curious how they were launched into the river. We speculated they were floated into the water during the flooding season. Certainly the boats we saw being built were too huge to be moved by mere manpower.

A bit of speculation as we daydreamed while cruising along: China with a population of a billion and a quarter people could have a 125 cities, each with a population of ten million. As of now, we knew Shanghai, Guangzhou, Chongqing and Beijing met this criteria. There must be more people living in the countryside than we had first imagined.

This morning, one of the older Chinese women came up to me and said, "Hello." To initiate doing this was very bold because the Chinese women, even more than the men, were very shy with Westerners. I said, "Hello." She asked where I was from. I told her the United States. She asked which state. I told her Idaho. She said she had been to "She-attle." Not quite understanding at first, I asked where? "She-attle," she replied. "I know where Idaho is. Thank you for talking to me." We smiled at each other as she left to return to her women friends.

We met a family from Singapore. They had a bright-eyed, intelligent eight-year old son. He spoke perfect British English and understood our English the best of any Asian we had met on the entire trip. He and his dad were playing tic-tac-toe using the dusty window panes of the lounge door for their chart. I asked if I could play a game with him. "Sure," he answered with a big smile. He drew a big tic-tac-toe form. We raced through. He claimed he beat me. I claimed I beat him. We both laughed and laughed. Such a good feeling, laughing together. I asked him if the boy with him was his brother. "No," he answered. "He's my cousin." I asked his age. He was eight, his Chinese age. I told him our grandson, Corey

Whiting, was that age too. They would have a wonderful time together. Perhaps he might enjoy meeting our granddaughter, Cameron Collette who also was his age—even though she is a girl.

Later, we had many conversations with his father. Sometimes the boy would be with him. We noted the son's English was better than the dad's and his accent was considerably more refined. We were not sure his dad appreciated this when around us.

We knew from the beginning of the trip that if the food was good, everything would go well. If not, every passenger would be complaining and bad tempered. After the first evening dinner, everybody was in a smiling mood, and this continued the entire trip. The ambiance of the dining room contributed to the feeling of good will too. Our table held ten people comfortably. There were three chairs opposite each other on the sides and two chairs opposite at either end. The back and seat of each chair was upholstered in a lovely bright orange brocade. They were high-backed Chinese style, and very heavy in weight, which made them difficult to pull up to the table. I was seated at each meal by one of the men and was very pleased by this thoughtful gesture.

Chinese Place Settings

The Chinese place setting on the table is always the same. Before each person's place is a small porcelain plate and to the left side a small bowl with a porcelain spoon. There is a small glass, holding a napkin—a paper one at noon and a linen one in the evening. The glass sits above the plate and to the right with a pair of chopsticks in their paper wrapping directly below. A large lazy Susan rotates in the center of the table. Always when we sit down, small platters for the beginning course are already on it. One never waits for any food.

The dining protocol was as follows: After sitting down, one immediately unwrapped his chopsticks. By nod or by request, someone took a bit of food from a platter with his chopsticks. He then rotated the disk, which signals everybody should eat. It was perfectly proper to use the porcelain spoon to serve oneself too. Lots of times, this was useful to scoop up liquid from a serving platter. The sauce was emptied into the small bowl to season the rice. It was proper to put food either on the plate or into the bowl, whichever was one's preference, although rice was always eaten from the small bowl. The bowl was held in the left hand, brought up to one's chin, and, with the help of chopsticks, the food was shoveled into the mouth—a delightful way to eat.

The order of the meal was thus: First offered were the cold, sweet, spicy and dry dishes, little bites served from small platters. Second were the foods with sauces. These were cut into bigger pieces. Probably they were fish and meat dishes and were placed on large platters. A bowl of steaming hot rice was put on the lazy Susan, then the vegetables, which were usually in a sauce. The last course, which we thought of as a sweet dessert or fruit, was a hot soup or noodles. The noodles were thin and floated in a broth, sometimes with a bit of green vegetable. One meal, a cold fruit soup was presented, but no one at our table enjoyed it. Chinese beer and Coca Cola was offered for drinking, along with hot green tea.

It would be impossible to describe the ingredients in any of the dishes, even if I knew their names. I can say at each meal there was a variety of fish, meat and fresh vegetables, which were simply prepared for that meal and were neither too hot nor too spicy. Everybody, including us, ate everything offered with relish, which was more than any of us needed. Without qualification, everything was delicious.

At the beginning of the trip, Simon asked if we wished breakfast Western or Chinese style. "Oh, Western," we replied. "Just a little fruit, toast and coffee would be very nice." The breakfasts actually presented to us were so unusual that I kept a diary of each one.

To set the scene, we were seated at a table by ourselves for these meals. No one wanted to eat with people drinking coffee, for goodness sakes. At first, curious as to why we were sitting alone, people casually drifted by our table. They would smile at us, shake their heads and go on. Our food was very amusing to them. As the days progressed, our breakfasts became interesting to everyone in the dining room. By the final morning, everybody said "good morning" and was openly observing what we were served.

Here is my record of what we enjoyed: The first morning our rotating Susan held plates of fresh apples sliced very thin, fried rounds of banana, two pieces of layered sponge cake, a platter of cold sausage, almond cookies, hot toast with butter and jam and a pot of hot coffee. We ate a bite of everything, and it was wonderful. The second morning, the offering was sliced cucumbers, cold fried potatoes, slices of fish sausage, scrambled eggs, layered sponge cake, almond cookies, hot toast with butter and jam and a pot of hot coffee. We ate this too with relish, although Mac did without the cucumbers and cold fried potatoes. The third morning, we were served fresh sliced tomatoes, cold fried banana quarters, sausage slices, scrambled eggs with diced mushrooms added, cocoa cake, hot toast with butter and jam and a pot of hot coffee. This disappeared quickly. Our last morning, there were fresh apple slices, cold fried potatoes, scrambled eggs, sausages like small hot dogs, yellow cake sprinkled with large crystals of granulated sugar, hot toast with butter and jam and a pot of hot coffee. What delicious food! Remember we had requested only "a little fruit, toast and coffee." All these meals were far more food than we ever ate for breakfast at home, but each morning we looked forward to them and enjoyed each one immensely. We never had a chance to observe what our Chinese friends ate at their tables.

Our table partners loved to tease each other. Soon they included us in their teasing. We liked that. Usually someone initiated a toast during the meal. Sometimes one was made to us. To toast, the glass was held in both hands with arms stretched out in front. Nodding his head to each person at the table, the toaster said a little speech. Instinctively, we knew the words were complimentary because the toaster was smiling. Holding our glasses in front like the toaster, we all nodded to him. Then, as one, we drank together. It was a nice custom.

As the cruise progressed, we found most of our table would speak a little English with us each day. They were still very shy about this. Every meal, we continued gently to initiate a little conversation. This was fun, and everybody laughed a lot. At our last meal, a luncheon, we toasted this, our last meal together. We teased one of the older men who had been playing mahjong that morning and had won money. He claimed he did not win much. He laughed because he won some. When Mac and I left the table after the meal, everyone waved goodbye. They waved again when we reached the dining room door. We returned their waves with big smiles on our faces. The nicest part of the trip was being with them. They made us feel very much at home.

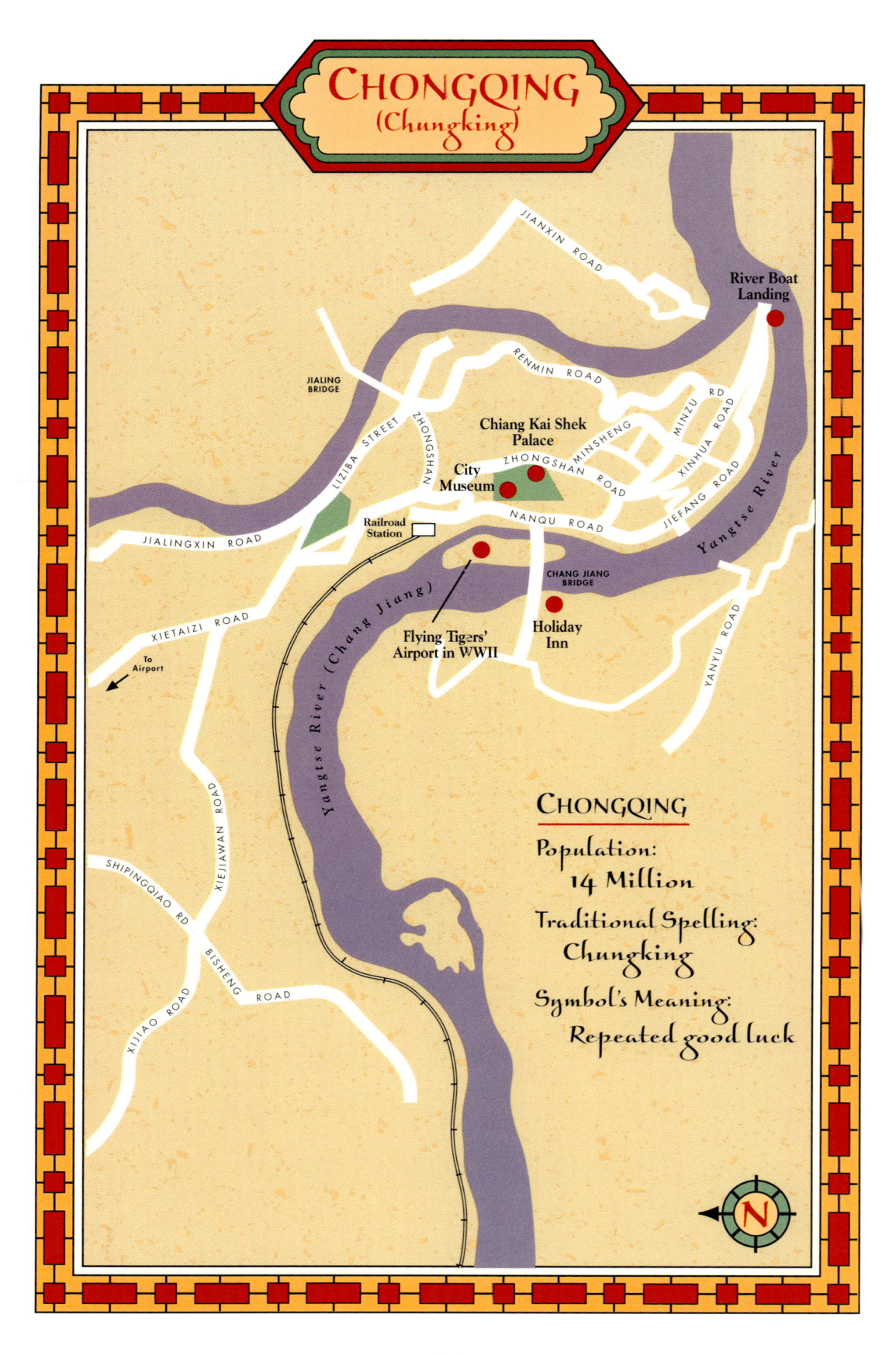

Chongqing
(Chungking)

Chongqing

Population:
14 Million

Traditional Spelling:
Chungking

Symbol's Meaning:
Repeated good luck

chapter 10

重 CHONGQING (Chungking)

Climbing up a long, wide staircase with no safety railing, our feet automatically stomped upward, like soldiers marching along in a military formation. The steps were too steep to take two at a time, and so narrow that we must watch each one, for fear of tripping on their short treads. We followed the three porters who were carrying our belongings. This was our introduction to Chongqing in 1993. Why climbing up a mighty staircase should be a welcoming event to a city, we did not understand. For us, it was an heroic effort.

At the top, a stocky, bright-eyed man came forward. "Mr. Whiting, welcome! You here. You late. We worry. I am Wu." He shook Mac's hand while his driver directed the porters in distributing our luggage into the car's trunk. Very quickly, we were under way to the Holiday Inn Hotel. It was located on the other side of Chongqing.

Before entering the car, we turned for a last look at the Yangtze Princess. What a handsome river boat she is! We enjoyed being aboard. We shall remember with fondness the interesting people who were with us. The sights we saw along the banks of the Yangtze were unforgettable. Our group will remain among the last tourists to have seen them, since the flooding for the new dam will destroy many of those remarkable scenes.

Chongqing was the furthest west and inland that we would reach on this trip. We might compare traveling from Wuhan to Chongqing like going from Montreal, Canada to Buffalo, New York. From Wuhan, we passed through locks in the Yangtze River to reach Chongqing, the same as one went through locks in the St. Lawrence Seaway to arrive at Buffalo.

Chongqing is divided into two distinct districts. They sprawl in and around very hilly mountains, with bridges to connect them. Only a small flatland lies between. This small piece of level land was developed into an airport before and during World War II and was used by a group of aviators known as the "Flying Tigers."

I was personally interested in this strip because long ago a young neighbor with a summer home on the shores of Lake Michigan volunteered to become one of those pilots. Seeing where he worked brought back memories of a lively young 20-year old who was a wild automobile driver. My parents worried for my brother and my safety when he and his older sister collided on our back road. This resulted in her convertible being seriously damaged by his much older model car. Perhaps his erratic driving prepared him for the kind of flying he would be required to do in the Chongqing skies.

The Flying Tigers

Recruited from the U.S. armed services to fight for the Chinese before the United States was at war, the Flying Tigers were 112 mercenary pilots called the American Volunteer Group (AVG). Traveling to the Orient for this work, they arrived as salesmen, teachers, tourists, musicians, vaudeville artists, bankers and baseball players. They were incognito because the United States was not officially at war with the Japanese. They fought as the AVG for over six months, then the United States declared war on Japan, and they became the core of the U.S. China Air Task Force's 23rd Fighter Group. It became part of the U.S. Fourteenth Air Force in March of 1943.

Under the command of General Claire Chennault, their mission was ferrying military supplies to Chongqing for Generalissimo Chiang Kai-shek, as well as chasing the Japanese who were conducting bombing raids on the city. While the Flying Tigers faced the dangers of fighting the Japanese and navigating their cargo over the Himalayas, familiarly called "flying the hump," the Allies were hastily building what became known as the "Burma Road." Constructed with enormous difficulty over some of the world's roughest terrain, when completed, its purpose was to transport military supplies for the Chinese Nationalists over a land route from India to China.

A longtime friend of our family, Russell Goss, was one of the soldiers whose service in the U.S. Army was to help in the construction of the Burma Road. In the early days of World War II, Allied successes were few and far between. Germany, Italy and Japan seemed unbeatable. The necessity of completing the Burma Road, plus the Flying Tigers' can-do achievements, became very important victories for the Americans.

In 1997, the Burma Road still was in use. Following the main road through Pyin U Lwin, Burma, a small resort town east of Mandalay, one came to the gateway of the famous Burma Road. It was a rutted, two-lane highway being used to transport arms. Now these were Chinese weapons coming south on Japanese-made trucks for the military government of Burma, to keep its citizens under strict control.

The Flying Tigers had to brave overwhelming odds against the Japanese airplanes which could turn and climb more than twice as fast as the P-40s the AVG had. The P-40s were used because they were deemed too heavy and inefficient for use in Europe. The Flying Tigers' tactics were taught to them by Claire Chennault who told the pilots to use their speed and diving power to make a pass, shoot and then break away. He used a chalkboard to demonstrate these tactics and scrutinized his pilots' flying skills through binoculars from a rickety bamboo tower.

The P-40s, painted with the eyes and jagged teeth of a shark, were quite the most colorful and deadly fighting aircraft of World War II. Their numbers and insignia were frequently repainted with new numbers and insignia to fool the enemy's intelligence. Pilots often altered their voices over the radio and gave orders to imaginary squadrons to create the impression of a much larger force, in case the Japanese were listening on their radios.

The total length of the Flying Tigers' runway was only 8,500 feet long, with a taxi strip on either side, plus several parking spaces for the airplanes. These were made from crushed stone bound together with clay. The Chinese government imported over 100,000 individuals to do this work. It was completed entirely by hand with a hammer, the only piece of equipment in use. The workers' families were there too. Everyone lived in the open, with no houses or shelter of any kind. When it rained, it pelted them. When the sun shone, it blazed down on them. When cold weather came, they shivered and continued crushing rocks with their hammers. Each was fed two bowls of rice and soup a day.

The ingenuity and teamwork of the AVG mechanics was legendary. They were under-supplied and frequently under heavy enemy bombing while fixing an airplane, but they worked with precision and would continue repairing aircraft during the raids. Since there were few spare parts, the mechanics often scoured the jungle for remnants from wrecked airplanes. Fuselages were rubbed down with wax to increase the speed as much as ten miles per hour. Makeshift air scoops and bomb racks were invented and attached to the airplanes. Claire Chennault's early warning network had Chinese all over the country reporting to him by radio, telephone and telegraph of approaching enemy aircraft. As a result, the Flying Tigers were rarely surprised by an enemy attack.

By the war's end, these men had made a key contribution to the Allied victory in the China-Burma-India theater (called CBI). They were credited with destroying more than 1,200 Japanese planes, with 700 probables. Their own loss was 573.

During the outbreak of hostilities between China and Japan, Chongqing became the capital of Chiang Kai-shek's Nationalist government. He and his army had fled there after the Japanese captured Nanjing, the original capital. At the same time General Joseph W. Stilwell, nicknamed by his troops "Vinegar Joe," was the commander of the United States forces in the China-Burma-India theater. He struggled from 1942 to 1944 to get Generalissimo Chiang Kai-shek's army to fight the Japanese and not the Chinese Communists. The Generalissimo's battlefield inertia and corruption were a source of constant exasperation in General Stilwell's headquarters. Chiang chose to ignore the pressure from the people and the democratic forces to organize resistance against the Japanese. Stilwell complained to General George Marshall, the Commander in Chief of the United States forces, that if Chiang was allowed control of Allied weapons and ammunition, the Generalissimo would use them against the Chinese Communists instead of against the Japanese. Stilwell saw his mission as defeating the Japanese, not fighting the Communists.

Although Chongqing was heavily bombed by the Japanese, it continued to grow in population. Industries were moved there to be away from the war zone on the eastern coast of China. The Communists were active too. Zhou Enlai, who eventually would become Prime Minister of China in 1949, was the manager of the New China Daily newspaper.

The "Xi'an Incident" followed. Chiang Kai-sek was visiting a hot springs spa in Xi'an to rest from his military campaign against the Communists, which was going poorly. There he was kidnapped by one of his own generals, a local warlord by the name of Zhang Xueliang. Zhang wanted to compel Chiang to sue for peace with the Communists, and then join with them in a united front against the Japanese. Chiang was forced to make a decision. With both Mao Zedong and Zhou Enlai intervening to save his life, Chiang agreed to join his Kuomintang forces with the Communists against the Japanese. That struggle lasted from 1937 to 1945. Afterwards, Chiang's conflicts with Mao's forces resumed, but he had lost the confidence of the people. Many of his Kuomintang forces had deserted and joined Mao's Communists. Mao Zedong negotiated a truce with Chiang's Nationalists. When Chiang understood he must forgo American assistance on Mainland China, he fled to Taiwan where he established the Peoples' Republic of China (or Nationalist China, as we know it). Chongqing came under the domination of the Communists in 1949.

The city of Chongqing was huge, with a population of some 14 million people. With no significant Western settlement, they were mostly Han (Chinese) people with some Mongolians, Russians, Tibetans and Thais scattered throughout. The city was situated in the Sichuan province of southwestern China where the Yangtze and Jialing Rivers joined. It was a major inland port and transportation hub. Lying 1,500 miles upstream from Shanghai and 650 miles southwest of Beijing, it was the starting (or ending) point for shipping and river boat excursions. Chongqing had rail service to Kunming, Wuhan, Shanghai and Xi'an. Its spanking new airport had scheduled flights to most of the major cities in China.

Now, the small Flying Tigers' landing strip had been abandoned. Chongqing's new airport and terminal was miles from the city. Just how far away we would find out when we drove to it for our flight to Xi'an. Passing through the suburbs today, it took over an hour to reach the very outskirts of Chongqing. It took us another hour of twisting through extremely congested traffic in Chongqing to finally arrive at the Holiday Inn Hotel. The hotel was situated in the newer section of the city known as the industrial/financial area. We never saw any of the steel, chemical, machinery or textile plants reported to be there, or any recognizable banks either, for that matter.

One of China's largest producers of motorcycles was in Chongqing. With technical and managerial help from the Honda Motor Company, the Jialing Industrial Group turned out a million motorcycles a year. In 1875, the company was set up in Shanghai to produce arms. It was moved to Chongqing before World War II broke out. After the war, the company decided the motorcycle market looked promising and went into production. They were assembled and individually packaged here, then shipped by barge down the Yangtze River to Shanghai. This took seven days. On the return journey, the barge brought sheet steel from Shanghai to be stamped into motorcycle fuel tanks and frames in the Chongqing plant. Undoubtedly, other industries will be developed in a similar manner.

Chongqing's mountainous topography was full of deep caves. Used as bomb shelters in World War II, they saved many people's lives during the Japanese air raids. There are adults living here today who, as children, remembered being shooed into them when the air raid sirens sounded an alert. They said the caves were dark and damp. To pass the time, the adults would tell stories. One story which scared all the children was about a certain bombing. It caused an avalanche that blocked the entrance of the huge shelter. Everyone inside suffocated. After hearing this tale, one could understand why a child might hate to be inside a cave. Today, many caves have been converted into stores or restaurants. One was a much frequented, well-liked disco. We would have liked to observe how the owners converted a cave into a commercial use, but there was no time. The government was actively encouraging individuals to scrape together enough money to become entrepreneurs, hoping to jump start a variety of businesses.

New concrete construction was everywhere we looked. The old housing, which we thought was very handsome, was being torn down and replaced with apartment complexes. Although new buildings were desperately needed, their architecture was extremely stark. They looked cold and uninviting beside the old Chinese quarters, but the new buildings would accommodate more people in safer living conditions. The old dwellings were made entirely of wood, with shingle roofs and bamboo poling inner structures. These homes were so tightly packed together along the mountain sides that they undoubtedly were fire traps.

The road through the city on which we were traveling was paved and transported an unbelievable mishmash of traffic. We noted tiny, bright red Japanese taxicabs like small red bugs darting in and out past cars, buses and heavy-duty trucks. Wu informed us that sometimes a man and his wife bought one of these. While she drove in the daytime, he took over the evening shift. Keeping the car in constant service helped them pay off its cost. Once they owned the cab outright, they then could run their own profitable business. We observed a few private cars with a driver. All drivers worked hard to avoid hitting bicycles and pedicabs. We noted there were not as many bicycles here as in the other cities we visited. Perhaps this was because of the difficulty of pedaling up and down the many hills. Adding to the traffic melee, many people walked on the sides of the road. No significant shoulder existed on either side, so the walkers mingled along with laborers pushing carts or shouldering long, jiggling bamboo carrying poles, with bundles dangling from the sides. Those poles were hazardous, as they stuck out into the road and could hit whatever vehicle was coming alongside. All the walkers competed for space with the mechanized traffic.

Somewhere along the line, we ran into an impasse, causing the already swollen traffic to jam together. A little further on, another even larger congestion developed when all traffic formed a single line and drove through a two-lane tunnel, the only way available to reach the side of Chongqing where our hotel was located. Once we were through this tunnel, there was another bottleneck at the first intersection. The quandary was in choosing which of the many crisscrossing streets to turn into, for heading toward one's destination. All trucks, vans and cars tried to avoid bumping each other at this turning point. We hoped none jumped out of line and caused an accident. That would stall everything. We slithered through onto a wider and less congested highway. We could see there was absolutely no space between any vehicles to permit passing. In the melee, it was not surprising that tempers erupted. Several policemen tried to keep the traffic unsnarled and moving, but there were so many vehicles and people that it was almost impossible to direct with any efficiency. Moving was slow going for everybody. Time and an enormous amount of patience was needed. Our driver seemed to have both, and we finally reached the Holiday Inn Hotel in one piece. Suddenly, we realized we would face this traffic when we went sightseeing. Won't that be invigorating the first thing in the morning!

Mr. Wu was born and raised here. He was a teenager when the Cultural Revolution began. He told us he and his three siblings were forced from their parental home and sent to farms miles from Chongqing. Each child went to a different one. Once settled, he said he worked hard to better himself. Only when he passed the tough entrance examinations for acceptance to the university was he allowed to leave his farm. Although he did not say, nor did we ask, he had to be recommended by someone as a good candidate for university training by the Party members of his commune. He was well versed in history, had a great sense of humor and understood English very well. He was the first guide we had who was willing to talk about the Cultural Revolution even though he, too, did so in a rather guarded way. People were still subject to severe questioning by the police for discussing anything political. For us, it was too confined to be in a car with one's guide, a stranger, and ply him with questions about his life during the Cultural Revolution. People just could not share this time with outsiders yet. He did acknowledge both his parents still lived in Chongqing. He had a son age 13, soon to be 14. This boy loved to make model airplanes. No Chinese guide ever admitted he had a wife, but one was hidden somewhere, probably developing a career of her own.

Mac and Wu discussed Chinese Communism and Western democracy quite openly. They talked about how Mac and Wu each perceived Communism in China and democracy in the United States. He was as interested in how our country was governed as we were in understanding how an individual lived under Mao's Communism. Interesting was the fact that his information about the United States was as limited as ours was about China. Mac and he probed the meaning of the word "comrade." To him it was a deeper, almost spiritual camaraderie, rather than simply a casual "pal." He acknowledged to Mac that its philosophy meant a total involvement. During the Mao regime, he was Comrade Wu, but he said with a grin, now he wished to be simply "Mister" Wu. He really grinned when Mac addressed him as Comrade or Comrade Wu. This made me a little uncomfortable, wondering whether being so jovial might be stepping on sensitive toes, but apparently it did not. Whether he was a Red Guard or not, we did not know, nor did we ask him. Wu is a very secure individual and probably would have told us, had we asked.

It was important to decide possibilities for our single full day of sightseeing. Wu needed to coordinate with our driver. Since everything was long distances apart and it would take more time to get from place to place than we realized, we made our choices with care. Upon Wu's recommendation, we settled on three places: a silk manufacturing factory to see production from cocoons to the final woven product, followed by a quick stop at an embroidery shop (of special interest to me). The day would end with a visit to a government-sponsored compound of artist studios. This intrigued us both, since people now had the freedom to express themselves openly with their paintings. We thought it would be interesting to see what they were producing. During the long drives to each of these places, we would observe a great deal more of Chongqing, which was our primary interest. The diversity to be found here was so different from the other cities we had been visiting. Chongqing seemed fresh and full of vim and vigor. We want to return someday.

For dinner, Wu suggested we might enjoy trying their native dish called "hot pot," a Mongolian speciality well prepared and enjoyed here. (It was Deng Xiaoping's favorite meal.) His description of it sounded so delicious that we decided this was what we should have for dinner. Wu promised to make a reservation at an especially fine "hot pot" restaurant. Apparently, there were many such places. At the same time, he volunteered to take our many rolls of film to be developed at his friend's "very good place."

The Holiday Inn Hotel was several stories high and up-to-date in every respect. It was no simple drive-in motel for overnight lodging, like most of our Holiday Inns in the United States. When we arrived, it was crammed with Western businessmen and Asian tourists. After settling in our rooms, we unwound just enough to become relaxed and changed our mind about going out for dinner. There was a convenient restaurant here which offered either Western or Chinese cuisine. It looked inviting.

From our bedroom window, we saw a lovely grassy park. It was just across from the entrance of the hotel. Established by the Holiday Inn Hotel, it was for the use of its employees, hotel guests and the adjoining community. This morning, several men and women were performing Tai Chi. While the pace of Tai Chi was slow, it was stimulating, with various stretch exercises to tone up the muscles of all parts of the body. One older gentleman's studied movements were a ballet in gracefulness. Looking beyond the park, there were several balloons floating above an office building. They were huge in comparison to the ones we saw over the Trade Exhibition Hall in Guangzhou. We thought those were large. Where are these marvelous balloons sold, I wonder? They would cause comment, but look wonderful, flying over our home in Idaho.

When Wu and his driver reappeared to take us for "hot pot," we urged them to go along without us. Before leaving, Wu handed us two large envelopes which contained all our developed film. What a speedy job that was! The photographs looked fine, but we sighed when we saw the negatives. They were in two or three large rolls and will be difficult to match up with their prints.

The next morning, Wu raved about how good the dinner was, but added he should not have recommended this restaurant, since no one there spoke English. Thus a very nice Chinese gentleman helped two Westerners save face for not going.

En route to the silk factory, we passed an outdoor food market. With an abundance of beautiful fruits, vegetables and other produce handsomely displayed, everything looked exceptionally delicious. The stalls were arranged so it was easy to walk through. We asked to stop. Wu replied we had a specific arrival time to meet at the silk factory, but promised to pause here on our way back.

The silk factory was a series of single storied buildings, each designed for a particular process. In the first, dozens of women stood in front of awkward-looking machines that appeared to have been manufactured before the 19th century. Their purpose was to pull threads out of the cocoons. The cocoons looked like small white peanut shells.

We were told a delightful story about how the first silk was discovered. It came about when a cocoon similar to what we saw here fell from a mulberry tree into the teacup of the Chinese Empress Hsi Ling-shi. She opened it and found inside a glistening thread that was the first strand of silk ever discovered. Since this happened long, long ago, the accuracy of the story might be questionable, but it made a lovely, romantic beginning to our visit. Up until the sixth century, the penalty for smuggling silkworms out of China was death, since silk was regarded as a precious commodity.

We walked into a room with many lines of young women whose average age was somewhere from the late teens to the thirties. Each was standing at a separate machine. Every woman had a basin with a pile of cocoons in front of her. The basin was filled with boiling water. The water softened the outer coat of the cocoon. The girl picked up a cocoon from the water with her bare hands and started pulling some stringy stuff away from the shell. When she found a thread, it was slipped onto a wheel above her pan. The wheel stretched the thread upward and rolled it onto a bolt. This string was as fine as a spider's web and was hard to see. The string from the bolt then wound onto a spool. This spool was twisted around until it was full. Once full, it was removed by the girl and replaced with an empty spool, and the process started all over again. A helper watched all the basins in the entire line and refilled them with more cocoons as the piles depleted. One pretty worker welcomed us to her station and explained this process to us. She said she spent eight hours each day standing at her station doing this work. I asked how old she was when she began at this factory. She said she was 13 years old. The legal starting age was supposed to be 16. Quickly counting the rows of women working in the room, I estimated there must be 20 or more rows, with at least that many women in each. Every worker was a female, while the foreman was a male.

From here, the foreman led us across the street into another large building, where the threads from the spools were made into even larger bolts. This process was hard to comprehend, but it seemed the thin threads from the bolts went through a procedure making them into a soft, glossy, thick material. That material was then dumped into large cardboard bins. The machinery here worked with sharp knife blades which cut up the threads and looked dangerous. If the machinery was handled incorrectly, the operator could lose a finger or cut an arm. Again, the entire process was "manned" by women. Their safety record was said to be excellent.

The final building was a huge, completely automated weaving room. The looms were very large and produced sizeable widths of silk materials. The shuttles operated so quickly that they were almost impossible to watch going back and forth. We observed no special safety guards on any of the equipment. The overhead lighting was dim, and none of the workers, who were all women, wore safety glasses. The foreman assured us his safety record was excellent. Beautiful cloth was being produced.

Our tour ended with a quick walk through their exhibition shop. It was possible to purchase a ready-made garment or order a length of beautiful yard goods to be custom-made. We told them how much we admired their products. We bowed and thanked them for showing us their factory.

To us, this silk factory in Chongqing was a perfect example of a technology totally disregarding people. Or, said another way, when the plant was designed, technology was thought to be more important than the people who ran it. Would it not have been a more efficient product producer, as well as a safer and better environment for the workers, had it been designed the other way around?

When we were comfortably settled and ready to drive away, it seemed something was wrong with our car. The driver could not start its motor. Mac and Wu got out, and along with the help of the foreman, pushed the car from its front bumper up a small hill so it would coast down, starting the motor. The sight was so funny that I quickly took a photograph. Wu and his driver were not at all amused with this happening.

We stopped at the farmers' market as Wu promised. It was a typical open-air, fresh food grocery store, with stalls for various foods needed by the residents of this particular district. The produce was set up in a narrow alleyway. Everything was displayed on individual tables with clean white tablecloths. There were so many tables that they curved all the way around to the corner of the next building. There were wide awnings to shade the food from the hot sun. At the end of each day, everything would be dismantled. New produce was brought in the next day, and the tables would be reset.

All sorts of freshly picked fruit and vegetables, plus nuts, cheeses and meats were attractively displayed. There were vast assortments of dried beans and lentils, thousand-year-old eggs, plates of tofu, various delicious looking patés, fresh cuts of meat and poultry, plus one huge basket full of eggs. I never saw such a large display of eggs in one pile anywhere. I wondered out loud how many chickens the farmer had to produce such a quantity. Perhaps they were not all fresh eggs? Maybe they were a collection over many weeks. I did not ask.

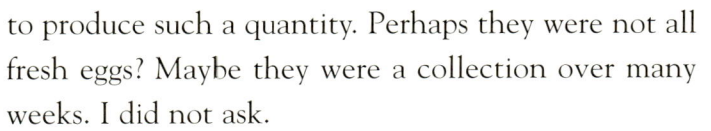

Everything looked delicious and ready to eat. We were suddenly very hungry. The farmers and their wives sold their own produce. They were a smiling, friendly lot with the wonderfully lined faces of hard-working people. They delighted in being asked the name of a particular fruit, vegetable, bean or nut. I had no trouble communicating and understanding their answers. It was obvious they were proud of their produce. Would I like a taste of this cheese or that pâté? Yes, I would, but not today. The fresh apples, peaches and pears were especially tempting. They could make a delicious afternoon snack. Would I like to buy? Yes, I would, but we cannot travel with them. Enjoying a bowl of hot noodles was very tempting. We had better leave.

Wu had to urge us back into the car.

The embroidery factory was a tourist attraction, but the men indulged me, since I was interested in watching how this work was accomplished by Chinese experts. We walked into a building which was a large room divided into two sections. One was a show room selling a variety of Chinese curios like carved jade objects, jewelry, wood carvings, Chinese tea sets and ethnic clothing. The smaller section on the other side was the factory to produce items for sale and also to demonstrate their technique of embroidering. All finished work was exhibited on several large panels in an adjacent room. It was possible to place an order for a special piece. Mac and Wu hurried through all this, while I stayed.

I walked toward one of the men working on his piece. "May I watch?" I asked. Nodding, he smiled at me. The man sat on a high stool beside his embroidery. His lunch plate and tea mug were on a table behind him. The silk piece he was embroidering was encased in a standing wooden frame or hoop. The frame was about a foot in diameter and the section he was working on was stretched very tightly in it. He smiled and turned toward his work. Bending over his hoop, he picked up a tiny threaded needle. The embroidery needle was pulled up through the silk, then pushed down to the underside of the fabric. This push-up/pull-down technique was how the entire piece was sewn. I recognized the particular type of stitch he was doing which was called a "split stitch." The part he was working had many shadings. He took particular care to keep the same tension on the piece so it would not pucker when loosened from the hoop. The design to sew had been pre-sketched onto the fabric.

I was fascinated by the size of the needle being used. Only as long as the last joint of my little finger, which is a little less than three quarters of an inch, it had an extraordinarily tiny eye. It was amazing to me that this man's fingers were agile enough to work with it. Although he did not wear glasses, he threaded it easily without this assistance. The piece of silk to be threaded was pulled from the large skein. It was deliberately kept short in length and was composed of two strands. Too long a piece would fray and knot as the sewing progressed. Undoubtedly, it took hours and hours of patient work to complete one of these designs. This man was a master in shading or blending the gradation of soft colors. I could hardly tell where a new shade started, which was what he was hoping to achieve. After watching a few minutes, I bowed and thanked him for sharing with me. He smiled and bowed to me. I hope he finished his lunch.

As I walked toward the show room, I passed panels of finished embroidery, and noted the various subjects of these pieces. They varied from faces of people to birds to landscapes to abstracts. Quite a range. All were quite beautiful, with even stitching and subtle blends of colors from the palest to the deepest of shades.

It was lunch hour as I walked into the curio shop. Many of the young women clerks were sitting on stools, hungrily chopsticking bites of food. Their individual pots of tea sat close by. The minute they saw me, the bowls were set aside, the tea was forgotten, and they were professional saleswomen once again. Quickly glancing at everything in the various cases, and nodding to the clerks to indicate how lovely their merchandise was, my mind was more on the beautiful embroidery I had just witnessed being made. I was not interested in buying, and Wu and Mac were certainly more than ready to leave.

One would never guess, as we drove down a tiny, one-car alleyway and turned around a blind corner, that we would come to a handsome wooden gate. This was where we stopped after a long drive from the embroidery factory. It was the entrance to a group of artists' studios. We were cordially invited inside and walked through an attractive shady garden to a reception room. Invited to sit down, we refreshed ourselves with a cup of tea, then wandered through the gallery. It was amazing to me, after so many cups of tea, how each tasted exactly the same as the one before. Drinking a small cup was a lovely welcoming custom, but we were becoming a bit satiated.

Originally, this peaceful compound was the home of a warlord. It was now a government sponsored workshop for a group of painters. We were never told how they were chosen, nor the length of their commission. Hung on large moveable panels was the work of the various artists who had studios there. Most of these works were done in watercolors and acrylics. There were a few oils. Why all the subjects were so similar was a puzzle. Perhaps this was planned. We observed no real spontaneity on the part of any artist. We recalled having the same reaction to the pictures we saw at the small art shop opposite the Friendship Store in Shanghai. These individuals apparently were simply happy to paint. In this lovely atmosphere, how could one not be so inspired?

Individual studios were spread throughout the garden of the compound. One climbed up narrow steps and turned around blind corners to find them. It was a charming ambiance. Today a few artists were working. One, name Wu (no relation to our guide), loudly invited us inside. He then put his arm across Mac's shoulders and asked me to take their picture. Artist Wu laughed loudly after I snapped the shutter. We left afterwards, forgetting to look at his work. Another artist was known for his cat drawings. He was an older man with a great sense of humor. This showed up on the expressions of his cats. We laughed aloud at many of them, which pleased him very much. He nodded and smiled and ha haa-ed with us. Very few artists did abstracts. Apparently it was not a popular technique. We noted everybody used a cake paint which they diluted with water to whatever intensity of color was desired. In this beautiful, quiet spot, with birds singing in the tree the only sound we heard, it was difficult to realize bustling, noisy Chongqing was just outside the gate.

Our stay in Chongqing was ending too quickly. We certainly should have scheduled more time here. We promised Wu we would return for more exploring of his fascinating city. We should remember the season we were here, which was late May. Each day had been bright with sunshine and clear of any rain. Chongqing's climate was sometimes called "the furnace of the Yangtze" because it was often hot and muggy with a lot of rain. Strictly by chance, we picked the right time to visit.

We both hoped we could meet Mr. Wu again. That would depend on whether we could find him and/or whether China Travel Service would help us in our quest.

FIVE YEARS LATER WE AGAIN VISITED CHONGQING.
THIS IS THE DIARY I KEPT DURING THAT TIME.

Monday, August 3, 1998:

We were met by our guide, Susan, after an uneventful flight. Chongqing was hot, humid and very foggy. It had rained hard the day before, canceling many flights. We were lucky ours was today.

The drive to the Holiday Inn Hotel was easy compared to the confusion we remembered in 1993. A whole series of new highways had been constructed since we were here five years ago. There was lots of traffic, but no road jams stopped us anywhere. All the lovely Chinese housing along the highway was torn down. We missed seeing it. Ugly high rise buildings had taken their place. None had a Chinese look. The little bright red taxis we remembered were in abundance. Susan told us all cars must be kept clean to drive through Chongqing. If one appeared unwashed, the driver would be fined. Later, when passing through districts outside the city, we saw many being washed.

The hotel was exactly as we remembered. Since this was not the tourist season, there were many rooms available. We were assigned two adjoining ones on the executive floor. There were only six guests there, and two of those were Mac and me. We appreciated our floor clerk. She was an excellent helper, since all the girls at the front desk always appeared too busy to answer any questions. She bowed us on and off the elevator, sent Mac's faxes, got us English newspapers and was a great source of information. Her face was as round and plump as a moon. This type of face is known as a "Buddha face" and thought to be very beautiful.

Wednesday, August 5, 1998:

Today we drove to the Chiang Kai-Shek Garden, entering by its courtyard. This elaborate garden was his private domain during his enforced stay in Chongqing after the Japanese forced him out of Nanjing. It was a beautiful place for him to rest and contemplate. He opened it to the public only on special occasions. During the Cultural Revolution, the Red Guards tried to destroy it. Restored now, it was open to visitors. Madame Chiang had her own separate quarters in the compound, because, as Susan pointed out, she was an important personage in her own right and liked to entertain special guests.

The garden was one of the most elaborate we had seen. After leaving the courtyard, we walked up steps beside a lovely pool with huge rocks carefully placed and meant to resemble mountains. Up another wooden staircase which zigzagged to the right, one walked into a gorgeous setting. We crossed a shallow pond by stepping stones and entered the garden proper. A large pond circled the entire garden. Small espalier trees, various shrubs and large rocks were around its edge. These reflected in the water. There were a few flowers in the garden and some water lilies in the pond. The walking path was curved. One could go deeper into the garden or walk up onto a veranda. There sat an elderly man reading a book. Another man was picking his toes while watching his grandchild play with a little car. From this veranda was a magnificent view of Chongqing.

We turned toward the house and entered Chiang's former reception hall where he received dignitaries. Now it was used as an art gallery to show and sell various types of Chinese paintings. Susan pointed out the differences in Chinese paintings. One technique outlined the subject and often had calligraphy. Another was painted without any outlining. A third method, and the more traditional one, had no boundaries or calligraphy. It seemed softer and more delicate.

We left the garden by walking over a wooden bridge. Underneath, a bull frog croaked noisily to his friend on the other side of the pond. One section behind the formal garden was a potting shed. We noted many bonsai in pots with large ceramic ones holding trees.

How distasteful this elaborate place must have been for the straight-laced General Joseph Stilwell. His home was nearby. His mission was to pursue the war with the Japanese. Much of the money that had been designated for those military purposes, Chiang used to build his elaborate establishment.

The Museum of General Stilwell was plain to the point of being almost shabby. It was an unimposing wooden building with many rooms, but no elaborate garden. He lived and worked there. It contained all sorts of memorabilia of his life in China. The walls were hung with original photographs of people who had served with him. Several of these showed the Flying Tigers. There were many glass cases containing his writing and personal belongings. One item we enjoyed seeing was a small box holding two- by four-inch cards. On each were Chinese characters with the English translation. This was how the General taught himself Chinese. He both spoke and wrote it fluently. He was the only United States general who had traveled extensively in China before any hostilities began. He knew the people and the country better than any other American at that time.

Chongqing was constantly bombed by the Japanese during World War II. Many bomb shelters were dug in the sides of the mountains where people hid during those raids. Chiang had his own private one built in the side of the mountain below his home. Inside, it was a series of cold, damp and dark tunnels and some larger rooms. Water dripped from the ceilings. Since the day was very hot, the coolness there felt good to us, but it must have been a cold and miserable place to stay in during an air raid.

With hostilities ended, many bomb shelters were converted into homes. Sometimes the family business was run from the sidewalk in front of it. I asked Susan if we could take a picture of one. The family I photographed thought this was great fun. They smiled and waved to me. I bowed and waved back to them and then took their picture.

That morning, we ended our sightseeing by visiting a museum of burial caskets. Having one of these was important to many elderly Chinese. It was purchased by the family before the person died. These seemed strange for us to see, but Susan thought we should understand an important part of Chinese culture.

Thursday, August 6, 1998:

Mac asked Susan to show us some of Chongqing's industries. We understood there were many. We assumed they must be along the river which would be used for transportation. That was incorrect. They were situated all around the city and not organized in either an industrial park or necessarily along the river.

First, we went to a steel mill. To reach it, we drove down an alley packed with vendors selling vegetables, wound around a narrow street and finally stopped at a barricade. After being paid a few yuan, the guard lifted the gate. We drove into a fenced community that happened to have the mill in its center. It looked very old. Susan told us 100,000 people worked and lived here with their families. Having them all in a single compound was considered good planning by the officials of the mill, since no traveling to and from work would be involved. There were apartment buildings as well as auxiliary shops to supply workers' needs. We passed official government offices, barber and beauty shops, TV repair places, a laundry with ironing boards, clothing stores, a section selling various food products, and one noodle shop with large pots of water steaming on top of a stove. In another side of the compound was a large swimming pool and an amusement park. No one had to leave the grounds. Susan told us government workers were required to take a three-hour lunch break while the factory workers only had a two-hour one. We inquired what they did with all that time. She replied that they probably napped.

The roads throughout the compound were built of clay. Since it had rained recently, globs of wet clay had fallen onto the main road. Many workers shoveled it to one side. Everybody found shoveling clay a normal happening as, either wet or dry, it fell often onto the road. We were stopped for a time by a truck stuck in the mud. Many men helped get it out. Even our driver offered his help.

A motorcycle/automobile plant was next. It produced Changan cars, as well as the little red taxis used throughout Chongqing. We were not allowed into this place, nor were women or children wearing skirts. A sign posted at the gate said so.

Driving out to the countryside, we saw a chemical plant. It looked deserted. The piping system that carried the chemical was a familiar sight to us, but it was so old and rusty. A paint job would have worked wonders and probably raised the morale of the workers. There was a large complex of apartments nearby. We saw no one in either place.

We stopped at a huge indoor farmers' market located in the middle of the city. It was full of fresh produce. It was enjoyable walking through it. Every type of produce was available. The variety of vegetables was probably three times as large as that in the United States. Included were many kinds of squash, varieties of mushrooms (the white, fluffy ones intrigued me), broccoli, celery, peppers of all kinds from mild to hot, scallions, some thinner and more fragrant than ours, lotus and bamboo roots, other native vegetables which I could not identify, peanuts and a variety of other nuts, a huge amount of fresh and dried fruit, all types of meat including innards such as tongues, throats, stomachs, intestines, hearts, and kidneys which people cooked and ate with enjoyment, ducks, chickens and other fowl, which could be purchased alive and quickly butchered, as well as another counter full of various chicken parts. All produce was attractively arranged on counters, with clerks ready to help the very orderly customers. The floors throughout were muddy and wet, having been hosed down that morning before customers arrived. Outside were a few flower stalls. Watches were for sale there too. Across the street, a group of men sat along the curb of the sidewalk. Behind them against a wall, long handled brushes and pails were lined up. Susan said these men were painters. They were waiting for jobs. We watched a man walk down the street carrying six bamboo chairs. Apparently, he wanted to sell them. Susan said they were old fashioned and worthless. She would not buy them.

We stopped at the Bank of China to acquire some yuan. Since Mac had not brought his passport, I presented mine. I requested yuan for $300. They gave me 500 yuan. The atmosphere was calm, efficient and well organized, unlike the street outside.

Today, we experienced some of the craziest driving ever. We were thankful our driver was highly skilled and could place the car within half an inch of an obstacle without brushing it. Apparently the right of way belonged to whoever got there first, no matter which side of the road it was. Every so often, one saw a lone auto driving on the wrong side in a solid stream of vehicles driving on the correct side. Not to worry, this is Chongqing. When street construction was under way, there would be no barricades. Workers must occasionally pause to allow vehicles to drive across the work space. Our driver had no hesitation to plunge into a stream of oncoming traffic. They invariably yielded.

Susan, Mac and I always conversed while being driven from place to place. On one occasion, we discussed China's policy on abortion. It was an accepted method of controlling the population. If a single woman became pregnant, giving birth to that child was not an acceptable solution. She was encouraged to get an abortion. "How could this take place if the woman did not want an abortion?" we asked. By strong pressure from her family, neighborhood and whole community to do so was Susan's answer. The only possible way she might keep the child was to marry the father, and Susan said those marriages never worked out. Should she withstand all pressures and a child be born, immediately it would be put up for adoption. Susan was very definite that single women did not raise children here. Abortion was the legal and accepted practice for illegitimate pregnancies. We did not ask what a family might do if the first child was a girl and not a boy. Did they raise her or place her for adoption?

Susan asked if we noticed the American couples in the lobby of our hotel with little Chinese babies. We began watching. While I was buying postcards, a young woman came to look at postcards too. She was holding a beautiful Chinese baby. Talking with her, I asked how old the child was. "Ten months," she replied. She held the little girl proudly. Then we sat near another older couple feeding their little girl in the cafeteria. All three of them were giggling and having a wonderful time. The beatific look on the faces of the new parents was wonderful, their happiness contagious.

One morning, there were several couples holding babies in the lobby.

Apparently, the Holiday Inn was a meeting place for many adoptive parents before they flew back to the United States. We were so happy the little girls had a home and did not have to spend their lives in a state run adoption home.

Friday, August 7, 1998:

This was our departure day from Chongqing. Before going to the airport Mac asked, no, he insisted, we look at a "red" building he saw earlier that morning when out for a walk. Neither Susan nor the driver knew where it was, so Mac pointed the direction. Around several corners, we were surprised by a huge skyscraper completely covered with red mirrored glass. It was glaring to our eyes and such a startling addition in a rather drab neighborhood that it was no wonder Mac wanted us to see it. We wondered aloud what it would be like to live or work behind red glass.

Adjacent to the red building, an entire city block was completely excavated. There was one huge, bare hole with no fencing around it. We speculated what its future might be. There were no billboards erected with an announcement.

We reached the airport to check in with time to spare. Our airline was not ready for passengers. We waited and fidgeted and stood in line. Finally, Susan was able to check us in, which was a huge relief. By that time, a long line had formed. Most of those people were part of a tour group. Saying goodbye to Susan was difficult. She was one of our best guides. About a half hour before the flight left, she waved us through Security. No one seemed to know which gate was ours. We asked several officials and each one gave us a different answer. We were reasonably sure this was our boarding gate. When the airplane arrived, all the passengers were let off to "have a rest." We Chongqing passengers had to stand in line until they were re-boarded. When the last one appeared, carrying many packages, she was booed for having made everyone wait while she shopped at the duty-free stores.

Our seats in the first-class cabin were appropriated by cardboard boxes piled high on each one. We were told to go to the coach section, where we luckily found space in the front row. The airplane was an Airbus. The airline seated as many people as possible in the smallest spaces. We were happy to be on our way, but had enjoyed our visit in Chongqing very much. What a fascinating city!

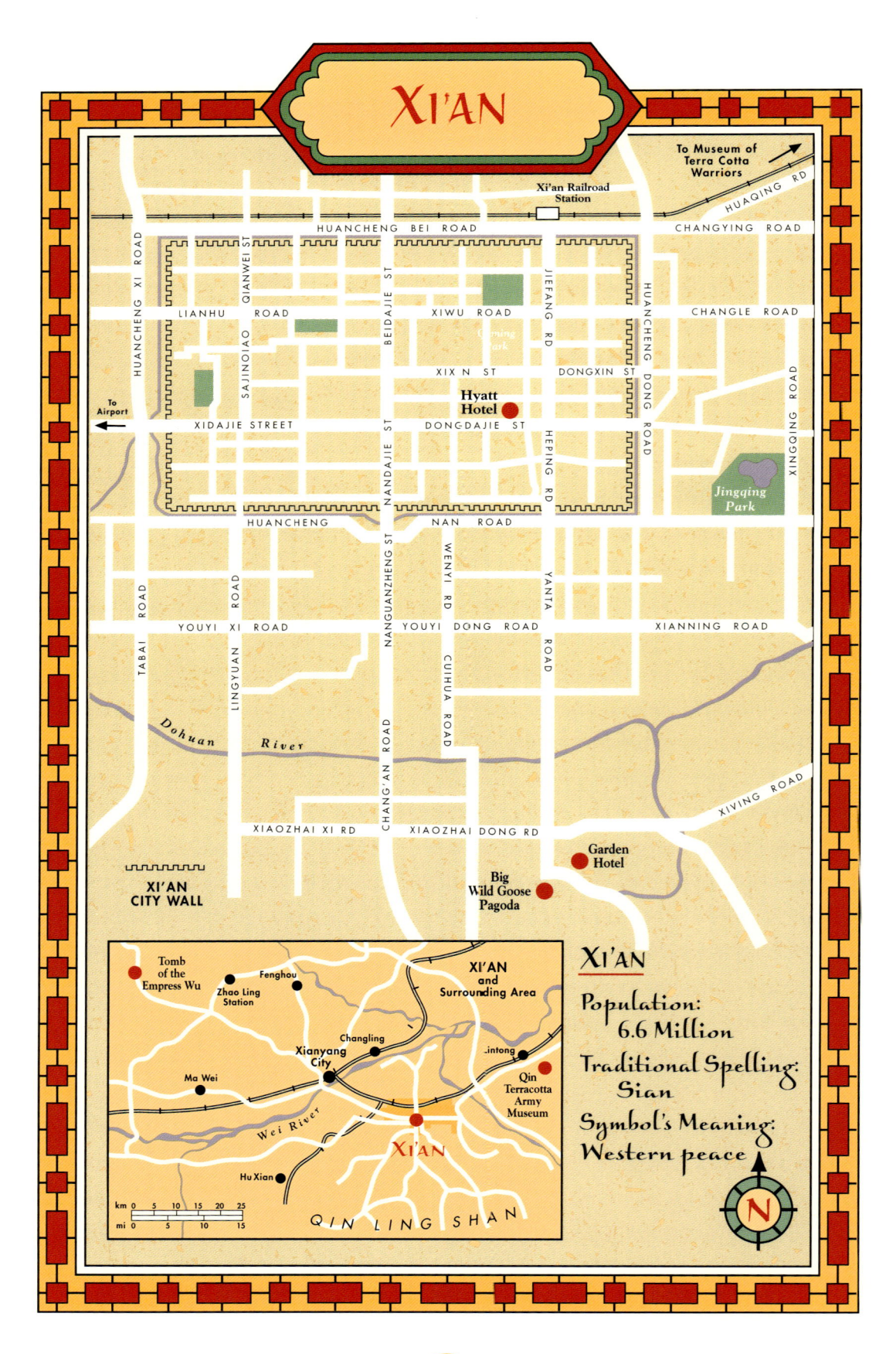

XI'AN

Xi'an

Population: 6.6 Million

Traditional Spelling: Sian

Symbol's Meaning: Western peace

chapter 11

西 Xi'an (Chang'an)

If one was to comfortably survive the seating arrangements on a Chinese domestic airliner, it would be helpful to be small in stature, have no bundles to store and enjoy having one's face inches away from the seat directly in front. That presumed the person in front did not incline his seat back. By now, we knew there were no first-class accommodations on any domestic Chinese airliner so these seats, 8-A and 8-C, to Xi'an were the best we could expect. Compensations on this particular airplane, which was a BAE high-wing China Northwest airliner, were a pretty and clean interior with two efficient stewardesses in attendance. The coordinated colors, in shades of pale blue, rust and chartreuse, revived us considerably, and one needed "reviving" when flying in China domestically. Since flight #107 from Chongqing was a short one, we should reach Xi'an full of energy.

On our arrival at Xi'an, a very dapper guide greeted Mac, offering his card while quickly escorting us through the terminal to the car. The card read Lui Lu. His family name was Lui, but he said we should call him by his given name, Lu. He had not adopted a Western one. He was full of fun and loved to laugh. His keen sense of humor colored every comment he made, be it a joke or a fact. With his habit of cupping his hand by the side of his mouth, everything he said seemed so private that we listened intently. After having had his say, he laughed joyfully, savoring his remarks with enthusiasm. This affectation was so funny we giggled. He reminded us of a friend who had this habit too.

Lu fancied himself a student of historical data, particularly of all the dynasties. He gave us more details about each one than we could absorb. Since our knowledge of Chinese history was sketchy at best, we accepted everything he said as the truth. Why should we question its accuracy? We wanted to learn as much as we could absorb of Chinese and Xi'an history, and this was an easy lesson.

Lu was a bachelor, born around 1968. He lived separately from his family in an apartment. He claimed not to know how to cook, so he tried to eat often at his parents' home in Xi'an. His mother was happy to prepare a meal for him, as long as he paid for it. She reasoned since she paid for his entire formal education at the university, and he learned very well, especially speaking English, he could now reimburse her for anything else he needed. She had very definite opinions. He hoped the girl he eventually married would be friendly with his mother. Otherwise, they probably will disagree all the time, Lu told us. He insisted he was in no hurry to find this wife since he had a nice girl friend. His philosophy of a successful Chinaman was one who ate Chinese food, had a Japanese wife and lived in an American-style home. Yes, Lu, we told him. We had heard this before. It seemed these credentials were the same for many a young Chinese bon vivant.

Xi'an

Xi'an, meaning Western Peace, was one of China's oldest cities. It was the capital of the Shenxi Province. Xi'an was called Chang'an in ancient times and was one of the six ancient capitals of China. Since 1136 BC, it has served as the capital for more than ten dynasties. It probably possessed more items of archaeological interest than any other place in China. The most important one for us was the Museum of Terra Cotta Warriors and Horse of Qin Shihuang, its formal title. We came here specifically for viewing this eighth wonder of the world.

Xi'an was very important during the Tang Dynasty as it was the starting point for what developed into the Silk Road. This was a trade route going through Central Asia and the Middle East as far as the Mediterranean, thus linking Xi'an with Istanbul, Rome and Venice.

The drive from the airport passed through a countryside full of strange, pyramid-shaped, grass-covered mounds. These were tombs that were not excavated. Xi'an became the fashionable burial grounds for emperors, their families and military entourage after the first Ch'in Emperor chose it for his burial site. It was some 30 or so miles from the airport, so we settled back to enjoy the unusual scenery. Driving along, we noted armed soldiers positioned on either side of the highway every so many meters apart and wondered why. Lu said undoubtedly some celebrities must be en route to the city. We hoped we could get there first and not have to stop for their entourage. He added that just this past week, the police caught and arrested drug smugglers along this same road. Xi'an may be more exciting than we thought.

Eventually, we arrived at the handsome new Hyatt Regency Hotel. The reservation manager was confused about our accommodations so the manager, Mac and I, with Lu trailing along, went on a search to see what rooms were suitable and available. What an ideal way to choose a hotel space! We were able to view several. We found two adjoining rooms, with all the amenities we like. They were newly decorated in a sophisticated, but simple, Oriental motif, with floor to ceiling natural bamboo Venetian blinds over the windows, restful earth colors throughout and just enough furniture to be comfortable, yet leaving the room spacious. Before departing, Lu cautioned us not to leave any valuables sitting around, since there was currently a lot of petty robbery in Xi'an. When the bellman delivered the bags, he hesitated by the door. Would Mac like to exchange some money at a very good price? Lu was wise to impress us about being careful.

Next morning, as we prepared for sightseeing, the telephone rang. I ran to answer, since Mac was in the lobby. A voice said, "Hello, is this Helen?" "Yes," I answered, "may I ask who this is?" We did not know a single person here. It turned out to be a Chinese-American friend who was calling us from Beijing. He had just arrived there, knew our itinerary and wondered if everything was going along well on our visit to China. What a nice surprise hearing a familiar voice. And wasn't he kind to be concerned about us?

Driving to the Qin Mausoleum on a different road from the airport highway, we saw more and more burial mounds. Lu said it was a Chinese custom to use one third of the family's wealth for proper burial accouterments. Driving through the shopping district of Xi'an, he pointed out stores selling clothing for this express purpose. I caught a glimpse of "a something" in purple satin. Perhaps this was a burial robe? Just imagine the costs entailed in the burial of an emperor.

We were en route to visit the Museum of Terra Cotta Warriors, the mausoleum of the First Ch'in Emperor, known as Qin (or Emperor) Shihuangdi. This consisted of a group of large scale burial pits full of terra cotta statues of warriors, some with horses and chariots from the Ch'in Dynasty. There were three pits to visit.

Historically, Lu explained, prior to the Ch'in Dynasty (221-206 BC), when a Chinese emperor died, he was always buried in the same tomb with his complete army of living soldiers, chariots and horses. The First Ch'in Emperor, Shihuangdi, born in 259 BC with the name of Yin Zheng, ruled as emperor from 221 to 210 BC, and put a stop to this practice. He was the first emperor to do so. Today, Qin Shihuangdi is remembered for creating this amazing tomb with its terra cotta soldiers that are look-alikes of actual soldiers from his own army. These were placed in his burial tomb. The tomb lay just outside of Xi'an.

Qin Shihuangdi

Qin Shihuangdi was an important, creative ruler. He united all of the various Chinese clans under the same system of laws and punishments for everyone. He abolished slavery. He built vast public works, including over a hundred palaces. He developed the region into counties, putting them under officials appointed by the central government. He ordered roads built to connect all the counties to Xi'an. A uniform Chinese script was organized. People of different dialects then had a means of communication for the first time. He established a standardized coinage with a fixed value so trade could be carried on. (The actual coin was a circle of copper with a square hole in its center.) The great fortification wall around Xi'an was reinforced to keep the hostile hordes from attacking the city. This construction was a long, tedious process and often convicts served out their sentences working on this wall. Because of Qin Shihuangdi's importance and burial in this district, Xi'an became the fashionable burial ground for future kings.

The discovery of the first burial pit, which later would become known as the Museum of the Terra Cotta Warriors, happened quite by accident. For years and years, the ground above and around the pit was used for growing crops. One day in 1947, a farmer started drilling for a new well on the property. As he dug into the earth, suddenly he came face to face with a terra cotta warrior buried deep in the ground. Imagine this farmer's shocked surprise. Its lifelike quality scared the wits out of him. To his credit, he stopped digging and reported the finding to the authorities. The local government took over and set about excavating the area. In 1976, pits two and three were discovered.

The Burial Pits

The entire excavated area is now more than 20,000 square meters or 216,000 square feet, (the mathematics converting square meters to square feet is 20,000 x 9 x 1.2), and is complete with terra cotta statues of 8,000 warriors and horses, all standing in a military formation, as if guarding the emperor. The entire project is considered the most important discovery in the 20th century.

More Specific Details About the Pits:

Number one pit covers an area of 14,260 square meters or 154,008 square feet. It contains about 6,000 clay figures and 40 war chariots. They are spaced in a rectangular battle formation. All seem alert and ready to march ahead. Most of these soldiers are members of the infantry. Number two pit covers an area of 6,000 square meters or 64,800 square feet with 89 chariots, 350 chariot horses, 116 saddled horses and over 900 warriors. They are lined up in a special battle formation and look very human. Pit number three covers an area of 520 square meters or 5,616 square feet with 68 warriors, a colorfully painted war chariot and 30 pieces of bronze weaponry. This pit was possibly the headquarters of all the pits. All three pits are absolutely spectacular to see. Seeing their dimensions makes one realize what a huge effort it was to excavate them.

It is the size of the warriors that makes them especially fascinating. Each warrior is 1.8 meters high or five feet nine inches tall, (using the following mathematics to convert meters into feet and inches: 1.8 x 39.4 ÷ 12), and probably weighs around 150 kilograms or 330 pounds (the mathematics converting kilograms to pounds is 150 x 2.2). The horses are 1.7 meters long or five feet six inches and weigh around 200 kilograms or 440 pounds. Each figure or horse was molded in clay, then baked in a kiln. Originally, they were colorfully painted, but over the years the paint disappeared and is no longer visible. Each warrior's face has an expression somewhat differing from the one next to him. Originally, each carried a bronze weapon, and the original chariots were made of wood. All these figures represent the Qin Army, which was made up of millions of warriors, as well as thousands of war chariots and cavalries. It was the Qin Dynasty's army that had been responsible for keeping the population unified.

When we drove up to the entrance of the museum and looked for a place to park, our driver was told by an attendant that he must put the car on the far side of the compound. No parking was allowed near the museum. Starting in November 1994, the Chinese local officials banned all vehicles from parking anywhere near the museum to help prevent damage from exhaust fumes to the figures inside.

Lu paid for our tickets, then we were permitted to enter the courtyard. The actual entrance to the pits was much further along. Looking ahead, we observed a series of huge buildings which covered the burial pits. Curio shops lined the walkways on either side of the courtyard. From these, anything could be bought, from Coca Colas and postcards to straw hats to shiny satin quilts sewn in gaudy, bright colors, to a variety of antiques. Walking up, then down steps through a temporary plywood tunnel, we saw many people leaning against an unpainted wooden barricade. We were inside an immense roofed building, easily the size of an American football stadium. We slowly approached the wooden fence. Suddenly, we looked out over a vast space, filled to capacity with soldiers, chariots and horses. The soldiers, some 7,000 of them, stand proudly, quietly at military attention. They represented the bodyguards for the afterlife of the First Emperor of Ch'in, Qin Shihuangdi. Their eyes seemed to be looking directly at us. Were they not the burnt orange color of terra cotta, we could easily believe they were alive. I shivered from the pure grandeur of the presentation. All we tourists became as quiet observing them as they were in viewing us. This atmosphere had an awesome, somewhat eerie ambiance.

We spent time studying the soldiers' faces, the positions of their hands and feet and the configuration of the battle formation. By design, each soldier varied in expression slightly from his neighbor. It was their large size that was particularly astonishing. One did not expect them to be so large, nor so lifelike. Each one was excellently preserved. It was difficult to appreciate that they were actually ancient terra cotta pieces because they looked so alive. They seemed to be awaiting a command to "forward march!" We noted one could walk around the entire exhibit because a wooden platform slightly above the pits had been built to accommodate this.

Later, Lu said more tombs would be excavated in the future, as soon as funds became available. We would like to see these when they are ready.

While we leaned on the edge of the wooden barricade, lost in the wonder of what was before us, a group of noisy sightseers disturbed our concentration. On a platform below, apparently used as a walkway for celebrities, a series of flash bulbs went off. Someone's picture was being taken. Then a television crew appeared. Who was here? Who were the dignitaries causing this ruckus? As celebrities, they were being allowed to view the statues on a lower level. The group sauntered by. Among them, we noted a distinguished-looking, white-haired gentleman who was accompanied by his plump, blonde wife. He, however, was the center of attention. Suddenly, we recalled seeing his picture in a recent newspaper clipping. He was Franjo Tudjman, the President of Croatia! Why would he be here, in remote Xi'an, China, with a war going on in his country?

With the battery of bodyguards surrounding President and Mrs. Tudjman, we two craned our necks outside the fence barrier to watch them walk past. They were almost close enough to touch. What a vulnerable position we were in. Should any disturbance break out, we would be in the center of the violence. Apparently, it was for the security of these Croatians that the armed soldiers were positioned all along the highway from the airport to this compound. Later, when we left the museum complex, President Tudjman was informally addressing a crowd of people before getting back into his limousine. His limousine was of Russian design, but Lu said it was built here in China.

President Franjo Tufjman

Back in his home base, this 74-year old man was a colorful figure. He was a former Yugoslav general and openly imitated the late Yugoslav dictator Marshal Tito's mannerisms. His office was a former Tito mansion, where uniformed guards snapped to attention when opening doors to escort visitors in to visit. Almost all of Croatia's business was determined by him, and he ran the nation as if it were his private domain. We guessed this visit to Xi'an was to solicit funds from the Chinese government for the war now raging in Bosnia. His visit was not publicized.

There was a large souvenir shop near the burial pits. Handsome terra cotta copies of soldiers, horses and chariots in varied sizes and poses might be purchased. While none of them were antiques, they were excellent reproductions of the ones we had been viewing. While I was trying to assess the huge variety, a smiling young saleswoman approached and said hello. Ignoring her merchandise, she said how pretty my blonde hair was. "What did you say?" I asked, completely taken aback. "The color of your hair, I like," she said again. Then she added its color was the envy of all Chinese girls. Very surprised by her forwardness, I thanked her for the nice compliment, adding I very much admired the dark color of Chinese girls' hair. "No, no," she laughed, then, remembering to be polite, said, "thank you." This was an unusually personal conversation, for most Chinese girls were not this forward, especially with a blonde, blue-eyed Westerner.

At another building nearby was a small museum displaying a series of antique individual terra cotta warriors. We went in to study the details of the figures up close. Since they were enclosed in glass cases, we were able to walk around each and see the minute details of the sculpturing. This museum had exhibits of each type of figure we saw in the pits. These figures were as amazingly lifelike close up as they were when viewed from the burial pits. We thought them handsome works of art. There were placards describing what type of soldier each was and what their jobs entailed, but nothing about the sculptors who created them. We wished something had been written about them.

While on our way back to the hotel on the outskirts of Xi'an, we spotted an open air herb market and asked Lu to stop. It looked fascinating. Under a huge canvas tent were burlap bags, baskets and barrels filled with every imaginable organic herb or substance that might be used for health enhancement and/or medical reasons. Each type was neatly assembled. It was possible to walk down spanking clean aisles and peer into any of the containers. We saw a variety of colored seeds, barks and fungus, dried flower blossoms and ginseng roots. I spotted some wood ears which were large and beautiful. There were baskets of insect parts, dried fish, silk worms, dried snakes and many varieties of shells. On top of two barrels of seeds were two precious little girls, sound asleep. They never blinked an eye as we walked by.

Anybody could come here to buy herbs. People usually brought their doctors' prescriptions, then picked out the needed assortment. A druggist in an adjacent building could immediately make up the medicine. We wondered why the barrels were so huge. Their contents must be used for more purposes than filling medical prescriptions. Perhaps much of it was exported. Lu never explained. Directly across the street, housed in a huge building, was a medical school specifically for the studies of Chinese medicine, sometimes referred to as holistic medicine. Medical training in Chinese medicine took as long to learn as Western medicine did. When ill, Lu said, many of his contemporaries used a combination of both Western and Eastern medicines. Adjacent to the medical school was the Jannsen Drug manufacturing plant. This was a joint venture between Sweden and China. What a contrast of cultures, with the Chinese herb market on one side of the street and the European drug company on the other side.

We left early the next morning to drive far out in the country to visit Tang tombs. Afterwards, we would leave for Beijing. On this two and a half hour ride, the morning grew hotter and hotter. There was much traffic, and we were delighted to reach our destination to get out of the car. Its air conditioning was not that good. Walking up a sloping clay road that was long and exceptionally wide, we came to a tomb at the top. Along the way, standing on either side of the road, were handsome eight-to ten-foot tall, massive stone statues. Each depicted a Chinese municipal official of that period. Just before we reached the tomb, we saw a fenced-off area with a group of clay soldiers lined up in a military formation. They represented the elite guard for the tomb. Looking closer, we stared unbelieving at what we saw; all their heads had been lopped off! This was an example of the plundering done by the Red Guards during the Cultural Revolution.

Tomb of Empress Wu

This was the tomb of the of Empress Wu from the Tang Dynasty (618-907). She became Empress by a circuitous route. When her husband died and their son proved ineffectual as a ruler, she became Empress in her own right and ruled successfully for many years. She was a skilled and able politician, but her murderous ways of maintaining power gave her a bad name among male bureaucrats. (Being a female, plus the ruling Empress, she probably scared them.) She retained the throne until she was 80 years old. She was properly buried here in her own large tomb. It had not been opened.

Lu decided we should quickly visit another Tang tomb on the other side of this district. It sat in a separate building, surrounded by a flower garden. Today, on the cement paving in front of it, were kernels of wheat spread out to dry in the sunshine. Upon walking inside the tomb, we descended a steep incline to the crypt which we saw mounted on a platform at the bottom. Viewing the tomb was not the reason why we came here. Rather it was to see the beautiful paintings on either side of the walls of the incline leading to the crypt. They were priceless works of art, worthy of all the unpleasantness of trying to keep our feet steady while we slowly but surely slipped downward on the damp clay floor. To stop sliding, we grabbed onto the metal handrails fastened on either side of the incline. The paintings were lovely scenes of hunting, playing polo, and watching a bird. Some other pictures depicted the everyday life of this little-known buried king. What a loving family he must have had to give him such pleasant remembrances for his afterlife. The colors in all of them were intact which was unusual since the tomb was musty smelling and quite cool. Still holding fast to the rail, we gradually worked our way down until we were at the bottom. It was a funny feeling to stand close beside a stranger's bronze crypt, actually touching it. Standing in the light from a spotlight in the vaulted ceiling, we felt his presence, but the atmosphere of this intimate place made one feel welcome and surprisingly at ease.

We had exactly an hour and a half drive back to the airport before boarding the flight to Beijing. As we turned onto the road to go through the village leading to the main highway, a youth was walking down its center. Our driver blew his horn, but the boy was unwilling to move aside to allow us to pass. As we slowed down considerably to miss hitting him, the young man suddenly grabbed onto the rear view mirror on Lu's side of the car. Lu signaled him to let go. The boy hung on, then lost his footing and let go of the mirror. Our driver speeded up to pass him. "Lu, what under the sun was that about?" we asked. "A crazy person," he replied. "Are you sure he was not trying to get money for drugs?" "No, no," he answered, apparently totally unconcerned, and fell sound asleep in the front passenger's seat. We quietly locked the back doors of the car.

While driving along on the main highway, we watched the traffic. Our driver was adept at maneuvering the car through all of it. We went by such a mishmash of conveyances. For amusement, I began to list on a piece of paper the different types of vehicles we passed. Along with the trucks, automobiles and bicycles, there were a variety of individuals walking on either side of this two-lane highway too. A man dressed in a dark city suit stood at a bus stop. When the bus failed to halt for him, he threw a stone at it. On top of one bus was a huge pile of baskets. We passed a tractor with a water tank mounted in back, and another tractor pulling a wooden wagon. Every person wore a straw hat to keep cool.

Buses were a pale green color. All were thickly covered with dust. There was a bus carrying a load of salmon-colored bricks. Although these Chinese bricks appeared to be slightly larger in size than our American ones, this type was exactly the same color we used to build our home in Michigan. Funny feeling spotting a selection of Chicago common bricks in a remote section of China! A motorcycle passed. There were not many of those here. There were no motorbikes. A small tractor carried a load of dark red bricks, plus three large adults. It was a slow mover. A bike had two huge baskets hanging on either side by its rear wheels, filled with sticks. Many people walking along the road held onto the hands of little children. Some men carried hoes with long handles over their shoulders. When they turned sidewise, this made an interesting traffic hazard. There were white, red and black motor cars. No other colors. A few of these were old Audis.

A group of villagers was sitting beside the road, trying to sell baskets of fresh peaches. The fruit looked delicious. At another village, everyone was sitting with piles of fresh garlic for sale. Further along, kernels of wheat were spread alongside the road to dry. In other places, raw straw was scattered to be dried in the sun and warm air. As we neared Xi'an, several modern gas stations appeared. One housed the tanks inside the building, while the gas tanks were outside at the others. There were donkeys pulling loads of about anything one could imagine. Sometimes a man walked alongside the donkey, but more often, the man sat on the wagon, even if it was an extremely heavy load. Horses pulled carts and wore complicated harnesses. Donkeys did not. There were multitudes of jeeps. Some were used by the military. Some small vans transported people. We saw a wheat harvester. It momentarily blocked the road. It was the only modern piece of farm machinery we had seen. We went around a van piled high with furniture. We passed many three-wheeled pedicabs loaded with melons. Three separate horse-drawn wagons traveling in tandem were loaded with sticks. Another pulled a wagonful of gravel. Here was a horse-drawn wagon carrying a family of four. This entire complexity of traffic headed in the direction of Xi'an. It moved mostly at a reasonable pace, and our driver was good about when or when not to pass. Nowhere had we seen such a variety of traffic on any road.

As we approached the city limits, policemen appeared and began to direct the traffic. Standing in the middle of street intersections on square plastic footstools, each policeman wore a walkie-talkie. The city became more crowded with vehicles and confused with people. There was much horn blowing as drivers tried to avoid hitting pedestrians. This noise woke Lu up.

Oops, there was an accident! As a bicycle rider waited in the center lane for his turn to cross the road, a taxicab collided with him, denting the bicycle's front wheel. Bystanders gathered. This was something out of the ordinary, worth watching. Angry words were exchanged, and we could see some people nodding and others shaking their heads. No one was hurt, but everyone had an opinion as to what happened. We went on past. Eventually the police would come, and things would settle back down to the normal affairs of the day.

The scheduled flight for Beijing never appeared. No one could give a satisfactory explanation why, other than that the airplane never took off from the previous airport. Since we were checked out of the Hyatt Regency Hotel, we needed rooms for the unexpected overnight. The travel agency would handle this. For a change of scene, we asked Lu if China Travel Service would reserve rooms for us at the Garden Hotel. Inside this Japanese-run hotel, we enjoyed Oriental surroundings, with a lovely stylized garden at the far side. There one could sip a cool drink beside a pool, while watching ducks lazily swimming past attractive greenery planted around its banks. There were interesting shaped rocks, through which a bubbling waterfall flowed. It was a very restful ambiance. We unpacked and enjoyed a quiet dinner. Afterwards, strolling through the lobby, we browsed through the gift shop and found interesting coffee-table books with beautiful pictures of Xi'an. Since books of this sort were hard to find in China and would not be available at all in the United States, we bought some beautiful ones for our library, as well as one for our daughter Susan, who expressed an interest in reading about Xi'an and its treasures.

When we checked out the next morning, a Tai Chi class was in session outside on the terrace by the pool. How much I wished I could join them, as I enjoy doing Tai Chi. It was very inspiring in the early morning sunshine to watch a group of men and women follow their lively instructor in this graceful exercise.

Lu asked how we liked this hotel as compared to the previous one. "It's not for Americans," answered Mac. "They do not understand English at all." He cited trying to get a receipt for our hotel bill. The clerk insisted on giving him individual copies of all our charges since arriving. Mac only wanted a receipt of the completed statement. I inadvertently added to his confusion when Mac handed me a 50 yuan note and asked me to buy two stamps. I asked the clerk how much two stamps cost. Not understanding my question and seeing the note in my hand, she answered 48 yuan. I took two stamps and two yuan back to Mac. He exploded. This was the last straw. "Helen, take this five yuan note to her and get my 50 yuan note back." That transaction was completely incomprehensible to the girl. She had not understood my original request, so Mac faced the girl himself to explain what he wanted. Telling this to Lu, he commented, "Well, this is a Japanese hotel, just full of Japanese." I giggled to myself. Who else but us would stay here? We knew the Chinese were not overly fond of the Japanese. Our accommodations were excellent in spite of this annoyance.

Before we went to the terminal, Lu announced he had arranged lunch for us at a restaurant in the neighborhood beside the airport. Down an alley, we stopped at an unimposing entrance that made us wonder what sort of restaurant this was. The owner, who was out front, bowed, greeted us with a big smile, bowed again, and then led us to a stairway. Mac and I went up and found a dining room full of tables, each set for ten people. No one was there except us. We were puzzled why we should be fed upstairs while Lu ate downstairs with the rest of the customers. A waitress bowed and directed us to our places. We were asked what we wished to drink, and Coca Colas were quickly brought. We sat and drank and waited. We waited and waited and waited some more. Eventually, three dishes of food appeared. Although he did not say, we guessed Lu must have pre-ordered the meal. We were never offered a menu. While we ate, the waitress stared at us, watching everything we did. This was very disconcerting, but the food was excellent.

What a complete bore it was to stand around a terminal waiting for an airplane to arrive. The masses of humanity walking around varied from several Buddhist monks in colorful robes, and Europeans of every size and shape, to traveling groups of Asians with all their relatives, who came to wave goodbye. Curio shops were investigated, and the beverage counter was well attended. A bottle of water tasted refreshing.

One couple looked very different from everyone else. We learned they were Brazilians from Sao Paolo. She had extremely short, over-bleached hair, wore a dark brown lipstick and rouged her cheeks a bright pink. It made a strange cosmetic effect because the colors did not seem to quite blend together. Her husband appeared as normal as she did unusual. He approached to ask if we were on the flight to Beijing. Affirming that we were, he wanted to know when it left Xi'an. Lu took over the conversation and told him everything he knew about the delay and when we were scheduled to leave. They were frantic to get on the Beijing flight to be able to continue their tour. Their problem was how their ticket was written. The difference between their ticketing and ours was that each leg of ours was a separate entity. This allowed us to reschedule, while theirs did not. Lu directed them to the China Travel Service office. Since they did not appear on our flight, we never knew how they solved their problem.

All three of us—Lu, Mac and me—were tired with waiting around, and Lu had other clients whom he must attend. We assured him we could get on the flight without trouble. Since the airplane never came yesterday, he preferred to wait and see us properly boarded. This was truly nice and the correct thing for him to do.

Finally, the loudspeakers announced our airplane had landed. Thoroughly harassed by now, everybody tried to go through Customs Control at once. What a crush of humanity, with everyone wanting to be first! Without any finesse whatsoever, Lu bodily shoved us into the more or less undefined line for the official checking tickets and passports. We three never had a chance to say a formal goodbye, but he knew very well how much we enjoyed Xi'an and all our adventures with him. Thoroughly crushed as we were squeezed into a single line past the official to an open door, we entered a large, airy lounge only to find we must wait longer before boarding the Beijing flight. We turned briefly to wave a final goodbye to Lu and saw he had already gone. Will he ever find his Japanese wife who will please his mother and himself? Will they live in an American house and enjoy eating delicious Chinese food? Maybe some of those plans will come true. We suspected right now he was much too busy living the good life to think about any such future nonsense. And what about us? We found a comfortable place to sit. Then we smelled the wonderful aroma of espresso and bought ourselves a cup. How it brightened our spirits before our Beijing flight was finally called for boarding!

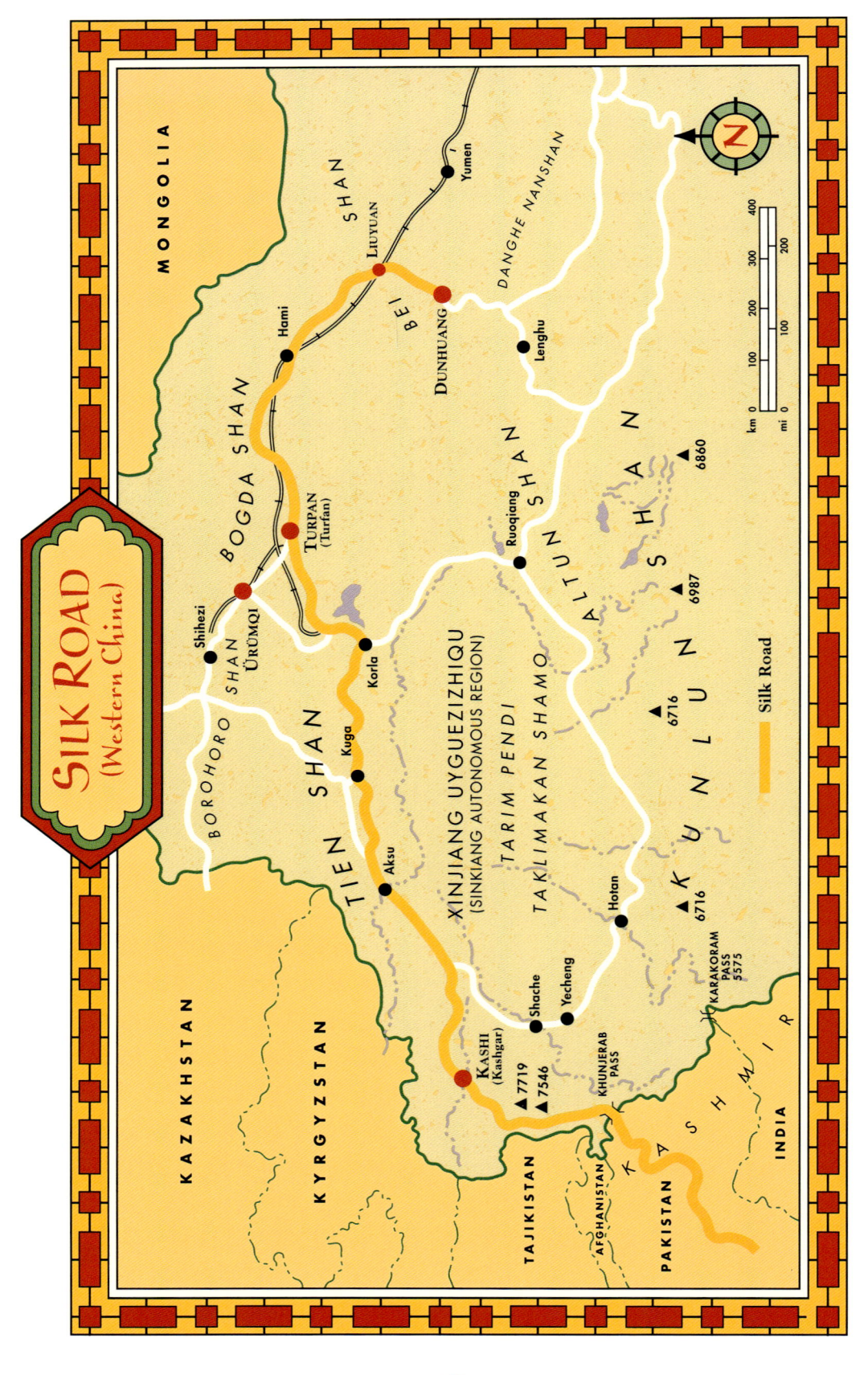

Silk Road (Western China)

chapter 12

絲路

The Silk Road (Western China)

NOTE:

Mac and I did travel into western China during the summer of 1998. The route we took was known as the Silk Road. In researching where we might go, we were surprised to learn there was a series of ancient caravan trails leading into the heartland of China. All of these were known as the Silk Road. Many were not open or ready for tourists. The way we went had been accessible only since 1983. It was known as the Southern Silk Road Route.

Since ancient times, all caravans started on the Silk Road from Xi'an, and so would we. Flying westward through the Gansu Province, our first stop would be Dunhuang, on the edge of the Taklamakan Desert. This desert was endless and had very dangerous sandstorm weather, sometimes called "black hurricanes." Caravans had always skirted around its edges. From Dunhuang, we would motor along the highway through the desert, passing several oasis towns. Our destination was Liuyan, where we would board an overnight train to reach Turpan. From Turpan, we would motor to Ürümqi, a city established and built with the support of the Russians, who wanted to have a foothold in western China. Then flying, our final destination was

Kashgar, a Muslim city in the farthest part of western China. It lay at the foot of the Pamirs Mountains. Had we continued on, like some merchants of old, our next stops might be Pakistan and perhaps even India or Iran. We will end our Silk Road journey in Kashgar, return to Urümqi, fly to Guangzhou and finally board a train on to Hong Kong. Unlike the travelers of old, we were happy to do this traveling by car, rail and airplane and not in a caravan of camels. It would take us approximately two weeks, not several years, as it did long ago.

Traveling along the Silk Road evokes tales of the mysterious Orient and those who made this route possible. It started when Emperor Wudi of the Han Dynasty (206 BC–AD 220) sent his General Zhang Qian to recruit the Yueh-chih people who had recently been defeated by the Hun of Turkish descent. They had fled to the western fringes of the Taklamakan Desert, but were looking for revenge and would welcome help from any ally.

General Zhang assembled a caravan of a hundred men and set out from Chang'an, then the Chinese capital, now known as Xi'an. Soon they were captured by the Huns in northwestern Gansu. They were treated well by the Huns, but Zhang and the remainder of his party eventually escaped and traveled west to Kashgar. There, and at other oases along the way, he found the Yueh-chih people comfortably settled. They were no longer interested in avenging the Huns. Zhang stayed with them for a year, gathering useful information for his Emperor, and began his return to Xi'an by the southern Silk Road. On this journey, he was captured by Tibetan tribes. Once again escaping, he returned to Xi'an, 13 years after his departure. Of his original party, he and one other were the only ones to complete this journey. He established the first route between the East and West, which eventually linked Imperial China with Imperial Rome.

Zhang fascinated his Emperor with stories of some 36 kingdoms in the Western Regions, some of which now are known as Pakistan, Persia (Iran) and a city called Li Kun, which was Rome. He told stories of the famous Ferghana horse, a fast and powerful warhorse, which was much superior to any others. An army using them would have the potential to defeat the

Huns. The Emperor sent General Zhang back to develop political contacts with foreign envoys, but mostly to bring back horses. The artists of the Tang Dynasty (AD 618–907) immortalized these horses in statues. We now see some of them in museums.

Silk was one of the trading commodities of the Chinese. No one in Europe had ever seen it. The Romans were fascinated by it. However, it was only a small part of the trade along the Silk Road. Eastbound caravans brought gold and precious stones, textiles, ivory and coral. Westbound caravans carried furs, ceramics, jade, lacquer, and cinnamon bark, as well as bronze weapons. Very few caravans completed the entire route between the capitals of the two great empires. Trading was done in many oasis towns en route. The prices rose at every stop.

The religious systems and arts of India, Central Asia and the Middle East came along the Silk Route too. Buddhism from India became the new religion and was taught by Indian priests to the Chinese Emperor. The Buddhist caves that we would visit in Dunhuang were built to ensure safe passage of the caravans and were sponsored by powerful families and merchants.

During the Tang Dynasty, Chang'an was a large cosmopolitan center having a population of nearly two million people. It was the departure point and final destination of travelers along the Silk Road. Interesting to note was the diversity of the population. There were over 5,000 foreigners from Turkey, Iran, Arabia, Mongolia, Armenia, India, Korea, Malaya and Japan. There were many temples, churches and synagogues.

The Ming Dynasty (AD 1368-1644) shut China off from the outside world, ending all foreign ideas and cultures. Islam replaced Buddhism, particularly in the far west, and brought a whole new set of ideas, the root of the culture of the Uighur people of the far west.

What follows are the notes Mac and I both took while on the trip.

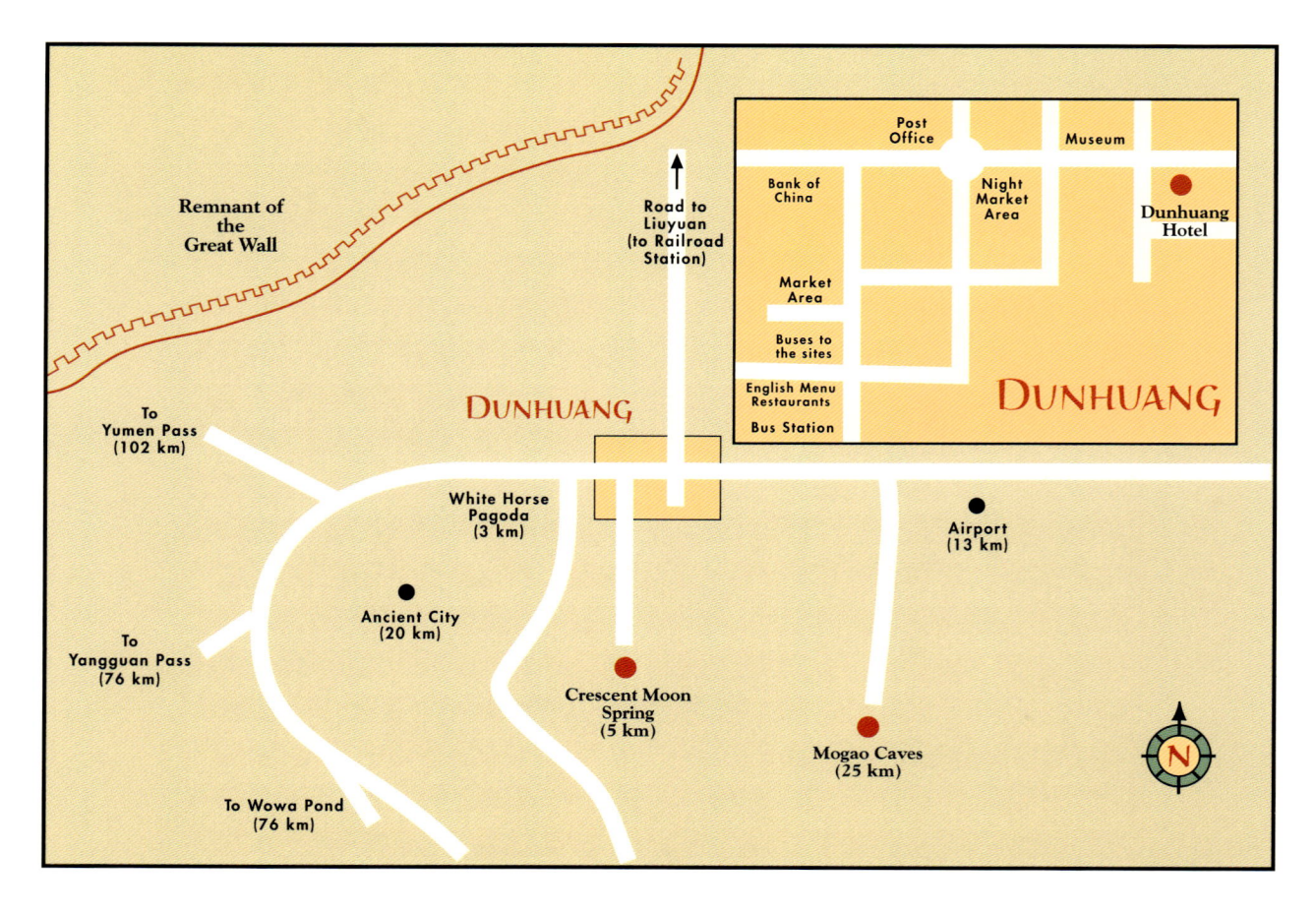

Dunhuang – Saturday, August 8

Accompanied by our guide, Lee, who would be with us during our entire trip into western China, we left Xi'an at 5:15 in the morning. Our driver wanted to be sure we got to the airport early. Mac and I got up at 3:30 that morning to be in the lobby on time. Along with Lee, we were driven to the airport in moonlight. There was hardly any traffic so the trip was fast. We three were the first passengers checked in for the flight to Dunhuang. After going through Security, we found ourselves in a pleasant waiting room with very few people. I noted the direction to the women's toilet and headed there. A cockroach greeted my entrance, and I had the choice of the three booths with holes in the floor and doors that would not fully close. They were clean, as all had recently been doused with a pail of water. That pail was just inside the room.

Dunhuang is located in the northwest desert corridor of Gansu Province, near the Xinjiang border to the east and the Qilian mountain range to the west. This 2,000-year old town was once an important caravan stop on the Silk Road linking Central Asia with China.

Our two-hour flight to Dunhuang went over a part of the Gobi Desert and a range of mountains called the Qilian Shan. Only a few passengers were on the flight. Lee told us they were mostly elderly people from Taiwan. How did he know where they were from? By their accent, and Lee said he could not understand a word they said.

The desert, from our height, looked very barren. It was easy to spot oases, as they were so green, and every inch of them was farmed. We learned the main crop was wheat. This was grown on instructions from the government, which owned all the land. The government doled it out to the farmers by mus, about a quarter acre. When the wheat crop was harvested, the farmer was permitted to plant another crop if he wished. He could market that one for himself. Usually this crop was cotton, as it brought a better price on the market than wheat. They raised a lot of corn too. We saw how each mus was laid out, with a mounded strip of grass between each one. Sometimes poplar trees were planted on the mounds. Sheep were herded along the strips to eat the grass. The cotton plants were fully leaved, some with pink flowers, and all had a bit of white cotton ready to pick. Machinery did that work. Harvesting occurred sometime in September.

We landed in Dunhuang on its long single, paved runway which served that city and its neighboring villages. A Ms. Miao greeted us and announced she would be our guide. Miao pronounced her name like "Meow." She guided us to a small Japanese-designed, but Chinese-manufactured bus. We had no idea we would have two guides and were a little puzzled by this state of affairs, thinking Lee would be the only one on the entire Silk Road trip. On further stops, a local guide with a car and driver always accompanied us.

Ms. Miao was very dictatorial in instructing how we should store our luggage on the bus. When she and Lee grabbed our computer bags and threw them in the front seat, Mac got angry. They laughed, a sign of embarrassment, and went back to the terminal for our big bags. Placing those heavy bags on the bus sobered them considerably.

A bumpy ride followed for about an hour, with Miao talking constantly about the surroundings and the history of the place. It was interesting that a flood in 1979 destroyed so much of the city that it had to be completely rebuilt. About two meters of water had fallen, causing the flood. Now all the small shops alongside the road through the town were new and clean. Water came from melted snow in the high mountains. These surrounded the city, although one did not see any mountain range from where we were driving. A reservoir supplied the town and made the electricity for Dunhuang. It was a town of about 50,000 people, small compared to most Chinese cities. We liked its neighborly appearance, with people going about their daily tasks on bicycles and others walking in the streets or along the sidewalks. This was a Buddhist center. We saw four monks dressed in long brown robes walking down a side street as we drove through the town. Tomorrow, we would visit a series of old caves in the Mogao Grottos which were created by their ancestors.

Such a bumpy ride! We had sat in the rear seats of the bus, which was a mistake. Those seats positioned us over the wheels, and we felt every bump the bus went over. Finally, we turned onto a road far from the town, in the middle of the sandy desert. We beheld a huge structure which looked like a mighty fortress. This was the Silk Road Dunhuang Hotel. We would stay there two nights and the better part of a third day.

The hotel was gigantic in proportion. Stepping across a high wooden threshold painted a strong yellow, we entered a huge reception room. On either side were sitting spaces sunk a foot below the entrance level. A very formal seating was arranged in each. Four straight-backed Chinese chairs were placed squarely around a small, low wooden table. Perhaps one could relax there and be served a refreshing drink. Straight ahead was the reception counter, made of a long, long piece of pink granite. There were huge murals on either end of the room. While Miao engaged us in conversation, Lee did the checking in.

It took two bellmen to carry our luggage. One of them smartly opened the pull-handles and easily walked with them. The other bellman carried his and stopped halfway up the stairs to catch his breath. There were no elevators in the entire hotel. Up two flights of stairs, we proceeded to walk down a very long hallway. Our rooms were directly ahead. The flooring in the hallway was made of bricks with no mortar between the joints. This feature interested us, as bricks must be well made to lie so flat without a gluing compound to level and hold them together. The bricking continued throughout the flooring in our rooms.

Our rooms were a large square sitting room and a bedroom, both with bathroom facilities. The living room was decorated with Chinese furniture which was placed against every wall around the room. A lovely Chinese Oriental rug with a subdued design of flowers in pale blues and pinks was on the floor. Four wooden chairs with wide seats and curved backs lined two of the walls. It did not seem possible for any human to sit comfortably in those chairs, as they looked so stiff and formal. Between each pair was a table with a lamp. On one table was a Thermos of hot water, and two covered cups and green tea bags. Across the room was a low wooden chest with drawer space. Placed on the rug was a low round enameled Chinese table with four matching stools. They sat low for me and were impossibly low for Mac. When he sat, his knees reached above the table. This grouping was a pretty addition to a very formal room. The bedroom was very simple with two beds, a night stand and a lamp. A chest of drawers was placed across from the beds. When we sat down on the beds, their mattresses were hard as a rock. We wondered how restful they would be.

We had agreed to meet Lee and Miao in the lobby so they could show us where lunch was to be served. We hurried back downstairs. The hotel restaurant was in another building. This was reached by a series of walkways. We passed by several buildings on the way. There was an interesting desert garden beside the walk. No demons followed us because we made many sharp turns as we passed each building.

We were seated at a table for two, while our driver and two guides sat on the other side of the room. We were asked the usual question, "Did we wish forks?" followed by a long discussion between guides, waitresses and finally, ourselves on what we wanted to drink. Our choices were beer, Coke, or 7-Up. Finally, when we were left alone, the food began arriving. A spicy soup was ladled into bowls. Then came platters with various foods. Using our chopsticks, we dabbled in each of the early arrivals, but when the eleventh platter came to the table, we stopped eating. Apparently this gesture did not stop more being presented to us. The food was a local cuisine and had no particular taste. It embarrassed us to leave so much food uneaten on the table. The waitresses never took any platters away. Suddenly, two young girls in long red satin dresses and fancy headpieces came into the room. They positioned themselves near our table, ready to sing. We quietly got up and left the room.

After a short rest, that afternoon we drove to the local museum in the middle of Dunhuang. It had displays of relics from the Han, Ming and Tang Dynasties. Probably they were not the best examples of those periods, but quantity made up for quality. We were told the British, particularly a Sir Aurel Stein, took most of the Buddhist texts written in Chinese, as well as collections of scrolls, documents, embroideries and paintings, back to London. Apparently the French and Americans took their share too. We spent a long time at every showcase. Miao was a history buff and knew a little about everything shown. Lee had presented each of us with a bottle of cold water. When Miao's lectures ran a little long, pressing the cool plastic bottle against one's cheeks kept us attentive. Every window in the museum was open and let in warm air. Almost two hours passed before we finished all the showcases, and by then we all were perspiring heavily, and our water bottles were warm.

Dinner was served in a private room adjacent to the main dining room. We were its only diners. The table was set with forks and knives. We were served Western food and drank a strange-tasting Chinese white wine. On my plate was a chicken cutlet with green beans and French fries, while Mac's had a pork chop and the same vegetables. Hot rolls came in a basket. On the table was a dish of sweet jam and one with dabs of butter. There was a bowl of sugar cubes and a small pitcher of cream. In it floated a dead fly. Serving us were a young girl and a man who took turns pouring tea, wine and shooing the flies away. We ate with gusto and enjoyed the Western food.

Our two guides and driver ate in the Chinese dining room, again totally enjoying the food.

On this visit to Dunhuang, our time will be spent visiting the Mogao Grottos. Named "Caves of the Thousand Buddhas," they are the world's largest and best preserved repository of Buddhist arts. We shall drive out into the Mingsha Hills to see sand dunes. It was said when the wind blew over the sand, the dunes sang. If we wanted, we might ride a camel to the Crescent Spring Lake in the mountains, a mere hour away.

That night when we closed the door of our rooms, both Mac and I looked at each other and shook our heads. How strange this place seemed. We laughed. We had waited months to come here, never realizing how different from our other China trips this one was going to be.

Dunhuang – Sunday, August 9

Today we awoke early. We dressed and went outside to enjoy the cool morning air and wait for the seven o'clock breakfast hour. I wanted to take pictures while the sun was still rising. The early morning light made the walls sparkle a golden color. The place looked like a desert fortress. It had wonderful high walls made of stucco. The stucco was mixed with large pebbles, making it unusual and quite handsome. High up on the corners of all the walls were lookout posts. Up there, one could see for miles.

Our entire morning was the drive to the Mogao Grottos and investigating the Buddha Caves.

On the way, Miao considerably softened her attitude toward us. She talked at length with me about her son, a five-year old. He had started going to school, much to the disapproval of her mother-in-law, with whom they lived. She thought her grandson was too young for schooling. Miao had prevailed. The little boy was one in a class of 50 five-year old boys and girls. The school had two classes with three teachers who worked with all the children. Miao said, after the first day, her little boy liked school and wanted to go back. She was pleased with his progress. They sang simple songs, learned how to draw—he became competent at drawing animals, particularly horses—and were told stories. At home, he especially liked to play with his cars. Last night, Miao had taken him shopping for a new one. Later, he begged not to have to take a shower so he could play longer with his new car. She was teaching him English. If she said something in English, she insisted he answer back in English. She was educated at the university in the next large town and was an English teacher. She taught high school teenagers for two years, then stopped when the government would not fund English in the school. Now English was a basic subject for any student entering the university because it was a basis for science courses. Miao was friendly today. Perhaps yesterday she was nervous meeting us.

En route through the desert we saw many lumps or small mounds in the sandy desert landscape. Miao informed us these were graves. Anyone could come here to bury their dead. People liked this spot because it faced south toward the Buddhist caves. We wondered how anyone found their ancestor's burial spot, since none of the graves was marked.

The Caves of the Thousand Buddhas in the Mogao Grottos were truly marvelous to see. When the monks lived here ages ago, they dug the original cave in the mountain side, then proceeded to use the clay to make Buddha statues which they placed back inside. They made drawings on the walls too. Some Buddhas were huge in size, others merely large, but all were very imposing. We climbed up many stairs to see inside several caves. The interiors of all the caves were completely dark, really black inside, as no electricity was allowed. The curators believed electricity would destroy the painting on the walls and on the statues. We were permitted to take flashlights and used them for viewing the walls and Buddhas inside the caves. Miao explained the meaning of the drawings. For the most part this was quite interesting, but became a bit repetitious. During one period, Russian soldiers were housed in some of the caves. Many of the paintings were ruined because the soldiers cooked inside their cave. We were not allowed to take pictures anywhere in this compound. Everyone was checked at the entrance by guards to see that no one carried a camera. Rules were strict here.

We must have walked up and down steps and along dozens of ridges to enter caves for three or four hours. The entire place was closed for the lunch hour. Everybody had to leave the compound. All gates were shut and locked. We enjoyed this adventure.

Dunhuang – Monday, August 10

Our big adventure this morning was going to Crescent Moon Lake, a very short distance from the hotel. We were let out a fenced street block leading to the entrance for the lake tour.

Along either side of this block were booths, each one filled with native souvenirs like hats, stuffed camels, and various bric-a-brac. We asked Miao how many hats or camels the merchant would have to sell in order to make any profit. She did not know and neither did Lee. The profit concept was an alien one to them. Most of the kiosks were unopened because it was still early in the day.

We paid our entrance fee at a booth beside an elaborate, tall, bright red Chinese gate. Then we walked through a small door built inside it. The first thing we saw were groups of camels sitting, standing or kneeling for people to mount their backs. So many camels! Up close, they were the strangest composition of contradictions. Each animal's oblong head was connected to a very crooked neck which swooped up toward the back. We were told these were Asian, not African, camels. Asian camels like these had two humps, while the African ones had one hump. The camel's legs were spindly and slender and did not seem strong enough to support its sizeable body. Constantly they flicked their tails in a nervous sort of way. These animals looked mean to us. We never encountered a happy one. They looked a person straight in the eye, almost daring him to climb on their backs. Some were tied together, making up a caravan. Many tourists rode them, but not us. Lee estimated that to buy a camel might cost its owner $30,000.

We were offered camel, jitney or foot transport to the lake. We took a jitney across a sandy stretch of desert to a parking lot, where we walked on a narrow clay path toward the Crescent Moon Lake. This lake, in the midst of sand dunes, was said to be very picturesque, but the sand dunes were spectacular. They were all along one side of the road on our way to the lake. Their crests had sharp peaks which created wonderful shading effects. We watched many Japanese tourists climb to the top of a sand dune and walk along the sharp ridge. Getting up there was a steep climb through heavy sand. Seeing them from where we were, down below, made the tourists look like Arabs from olden times, tramping through the desert. Once on top, many slid back down on a toboggan-like sled. Pity the poor concession people who handled those sleds. They had to climb up with them and wait for some tourist to rent one. We noted two or three sets of steps built in the sides of dunes so a person could walk up instead of trudging through the sand. Lee said he did this type of sledding in Mongolia and it was great fun.

We walked toward a large pagoda in the distance. Along the way, we watched workers assembling equipment for drilling a water well. One man was on a shaky ladder trying to catch, by hand, a rope thrown up to him. After about three tries, the man below threw the rope high enough, and the person on the ladder caught it. Working with safety rules was not practiced here.

Finally we were on the platform of the pagoda, viewing Crescent Moon Lake. What a disappointment! There was hardly any water in it. It was surrounded by tall grasses. We were told the fish in it had died when they connected the lake to a pipeline carrying water from another lake. Apparently that polluted water killed the fish.

We ambled back to the parking lot.

The rest of the day, we organized our packing for leaving Dunhuang and driving to Liuyuan that same evening. There we would board a train for a nine-hour overnight trip to Turpan.

Checking out took time. Mac and I went to the lobby early to do it, but the girl had trouble making her American Express machine work. Fixing it took more time. By then, both Lee and Miao had appeared and added to the confusion. Miao grabbed our bill from Mac. He told her in no uncertain terms it was "our bill, not hers" and not hers to read without first asking us. Sometimes guides can be too helpful.

Dunhuang was certainly a tourist attraction. The hotel, while handsome in architecture, needed practice in serving its foreign guests. We thought adding a shuttle between the hotel and the town would be an interesting diversion, as the town was small enough to amble through with ease. This place had all sorts of possibilities for tourists.

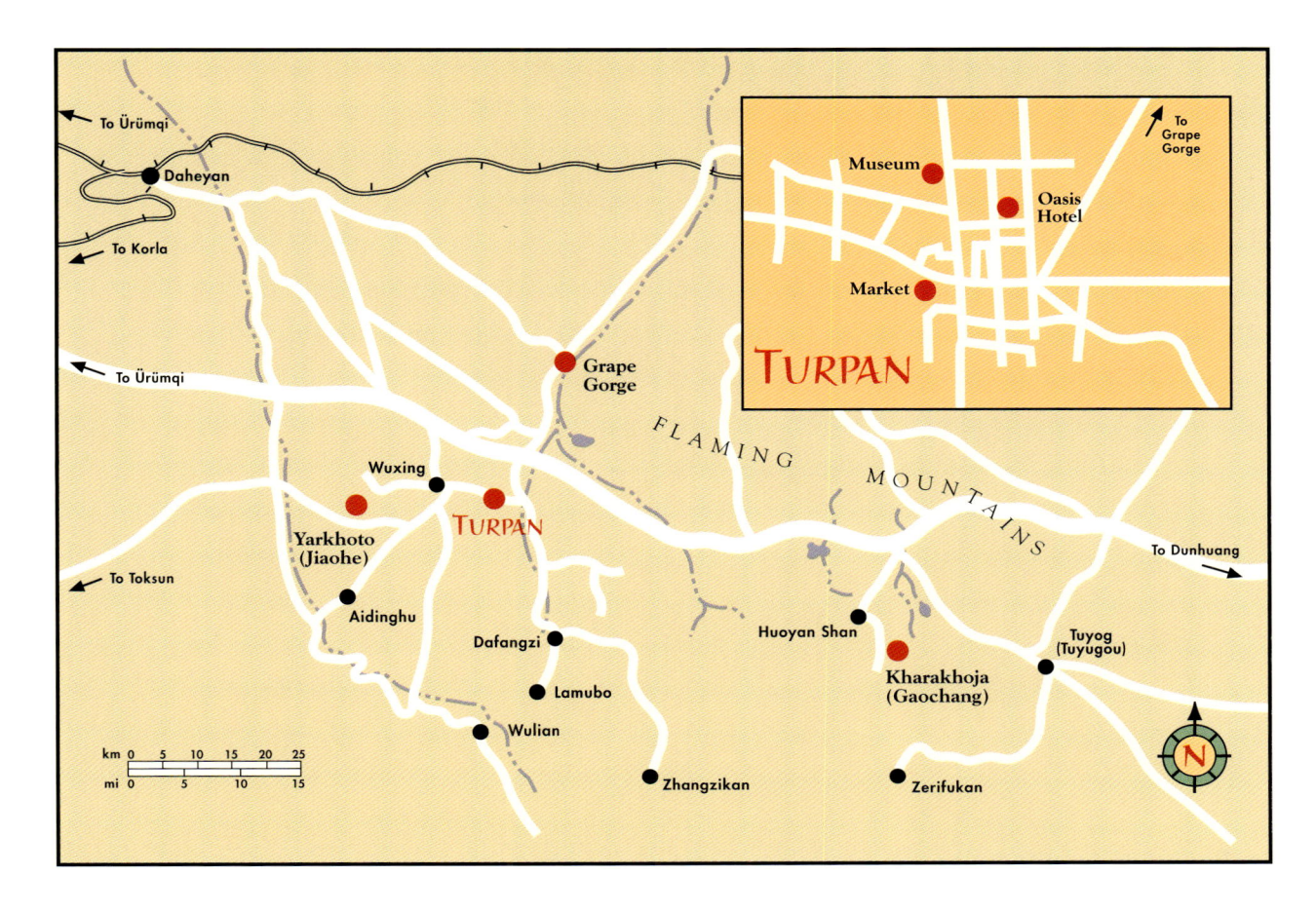

Turpan from Dunhuang – Tuesday, August 11

Our drive to Liuyuan for the overnight train to Turpan was a good two hours long. We swayed and bumped over less-than-smooth roads at speeds greater than the driver should have been going. Never again would we agree to an old vehicle like this if anything else could be rented. Mac told Lee he would be pleased to pay a taxi to follow us with all our luggage if this was the only solution. Unfortunately, no changes could be made.

En route, we experienced a small sand storm. We saw it coming far in the distance, a black cloud moving across the desert. The wind whipped sand smartly over our road making visibility difficult and sometimes blinding us. This was a small example of a dust storm. We saw and felt how dangerous one could be when visibility became non-existent on a traveled highway. There were some vehicles on the highway today besides us. Everybody came to a complete stop when the storm was at its height, but our driver kept moving slowly. As suddenly as it came up, it blew over. Everything was covered in sand. We continued on at a faster pace. Blue skies appeared and lasted for a while, then black clouds and rain. That was not quite as bad as the sand, but it did slow down our progress.

We reached the train station ahead of time. Miao got our tickets and proudly announced they were for cabin number one. Lee emphasized this accommodation was strictly private—only for us. We did not have to share it with strangers. Other accommodations on the train were not as private. In the other cars of the train, we could see bunks with no curtains in between. They seemed filled with passengers. Later, we learned Miao had purchased all four bunks in our compartment. That assured us the entire space and our privacy.

After much standing around, it was time to get the luggage out of the bus and up the station steps, and to stand in line to have our tickets checked. People suddenly emerged from everywhere and crowded into a tight line to present their tickets to the official. We finally squeezed through and made our way to the train platform. There was the train, but our car had not been connected to it. Miao grabbed Mac's small bag and walked ahead of us, while talking to a friend. Ever since we had arrived, she had acted aloof and had actually left us when she spotted a friend on the other side of the parking lot. Now she was walking with another friend, totally ignoring us. Previously asked if she really wanted to make the long journey from Dunhuang to Turpan, since we were perfectly capable of getting on the train by ourselves, she replied she always saw her "guests" on board. Now she was paying no attention to those "guests," and we wondered why she had bothered to come. We suspected she was trying to find a ride back to Dunhuang with a friend instead of in a public bus.

Suddenly, around a bend in the tracks, we saw an engine pushing a Pullman car toward our train. Standing on its front bumper were six train employees. When the car locked on to the rest of the train, they jumped off. We passengers were asked to board. A Japanese group pushed ahead of us. Once they boarded, I hoisted my bag up to the large female train attendant, and she grabbed it. I got aboard with her help, as she half pulled me up onto the platform. Lee yelled to go to cabin one, which I did. To Mac's displeasure, both Lee and Miao assisted him with the rest of the luggage. Both of them were in his way when he tried to place it in our small compartment. It had to be lifted up onto the upper bunks, as there was no other space. Our compartment had four bunks that were bolted to the side walls. A large window was at the far end with a table underneath. A sliding door, with a mirror on the inside, opened onto the corridor. I asked where the Western bathroom was. "At the far end of the hall," answered Lee. Miao breezed off as soon as the luggage was aboard, without saying goodbye. We never saw her again.

Our luggage fitted very nicely on the upper bunks, leaving the lower ones for Mac and me. When we found out Lee was sharing a cabin with a Japanese couple, we invited him to store his luggage on the bunks with ours. He appreciated that very much, as there was no room for his bags in his compartment. He advised us to lock our door, then bid us goodnight. Soon a train attendant appeared with a large Thermos of hot water, which we politely refused.

With a shrill whistle from our coal-powered train, we were off. It was exciting to be moving and on our way to Turpan. We looked around our cabin. At the end of each bed was a neatly folded blanket. A small hard pillow was propped at the opposite end. We quickly availed ourselves of the Western facility. This was a good idea because, when we got there, a young Japanese man was washing his face in the communal sink, and a young Japanese girl was using the "Western." That facility was more Asian than Western, but it served its purpose and was reasonably clean. Back in our compartment, we locked the door as Lee had advised.

We breathed the nice cool air from our open window. Mac asked me what to do with the bath towel at the end of his bed. I laughed and told him it was his blanket. We switched our pillows from the window end of the bunk to the door end so we could look outside. We removed our shoes and lay down and watched the passing scenery. Daylight turned quickly to dusk and then a black night. Lying down felt good on our backs after the bumpy two-hour drive from Dunhuang.

All was quiet except for the train's wheels on the tracks. The cool breeze coming in the window felt pleasant. We had just reached the stage between awake and asleep when a train went past. A violent swish of air came in our compartment and a loud banging rattled our window. We were jolted awake. Its engineer tooted a shrill horn as it passed at great speed only inches from our window. The whole cabin shook. Mac got up and closed the window. He removed the plastic tablecloth, torn apart from the blast of wind, from the table. We both settled down again to sleep.

At least twelve times during our nine-hour ride some train went by. Each time, our cabin shook and rattled, and we both woke up. Finally around two o'clock Mac decided to go to the Western. When he returned, the train attendant tried to place a passenger in our cabin. Mac showed her our luggage piled on the bunks and told the attendant we had no room. Actually, we never should have been asked since we had paid for all the bunks. Sharing everything with everyone, was this Communism rearing its head? That philosophy was so well ingrained.

In our little compartment, we came back to life in the early morning light just after passing one of China's major oil fields. It lay at the foothills of the Bogda Shan range. At seven, we opened our cabin door. There was Lee standing in the corridor just outside our compartment. He had been up since 4:30, unable to sleep in his compartment because it was so hot. The Japanese couple with whom he had shared it were fast asleep, having closed the window when they went to bed.

The train arrived promptly at 7:20, as advertised. We hoisted all our luggage off and pulled everything toward the station, which was some distance away. There our smiling Turpan guide met us and led us to a very comfortable VW microbus for the trip to the Silk Road Oasis Hotel. What a joy to have the smooth-riding, powerful van carry us on the 45-minute trip to Turpan and the Oasis Hotel. The highway was the best we had encountered in China, except for the freeways. We were tired after the train trip and happy to be here.

Once, Turpan was an important way station on the Silk Road. It is situated on an oasis at the edge of the vast deserts of the Xinjiang Uighur Autonomous Region.

At the hotel, we were shown to the coffee shop for breakfast, while Lee and our Turpan guide negotiated acquiring our rooms. While they were being made up, we relaxed and enjoyed eating breakfast. Freshly squeezed orange juice, tea and bottled water first quenched our thirst, and cereal and toast with jam followed. We ate and drank with relish. When the rooms became available, we unpacked, bathed and rested until time for meeting our guides downstairs for a Chinese luncheon.

The Chinese restaurant served a Muslim-type Chinese food with many vegetable and bean dishes. Dishes kept coming and coming to our table, until we counted over 15 platters before they stopped. The food was delicious, but we did not do it justice. The melon was particularly sweet.

That afternoon, our local guide planned to escort us to an irrigation museum, as well as to the ancient ruins of an old fortress, plus a grape vineyard.

After lunch, we took another short nap, thus avoiding the heat of the noonday. We planned to meet later in the afternoon.

The museum showed an outlay of the irrigation system in this district. It captured water or melted snow as it flowed from the Bogda Shan Range. The water was collected through a tree of unlined conductor tunnels that fanned out about twenty miles in distance to the vineyards of Turpan, which were below sea level. This system, called "karez," fully deserves to be classified as one of the ancient wonders of the world. It was created by the Han Dynasty and was used until destroyed by Genghis Khan in the 1300s. Recently, it had been recommissioned. Melon and grape culture flourishes under this system and, along with tourism, supports the economy.

A short distance away from the museum was a fortification called Jiaohe, created in the Han Dynasty. This amazing fortification complex was carved out of the soft rock high above two rivers. A good pathway allowed us to leisurely stroll upward and enjoy seeing the huge boulders which had been the fort. Substantial dwellings and other military building existed until destroyed by Genghis Khan.

Grape Gorge (Putao Gou), in another nearby district, was famous for its green, elongated grapes. Our guide selected a vineyard and we parked the car in an overcrowded lot. Mac and the guide walked to the vineyard, but I remained in the car. It was an education to sit there and watch the maneuvering of the traffic in and out of that small parking lot.

This was a long day. We were happy to have a quiet dinner by ourselves in the Western café and then go to bed.

One thing that was hard to get comfortable with was the large entourage we acquired on each stop. We always picked up a local guide, as well as a car and driver. This was customary on this sort of a trip and worked well, but it required a large vehicle for five people with luggage. Those vehicles never were quite the right size. Most were not very comfortable. Lee was helpful getting us to trains and airplanes on time and meeting local guides. If we had a problem, he was quick to understand and correct whatever bothered us, usually asking the local guides not to hover around us. When traveling, we were satisfied with this arrangement. However, once settled in the hotels, it was most disconcerting to have Lee and the local guide monitor our dinner checks, stay around to see if we enjoyed the food or even help us order it, unless we asked. Our private time felt violated, and we did not like that. We worked to diplomatically correct this.

Turpan – Wednesday, August 12

This morning, we left the hotel at nine and drove to Gaochang via Wuxing. It was only 20 miles east of Turpan, and the highway there badly needed reconstruction. Our route involved several detours full of unavoidable potholes. We were well shaken on our arrival.

En route, just outside Turpan, we fueled up in a thoroughly modern station under a canopy supported by golden arches of McDonald's quality. Further on, we passed an oil field with antique-looking pumps operating on five wells. A flare was disposing of the associated gas.

Wuxing, populated by Uighur (pronounced wee-grr) people, was a typical Central Asian place with donkey carts, busy open-air markets, adobe brick housing and a Muslim population. This was immediately noticeable in the women's clothing. They did not cover their faces, but wore scarves wound around their heads and long dresses. This looked very attractive on them. Every family here had its own home. These dwellings were built close together. We noted some families had items for sale in their front yard like fruits, lumps of coal or a few household items. Because it was so hot and dry, people placed their beds outside their homes in the yard or in a vacant lot. Besides sleeping, these double-sized beds were used as meeting places for all sorts of communication. On one, we saw a group of women sitting together playing cards. On others, women were enjoying glasses of tea. A group of larger children chased each other around one, while smaller children sat underneath quietly playing. On still another, an adult slept while a group of men gossiped near him. We noted the mattresses on them were thin, quite filthy and more a covering for the spring coils. No covers seemed to be used at any time.

All the double-sized beds were identical, made of iron with long legs that held them high off the ground. At the end of some were bundles of nondescript looking blankets rolled up in a round ball. Perhaps this bedding was used during cooler weather. No one was concerned that rainfall might interrupt a night's sleep. Here, maybe an inch fell a year, and it was very dusty. During this hot season, everyone slept outside, unconcerned about being disturbed. In the winter season, the beds were pulled inside the house.

Driving through the village, we noted new housing built of adobe bricks. These new buildings looked modern and clean with open spaces for windows and doors. Next to some were structures with many openings in the walls. They were used for drying grapes to make raisins. Grapes were the main crop here.

We passed a huge open-air market full of people, and drove onto the single lane of a disintegrating bridge. This bridge was the entrance to and from the town. It crossed over an irrigation channel and had no railing on either side for safety. When we were ready to cross, two men stood on one side having a serious discussion and never moved or noticed us driving across. They made our crossing space even narrower. Adding more confusion, the clay holding the bridge in place had eroded seriously on one side. We held our breath as we slowly drove over it, hoping the whole structure would not collapse. Driver, guides and passengers were very pleased to reach the other side.

Our goal from there was Gaochang, the ruins of a huge ancient city built for protecting the people from the unfriendly hoards. Its entrance was a noisy market where cars, buses and vans with their tourists parked in no particular order. Most of these tourists were Japanese and Taiwanese. We got out in the middle of this milieu and saw several tables set up for selling canned drinks, native hats, books and postcards. One of the merchants asked me if I wanted a Coca Cola, 7-Up, coconut juice, Gatorade, red beer, water or lime juice. Such a wide selection. All drinks were in cans or plastic bottles.

Transportation to the fortress was by donkey cart or on foot. Very small donkeys were harnessed to carts that were nothing more than platforms, each covered with several colorful rugs. A cloth awning, held up by poles, attached to the cart's sides and covered the top. About ten adults sat on the sides with their feet dangling over the edge. We watched the driver swish a rope whip over the donkey's back to keep the cart moving. We elected to walk to the fortress instead of riding on one of these. Several went by us as we walked along. We waved "hello" to people as they passed. Only the Orientals seemed to enjoy riding.

It was a perfect day for strolling along the twisting clay road to the ruins. The sky was overcast, with a threat of rain. This did not worry us. As we approached the ruins, we saw the fortress constructed of huge boulders made from the local clay with straw reinforcement and baked solid in the sun. There were enough of them still standing to visualize a large city fortress which once housed 50,000 people. The fortress was destroyed in 1300 AD by Genghis Khan. He did an incomplete job, so many of the buildings were still standing in eroded, but recognizable, condition. Some were very large structures with domed roofs. All the buildings were remarkable for their variety and excellent state of conservation.

They said it never rained here. However, on our return to Turpan, we noted drops of a strange transparent fluid on the windshield.

That evening, we took a walk around the large block of our hotel. We thoroughly enjoyed seeing the people in their home settings. Many waved and greeted us with smiles as we passed. We observed the heavy traffic at the intersection of our block. We proceeded down the long city street, observing the stores and people, and turned at the corner into a quieter neighborhood. It was fun seeing children playing, men at chess boards, people preparing barbecue dinners and everybody outside enjoying the coolness of the evening.

The next morning, we enthusiastically told our adventure to Lee and the local guide, whose name turned out to be Tang. They both were horrified we had gone without them. They both felt it was dangerous and asked us not to walk alone again. Regretfully, we did not.

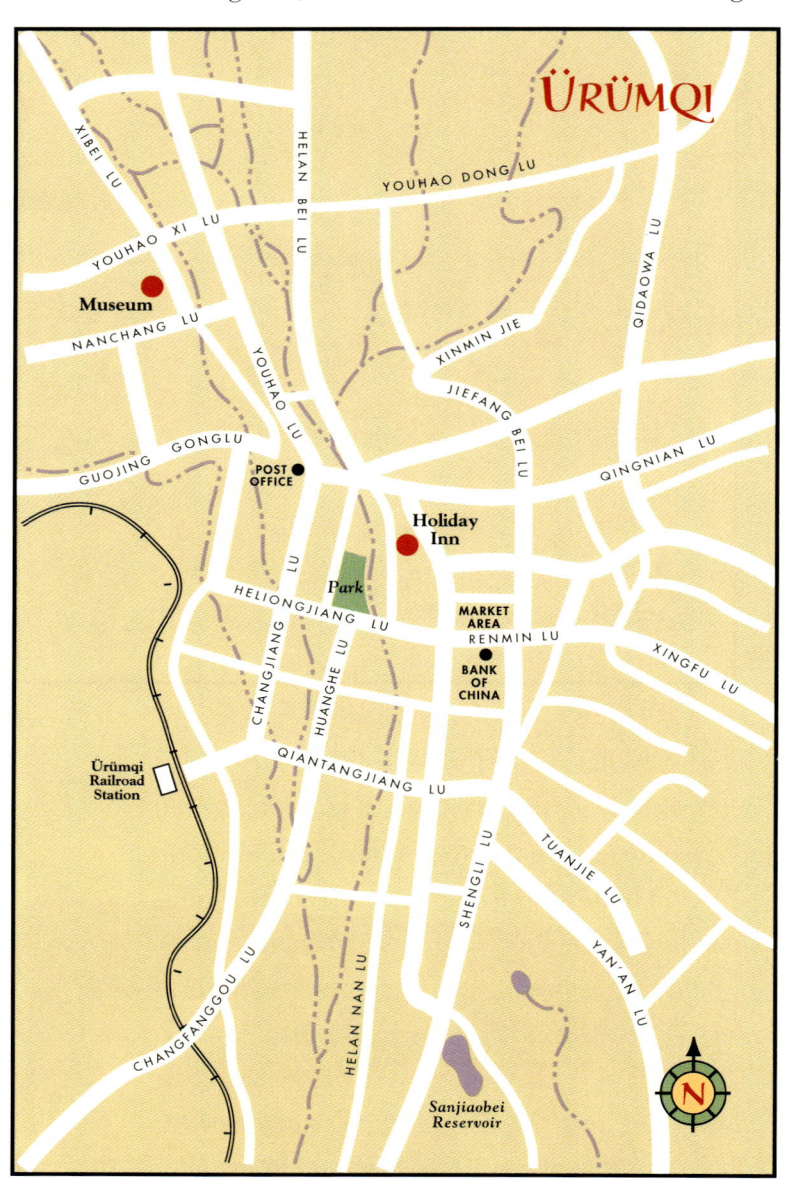

Turpan to Ürümqi – Thursday, August 13

The drive from Turpan to Ürümqi would be at least a four-hour trip, or so we were told. At nine o'clock, we were standing in the lobby with our luggage, hotel bill paid and ready to depart. Soon Lee appeared, then Tang, our local guide, but no car or driver. Tang went to look for him. As we stood there outside the hotel's entrance, a group of about eight Italian couples appeared. They stood in the dead center of the driveway talking animatedly among themselves, but totally blocking the driveway. They looked over at us and stared, probably surprised to see any Westerners. Our driver appeared and drove the van around to the entrance, trying gently to move the Italians aside so we could load our luggage and be off. That caused the Italians to really stare, as if wondering who we were with a private car, driver and two Chinese guides. It amused us.

Off we went, down the tree-lined boulevard onto the main road out of Turpan. We settled back. Tang asked me if I slept well—his usual morning greeting only to me, and I replied "wonderfully well"—my usual reply to him. That let him brood for a while on what exactly I had meant by "wonderfully well." He was a great one to ponder and ponder a thought, especially one in English.

Suddenly, just outside Turpan, the driver stopped beside some roadside grape vendors. Both our driver and Tang got out of the car, and Lee started to chuckle. These two men were bargaining with the vendors to buy some local fresh grapes, known to be particularly tasty. We thought they would each buy a large clump. To our surprise they were negotiating how much a box would cost. While we sat, they bargained and bargained a price. Finally we saw some money being exchanged. "Good," we thought, "now we can be on our way." Not a chance. The three boxes they bought had to be tied with string, so more haggling went on over the final price. We learned the vendors wanted thirty cents a box. Our local guide and driver thought they should pay less. In the end, they saved less than fifty cents between them while we were delayed for twenty minutes. When the van's door was opened, we saw three large boxes which we were to transport to Ürümqi. "Do you suppose they will settle them on top of the luggage?" I asked Mac. "Not a chance," he replied. "I don't want those sticky grapes dripping on our bags." But it took Lee, Tang and the driver to move various tote bags and other paraphernalia to establish a space behind the driver's seat to place all three boxes. Then we were on our way to Ürümqi.

We started out on the new westbound highway, which would be formally opened the next week. It was smooth and pleasant riding. One more stop. This was for gas, and probably a smart move. There were very few, if any, gas stations along the highway.

Soon we were diverted from the highway onto an old rough road. This was where the "new" highway stopped. The rest of it was not finished. There were several flood flows across the old road, which we had to ford. Already, some large trucks were stalled in mid-ford which alarmed us.

Halfway along the four-hour journey, we entered a magnificent canyon through which flowed the rain-swollen stream carrying water out to be "lost" in the desert. There were colorful rock faces and deep side canyons creating a strong backdrop. Along the other side of the canyon ran the paved, beautiful new highway as we veered back and forth on the bumpy old one. This canyon divided the Tian Shan from the Bogda Shan, the huge mountain ranges.

We emerged from the upper end of the canyon onto the Ürümqi plateau. The driver had to stop at a small town to visit the washroom or perhaps it was a girl friend. It was a mystery. Then we passed a salt lake filled with water trapped on the plateau. Further on, we went by a field of wind generators, all their blades turning in the wind. Still further on was the first industrial complex we had seen, indistinct in the haze.

We entered the modern city of Ürümqi. With its wide paved streets and high-rise buildings, it had a population of two million. There was a strong Russian influence on the buildings, industry and monuments. The Russians wanted to build something accessible for them should they decide to invade China. Today, they had a large army posting, near the border with the old Soviet Union. The traffic flowed more smoothly than in other cities we had driven in. Ürümqi is the capital of the Xinjiang Uighur Autonomous Region, China's most western province.

After settling in our rooms at the very modern Holiday Inn Hotel, we went to the Ürümqi Museum with our guides. The display had a very interesting time-line showing mixed objects and starting before 1000 BC. The silk on display here was far better preserved than silk we had seen in other museums on the trip, thanks to the dry climate of this region. The brass objects were of a distinct form versus those of eastern China. There was a room off the main museum which held mummies. I did not want to go in there, but was persuaded by our group to take a short look. I was appalled to see not only dark bones, but complete skeletons of mummified people—men, women and a few children lying there in open caskets. Staring at them seemed sacrilegious to me. After quickly walking around, I left the room and was teased a bit for doing so.

Ürümqi – Friday, August 14

We drove many miles out of the city over roads in various states of construction and maintenance. The sights were minimal, as the suburban industry looked obsolete and the farmland was marginal. Our guides thought we would enjoy seeing a settlement of Khazakh nomads and their yurts on a mountain side. They herd sheep and cattle on horseback and move their camps as the seasons change. These people are small, and so are their horses. On this same site was a waterfall from the melted mountain snow of the very high surrounding Tian Shan range. We planned to drive up to see it. First we took a short walk through the yurt village. Some yurts were very large tents. All the smaller ones had cooking facilities outside. Some had paintings over their doorways. The grounds around all were scrupulously tidy. I saw a small boy sitting in the doorway of a large one, obviously his home. Waving to him, I noticed the room inside the flap opening. There was a big television set. It seemed all wrong in this nomad setting.

We could drive up the mountain sitting on one of the nomads' wagons to see waterfalls, or, if asked, could ride bareback on one of their horses. A tiny young woman asked me to go with her. I shook my head. Her horse looked too lively. Back in our car for the drive up the mountain, we were stopped by a uniformed official. He told us we could go no further because some "big potatoes" were visiting that day. (Lee said this was an exact translation of what he had said.) Lee and Tang negotiated with him and eventually we were allowed to drive on, while other tourists were detained.

The road was extremely narrow and twisty, more for wagons than automobiles or buses. It proceeded upward beside a rushing mountain stream. Suddenly we saw magnificent falls, dropping perhaps a couple hundred feet from a cleft in the rocky peak above. The flow was just the size of the narrow canyon. A lot of mist produced a lovely rainbow at the foot of the falls. Mac and Lee elected to walk up to its top on a slippery path beside the stream. Tang was torn between leaving me alone in the car, but afraid "Mr. Whiting might slip and fall if he was not there to hold his arm." I knew Mac did not need such help, but urged Tang to go on. Mac and Lee were already coming down by the time Tang reached them. Time was important. They wanted to avoid causing a traffic jam when the notables were being driven up. As it happened, the tour buses were approaching the entrance of the road when we came down. We wondered how several buses could possibly turn around in the small space at the falls. Their problem, not ours.

The same bad road conditions on the way back to the hotel left us with neck pain. We spent a quiet afternoon in our room. We were advised not to venture out on the streets of Ürümqi alone, much to our disappointment.

Ürümqi was not as quaint as the tour books would have you believe. There were no Uighurs in native costumes and no souvenir salesmen working the streets. Souvenirs could be bought at department stores. Ürümqi was industrialized and modernized. Our hotel, a Holiday Inn, was as up-to-date as any American one. Our rooms had all the amenities we could possibly want. Our meals at the Chinese restaurant were especially delicious. Noontimes, we ate at the Western one, which offered either a buffet or menu service. Our stay in Ürümqi was most enjoyable.

Ürümqi to Kashgar (Kashi) – Saturday, August 15

Lee and Tang wanted us to drive up the 5,000-foot high Bogda Mountain, a part of the Tian Shan Range, to see the Heavenly Lake. There was a restaurant for lunch, then we would take a walk around the lake and watch a rodeo. Afterwards, we would drive back to Ürümqi's airport for our flight to Kashgar, more familiarly called Kashi.

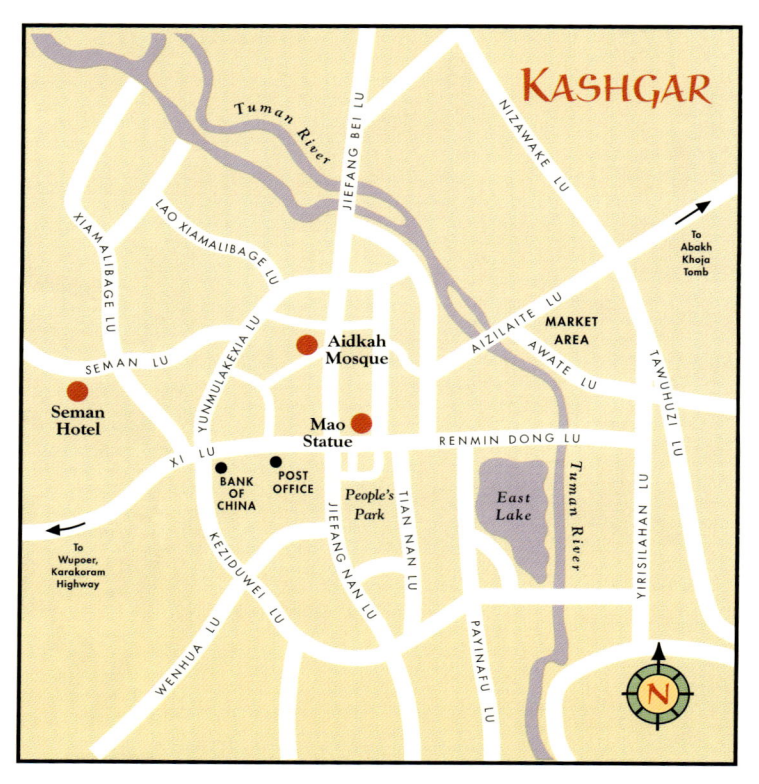

We thought this sounded like an ambitious plan. We wondered why we were consenting to such a long day of driving. The bumpy roads made my back ache and Mac's neck hurt. Lee assured us the trip up would only be two hours or so. We agreed to go. When we were ready to go, as were Lee and the driver, no Tang was anywhere to be seen. Eventually Lee found him working on something for his personal travel plans, totally unaware of the time.

The drive to Heavenly Lake resulted in many detours, switchbacks, and bumps until Mac asked the driver to slow down. We passed some obsolete-looking industrial chemical and petroleum complexes on the way. We saw some attractive new housing for workers, who would be moved from grim little shacks. There were marginal coal deposits on the way up to the lake. Two hours became three until, four hours after leaving Ürümqi, we approached the base of the mountain. No two hour trip was this.

What a jumble of cars, large buses, vans and trucks were at the entrance. Mac and Lee got out to stretch their legs and walked along the side of our van. Tang went to buy our tickets while the driver maneuvered through the traffic to the entrance gate. Tang was waiting at the entrance with our tickets. Up the mountain we drove, with many, many switchbacks. We passed the lovely Little Heavenly Lake nestled among the steep mountains. It was turquoise blue and shone like a mirror. We followed a river which alternately was small and large. As we went higher, the road got steeper and eventually the pitch was very steep. Our aggressive driver succeeded in passing every slower-moving vehicle, including one pickup truck that was stalled. That caused a backup all the way down the mountain. More switchbacks and then we came to the summit, 5,000 feet up from the entrance gate. It looked down on the beautiful large Heavenly Lake. It was crawling with visitors.

Our travel agency had reserved its own spot to park on top of a mini-peak. We found and used the very dirty and primitive facilities, but enjoyed a nice "snack" of about ten dishes at the restaurant. We had persuaded the driver and guides to eat with us, and they agreed reluctantly, not liking to sit with their clients. The meal began with soup and ended with a big bowl of freshly made noodles. They were very long and slippery, but hot and delicious. The fine technique of eating noodles with chopsticks was one I needed to learn. Our group delighted in teaching me how. My effort was effective, but not very graceful. The noodles tasted so good.

We wandered around the grounds afterwards. The lake was beautiful. The crowds of people were interesting to watch. Everybody was in good spirits. We began to wonder when the rodeo would take place, as time was passing. Neither Lee nor Tang were anywhere around. Mac looked at his watch, shook his head and decided we never would have the time to see a rodeo, then drive back to the airport to make our flight connection. Finally our car appeared with Lee, Tang and an unknown man sitting in front beside the driver. We caused quite a commotion by saying we preferred not to stay for the staging rodeo and immediately wanted to return to Ürümqi. They all were very disappointed, especially the stranger in the front seat. It turned out he was responsible for the rodeo. We hoped a slower drive back over all the bumps might save our necks and backs. The driver grudgingly agreed and gave us a very soft ride. Later, he said he had a hard time staying awake.

What a wise decision. It took a good three hours plus to reach the airport. Passengers were standing in line at our check-in counter when we entered the terminal. Luckily, the airplane was late. We had time to observe the crowd. There were lots of Orientals, but no other Westerners. We bid Tang and our driver goodbye. Tang promised to meet our flight when we returned from Kashi.

The airplane to Kashi was an old Russian airliner run by a Chinese company. It was air-worthy, but short on amenities. When we boarded, the inside was hot—extremely so. There was no air conditioning or air of any kind and the airplane was completely loaded with passengers. When the engines started, we were told, it would be cooler. Meantime, all the passengers were perspiring and fanning ourselves and getting impatient. When started, the engines sounded so horrible we wondered if the airplane would get up in the air once it left the runway. We fervently hoped we did not have to take this same airplane back to Ürümqi, where we would be returning in three days.

A severe windstorm greeted our arrival in Kashi. It was blowing so hard that it was difficult to walk the short distance from the airplane to the terminal. Mac ran ahead and I followed, buffeted on all sides.

Kashi, or Kashgar, as it is also known, is the westernmost urban city in China. In 1955, the People's Republic established the Xinjiang Uighur Autonomous Region, with Kashgar as the principal city in the southwest. It is more than 1,000 miles from Beijing and some 600 plus miles west of Ürümqi. It is less than 100 miles from Russia. It was closed to foreign visitors until 1985. It is bounded on the north by the Tian Shan (Celestial Mountains), on the west by the Pamirs Mountains (Roof of the World) and on the east by the Taklamakan Desert. Kashi is watered by streams from the snow of the mountains. The minority population is made up of Muslims. Uighurs constitute the largest segment, outnumbering the Kirghiz and Kazakhs, as well as the Han Chinese. The People's Republic has tried to encourage preservation of the minorities. Uighurs were not restricted in the number of children they might have, as were the Han Chinese. They were allowed to worship freely at their mosques. Uighurs were known throughout China for their fruit growing, craftsmanship, and spirited singing and dancing.

Our local guide, Lloyd, met us. Lloyd was a tall, handsome young man who was born in Kazakhstan and raised here in Kashi. He was locally educated and spoke excellent English, the best of any of our guides. He said he had been taught by an American priest. He was married to an Uighur woman, a school teacher. This marriage caused a great commotion in his family and was considered unsuitable. It was known that the Uighurs never intermarry. His father's very large family was verbally giving Lloyd and his wife a hard time. Lee and Lloyd spent time discussing this situation.

We drove through beautiful green farmlands on our way to the hotel. Corn, wheat, cotton and rice was grown here, as well as melons, grapes, peaches and many different vegetables. There was plenty of mountain water for irrigation.

The Quiniwake Hotel was modern, but our rooms had no air conditioning. There was only a small fan to use, which was in the bedroom. In the evenings, we opened the windows and cool air came in. We slept well. From early afternoon until it set, the sun shone in our windows and made the room uncomfortably hot and stuffy. Occasionally, we left the door open into the hallway, although this was not practical most of the time. Out there, it was cooler by far than it was in our rooms.

For reasons we never understood, the bathroom had no hot water. Lee remedied that by speaking to the staff. One day, the water was completely turned off. In this place with an abundance of water for irrigation, it seemed strange that the hotel had water problems.

All meals were served in the hotel's dining room. Upon entering, we picked up plates, glasses or cups and chopsticks at a buffet table. At the noon and night meals, we were always served at our tables by waitresses. Breakfast was always cafeteria style and often included leftover dishes from the previous day. The food here was a Muslim cuisine, not at all like any other Chinese cuisine we had eaten. Because of the Muslim religion, there was less meat and more beans and vegetables. These were cooked until mushy. Some dishes tasted good, but others were marginal. Mostly, we could not distinguish what was what, except fish, which always looked like fish, no matter how they cooked it. We sat at a table for two while almost everybody else was in larger groupings. Usually those people were either in tour groups or business personnel having a conference at the hotel. All our food was presented on small platters. We never saw a menu, which was probably fine, since it would have been in Chinese with no translation. Usually when about 11 plates were on the table, we asked the waitresses to bring no more. They would smile and continue, because this was what they were told to do. We learned the dishes would stop coming when the buns were served. These were good, and like everything else, we ate them with chopsticks. We tried drinking Chinese wine which, when poured, was warm because the bottle had not been put in the refrigerator. No one else drank wine, only beer and Coke. Lee amused us at breakfast. His meal consisted of a very watery millet cereal and pickles. "Pickles for breakfast, Lee?" we asked. "Sure," he replied. "They taste good, and I always have them at home for breakfast."

It was a totally different atmosphere in this town. It seemed more rural and picturesque than the others we visited. Lee asked us not to wander outside the hotel compound alone. He would be happy to go with us any time. Later, after we left Kashi, Lee informed us that a policeman had been stabbed to death near our hotel compound. He was a Han, like Lee, and that episode made Lee nervous. The Uighur people are not fond of the Han Chinese.

Kashi - August 16

We awoke perspiring and thinking how nice it will be to get to Hong Kong with its many amenities. This was after another night in a hot, stuffy room without air conditioning or a breath of air coming in the windows. Breakfast included parts of last night's dinner, plus some undistinguished breads and unusual eggs, actually eggs fried in a batter and served cold.

We were looking forward to visiting the famed Kashi Sunday open-air market, which served some 10,000 people every week. Vendors driving donkey carts came from as far away as 200 miles to offer their wares. Most were farmers bringing along their entire family.

As we approached the grounds, the streets into the market were jam-packed with people. There were donkey carts, buses, animals on tethers, cars, bicyclists and many others on foot. Our driver had to go very slowly so as not to hit a person or an animal. We wondered, in all this mass, where he would park the car. Soon he turned into a small alley with a gate. It was opened and, luckily, a parking place had been reserved for us. From there on, we walked.

Sauntering down the earth road as we entered the market, I was trying to see everything at once. So much activity! It was hard to absorb. We passed by the meat stalls with lots of red slabs hanging from hooks. Various sharp knives lay on the counters, ready to cut meat into any portion the customer wished. "Pushi, pushi," someone said behind me. "Pushi, pushi!" Lee shoved me onto the side of the road, an unusual thing for him to do. The person saying "pushi, pushi" meant "make way, make way." Naturally I did not understand until a donkey cart full of people went past. I was very glad I had "made way." Another donkey wagon came behind the first. I noted the woman had on gold dangle earrings that looked lovely against her bronzed skin. Most of the women covered their hair with colorful scarves but not their entire faces, although all were of the Islamic faith.

This market was huge, with stalls everywhere. It covered several city blocks. We began walking through the displays. We saw rugs woven in brilliant colors, predominantly reds, purples, greens and yellows. We passed stalls with varieties of clothing for men, women and children, others with beautiful silk scarves, and some with nylon stockings in unusual shades of beige, pink, blue and red, pinned with old fashioned wooden clothespins onto rods mounted high above the stall. The breeze waved the stockings back and forth. There were varieties of pots and pans, many of them handmade, plus donkeys for sale, roping made from various materials including horsehair, calculators and displays of knives and daggers in various sizes and shapes. More than one salesman pointed out the small ladylike daggers to

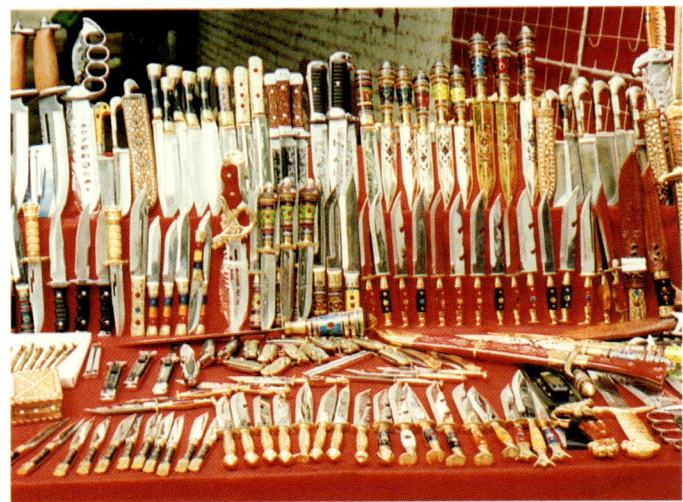

me as I passed. They looked lethal. This place sold a real diversity of items. We were fascinated by such wide choices. We watched horses being demonstrated by young boys who raced them up and down a small earth alley. That was a bit scary as the horse came running directly at the crowd we were in, turning at the last moment. Little round hats which sat on the back of the heads of almost every Uighur man we saw, were an important item. Each represented the vocation or age of the man who would wear it, a very important distinction in this locality. We walked by stalls loaded with varieties of melons, overloaded spice booths, and an outdoor beauty parlor offering haircuts for the men. Candy and ice cream stalls were full of children. Tires for trucks and automobiles were there, as well as many baked goods. When bought live, chickens were immediately slaughtered behind the stall. Vegetables had been picked early that morning and brought fresh to market. Dried beans and grains, beer, gold, silver and plastic watches of various manufacture were all available. Live sheep and goats in groups of six or eight were tethered and walked through the crowds causing great confusion. Apparently, they were sold in groups. Other sheep and goats rode to market in the back of trucks with a man swishing a rope whip over them to make them keep their heads down. We could have bought a variety of herbal remedies. The local refreshment was iced milk. The most curious things we saw were red dyed eggs lying on blankets in front of women. We asked about them, having never seen a red egg except those dyed for Easter. Apparently, these too were dyed and given as presents by the parents of newborns to visitors when they came to see the new child. This was a local custom. The only unavailable things at this market were narcotics, alcohol, tobacco and major hardware, cars and tractors. Everything perishable must be sold by sundown, as the stalls needed to be emptied. A person shopped early for selection or late for bargains. The next morning the market moved on and was set up in another city.

This Sunday market was truly spectacular, a sight not to be missed. There were some European tour groups there, but we encountered only one American. Actually, we heard her. She said very loudly to a local, "No, I am not English. I am an American." "Where are you from?" we shouted, as she continued down a pathway opposite ours. "Texas," she replied and disappeared into the crowd before we could reach her.

After a long walk back to our car and a comfortable ride back to our hotel, we decided this had been quite a day.

Kashi - Monday, August 17

This morning we did a complete city tour.

Our first stop was at a mosque, which was an exquisite private tomb of the leading family of Kashi from 1640 to 1820. It was one of the most beautiful examples of Muslim architecture, very heroic in style and symmetrical around its huge entry. A large dome was on top. The outside of the mosque was covered with handcrafted tiles of blue and green set on a white background. A large formal garden lay in front. The entire family, some 58 people, was buried inside. Each had their own raised tomb, draped with a silk cloth. By the size of the tomb, one could tell whether it held a man, woman or child. Originally, this mosque was built for the founding member of the family. When the last member died, that was the end of the entire family.

Many tourists were inside when we got there. In the hushed atmosphere, looking at the many draped tombs, I was shocked, but not surprised, when a Western tourist speaking German started taking flashbulb pictures. Somehow, in this religious atmosphere, this was very insensitive.

From there, we walked up to the "Fragrant Concubine's Tomb" which had a little mosque in front of it. The mosque was small and delicate, with handsome wooden columns. Each column was painted differently and looked very feminine to us.

The Fragrant Concubine

There was a story about the Fragrant Concubine. She was a Uighur woman that the king dreamt he saw holding a bouquet of flowers as she sat on a monster. Falling in love with her, he sent his messengers all over the kingdom to find her. They searched far and wide. Finally they saw a girl sitting on a mud fence, holding a bouquet of flowers. Since the fence looked like the monster the king had described, they took the girl to the king. He made her one of his concubines. When she died, the king had her cortege taken back to Kashi, her home village. That trip took three years. This mosque was built in her memory. There was a picture of her in the courtyard outside the mosque. She was very pretty.

We had a nice drive along a tree-lined road to reach these mosques. It wove through a neighborhood of very substantial Uighur homes. Each had a courtyard, mostly hidden by a high fence. All had a single front entrance from the street. Most of these were closed, so we could only occasionally glimpse inside a partially opened one. Obviously, these were upper class Uighur homes. The tourist agency had arranged for us to visit one of them. We refused, not liking to walk into anyone's private home without being invited by the family.

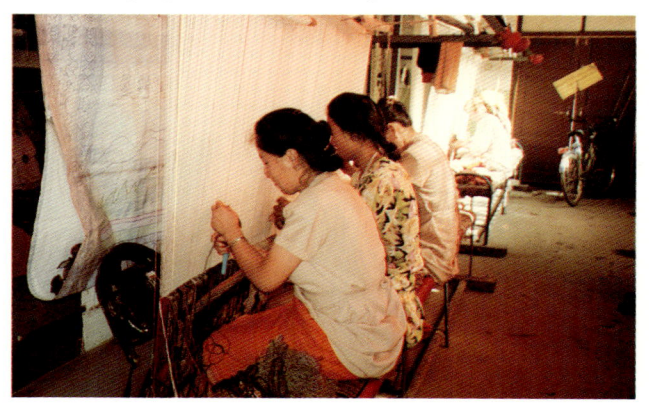

There was a handicraft guild in Kashi, sponsored by the government, showing tourists various Uighur crafts. On upright looms, the girls were taught rug knotting using Oriental designs, while the boys learned to shape wooden musical instruments from a master in this craft. Every Chinese city we visited had a handicraft center such as this one in an attempt to kept these crafts alive. Nothing original was ever produced. Usually the place was dirty and the workers seemed uninterested in developing their craft.

There was an important mosque in the city. Called the Idkah Mosque, it was said to be the largest in China. Originally built in 1442, it dominated an entire center square in the city. Around it was a lovely garden, full of leafy green trees, with a wide walkway leading to the mosque. Wooden benches filled the yard on either side of this main entrance. They made a quiet, peaceful place to sit or pray. We were told as many as 10,000 people could be accommodated here at one time.

We removed our shoes in order to enter. Inside, all the floors were covered with Oriental prayer rugs, each a rectangle for a single worshiper. As we walked toward the center of the mosque, we were sickened to find a small group of young Japanese tourists sitting on and posing for pictures beside the Holy Chair. This chair was only for the Izmir to use. We stared at them, not believing what we were seeing. They continued taking pictures, always a no-no inside any holy place. An official appeared and told them they were defiling sacred areas. He asked to them leave the mosque. Our guide told us the Ayatollah Khomeini preached here during a state visit. The huge and beautiful grey Persian rug in front of the Holy Chair was a present from him.

When we came out of the mosque, a young boy had moved our shoes to a different spot and was ready to help us put them back on.

Walking out into the street toward our car, we saw a policeman scolding a man who had drawn a large square with white chalk on the pavement in front of the mosque. The chalk square indicated the area for his kiosk. The policeman insisted the man erase those lines. The man was rubbing the chalk off the cement with a broom and the work was going very slowly. The policeman kept at him until every line had almost disappeared. Then the man was allowed to depart. Apparently merchants chalked off sections of the pavement for selling their wares, but this merchant drew his lines too close to the mosque.

Back at the hotel, we walked to the end of the compound behind our hotel, where the British Consulate had been. It had a nice grassy park, full of trees, where a group of children was playing. What a nice cool place for them in this hot weather! What caught our eye nearby was a rickety Chinese bus loading passengers. This was in preparation for a trip across the mountains to Pakistan. That trip would reach an elevation of 15,000 feet before arriving in Pakistan. During the previous two days, trips had been canceled so there was an over-capacity crowd claiming seats. More than half of them were young Europeans. All were trying to get aboard. It was a tense situation with lots of passionate discussion with the five or six employees who were trying to help. We identified French, German and other Europeans, Pakistanis, bearded old Muslim men and other nationalities we could not place. After all the passengers were aboard, the bus sat in the driveway for almost an hour while tickets were checked and rechecked. One passenger, a nice looking young woman, was trying to get aboard. She stood by the door opening, but was not allowed to climb aboard. After an hour, when the overheated passengers inside the bus started pounding on its sides, the officials finally decided there was no seat for her. In the United States, such a long wait might have precipitated a riot. We enjoyed the tense scene, which perplexed Lee as he politely sat with us, not finding it interesting or amusing.

In the course of the boarding, we saw a tall, husky, young man put an old wooden chair up beside a back window on the opposite side of the bus from its entrance. He stood on it, braced his hands on the open window, hoisted himself up and crawled in the bus through the window. Thus he was aboard. It was quite a feat. The conductor never threw him off. We shall always wonder if he took the seat meant for the nice looking girl who had so patiently stood by the entrance.

That evening, Lee entertained us at a Chinese restaurant he had tested, across the street from our hotel. It was a delicious dinner and was our final one in western China. It was a happy ending in a fascinating place.

As our trip comes to a close,
we visit the nation's Capitol Beijing,
and the fascinating Great Wall of China.

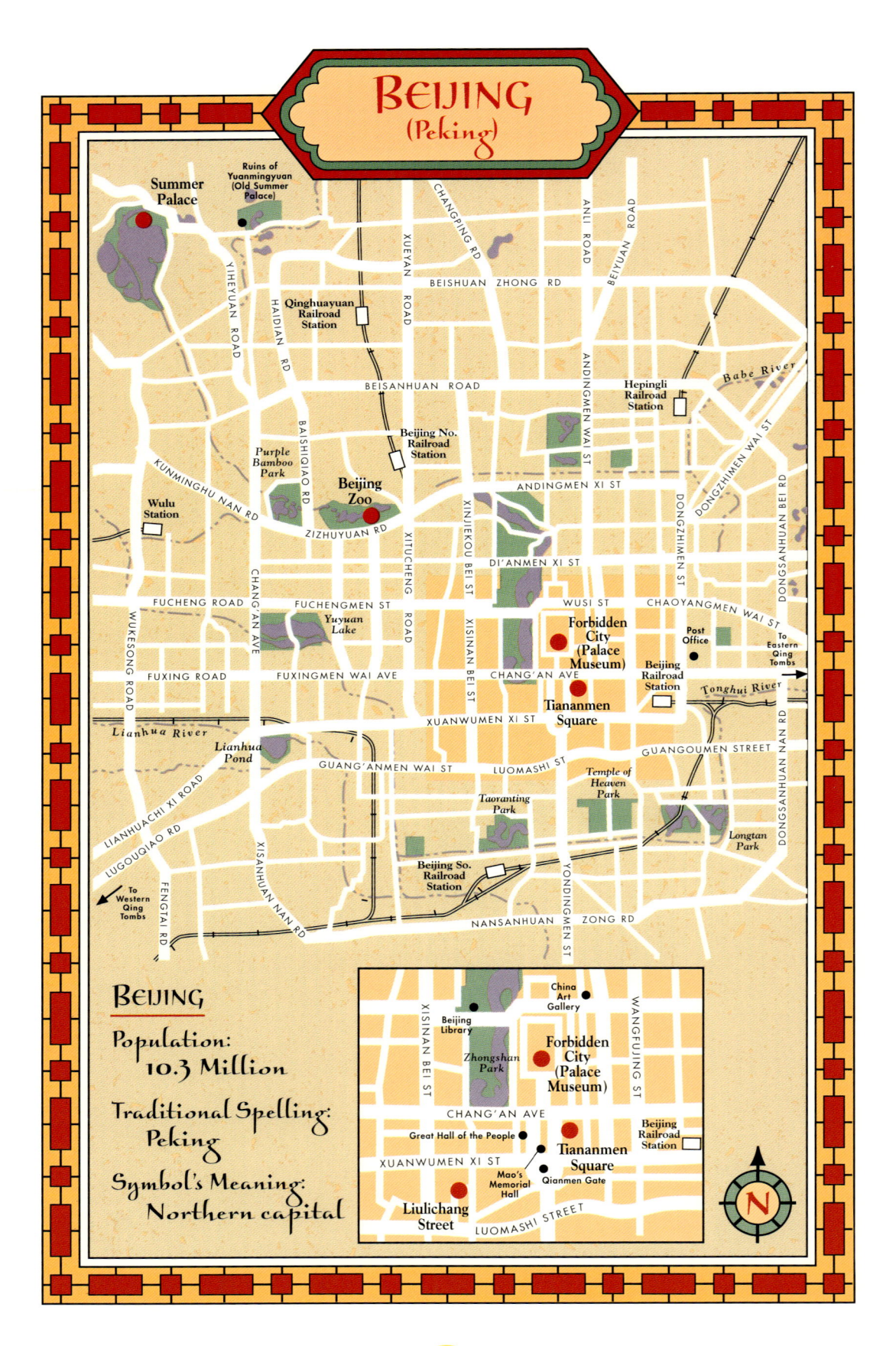

Beijing (Peking)

Beijing

Population: 10.3 Million

Traditional Spelling: Peking

Symbol's Meaning: Northern capital

chapter 12

北 Beijing (Peking)

On to Beijing, the final stop of our 1993 trip.

We climbed a wobbly steel staircase to enter the airplane, stepped over a high transom and showed our seating assignments to the stewardess. She indicated they were in the back, one seat by a window and the other in the center of a row for three. This was a Russian-designed airplane, and these were known as "bucket seats." Their backs folded completely down on the seat cushions when not in use. When one sat on the seat, its cushion sagged perilously close to the floor, making it most difficult to get back up. In our opinion, this airplane should either have been modernized, or better still, simply retired. Happily, this was our last flight on a Chinese domestic airliner. Shortly, we would be flying back to the United States on United Airlines from Beijing. We were weary of being cramped on Chinese airplanes with their small quarters and never any elbow room, no matter who the manufacturer was. Perhaps we were becoming weary travelers too, as we finally boarded this flight from Xi'an to Beijing.

Once airborne, the airplane creaked and groaned with every bump of rough air, but we reached Beijing exactly on schedule. When we walked into the terminal with our luggage, a girl at the gate waved a sign with our names.

Her name was Helen, and she was the youngest guide we had been assigned on the entire trip. When the car was loaded, she told us the drive into Beijing was about an hour in length. During that time, we would discuss sightseeing possibilities.

Beijing was a strange combination of two cities. One part was official Beijing, the capital of China. Its stately buildings were the headquarters of the nation's government. Tiananmen Square was a concrete square park, around which these buildings were situated, with Mao Zedong's tomb and the Great Hall of the People at one end, the wall shielding the Forbidden City on another side and many government buildings opposite it. The Gate of Heavenly Peace, a reviewing stand for official government rallies scheduled in Tiananmen Square, dominated the entire park. Except in the afternoon, when everyone wandered through the Square or queued up to see the yellowing, entombed Mao, there was no sign of life here. Undoubtedly, serious affairs were being discussed inside the austere government buildings lining the wide, tree-lined boulevards. These decisions often made world-shaking news.

It was true that every person, organization, municipality and province in China was controlled by decisions made in Beijing. The leaders live here but are invisible. They decide future plans and speak in one voice for everybody. Their edicts and pronouncements generally come through the government's news organ, the Xinhua News Agency. When any newspaper carries an item from China with a by-line saying "as reported by the Xinhua News Agency," this means it had the government's stamp of approval.

The other section of Beijing, in the opposite direction from Tiananmen Square, was alive with a variety of shops and street vendors. Dresses for sale swing on hangers along the sidewalks. Vendors push carts down the street, loaded with Coca Cola and cans of other familiar brands of soft drinks. Portable book stalls are set up along the curbs. A more formal bookstore that we found above a record parlor, shared a room with a clinic for birth control information. Small spaces for parking automobiles or bicycles are down tiny alleyways. The parking is organized by either a man or woman. Those attendants have the ability to squeeze more vehicles into less space than could be imagined. McDonald's is a presence and constantly busy. Several acupuncture parlors operate, as well as family clinics. This jumble of services meld together to serve the neighborhood very well. People lived here and walked along smiling or stopped to converse with friends. Perhaps they were making a deal or simply gossiping. This was quite a different ambiance from the governmental section, where the only sign of life was the black limousines ferrying top officials, members of the diplomatic corps or businessmen keeping official appointments.

On this short visit to Beijing, every minute was important for sightseeing. The sites we wanted to see seemed to be miles from the city proper, as well as several miles from each other. While in the city, we especially wanted to walk in Tiananmen Square. Having watched its recent notoriety on television, we knew it would be interesting to be there ourselves to visualize those happenings. The Forbidden City adjacent to the Square was certainly a must. The Summer Palace would be interesting, but a chance to walk on The Great Wall was a priority. Helen said there was a park especially built for panda bears which was en route to The Great Wall. Should we stop? Of course! We could not miss them. She would consult with the driver on how to coordinate these stops. She always consulted with him before agreeing on any course of action.

The drive into Beijing was long. The day was hot. Beijing was experiencing a heat wave. We were thankful the car had good air conditioning. To divert us, Helen pointed out a series of new trees recently planted along this newly constructed highway leaving the airport. A group of retired citizens accomplished this as a civic project. The elders wanted the approach to and from the airport to look nice when the 1996 Olympics came here. To have Beijing chosen as the city for these games was a dream every Beijinger hoped would happen. (It did not.)

A Short History of Beijing

As we drove along, Helen began to tell us a short history of the city. "Beijing had been the strategic northern outpost of the Chinese Empire, as well as the capital of China, for well over a thousand years," she said. "Through centuries of strife, it was Genghis Khan, founder of the Yuan Dynasty (1271-1368) who organized the construction of palaces, boulevards and even a canal. This was built to link with the Grand Canal so that tribute ships could sail directly to the capital. When this dynasty was overthrown by the Ming Dynasty (1368-1644), the new leaders spent vast sums of money constructing new palaces and temples with gardens and lakes, making the city into one of great splendor and beauty. Overthrown by the Ch'ing Dynasty (1644-1911), the Manchus made service to the imperial government a requirement for citizens. After China became a Republic (1912-1949), there was little development in the city. The Republic floundered, and Mao became the head of the government, declaring the Peoples' Republic of China (1949-1976) which ushered in the Cultural Revolution. During this time, many historical and religious monuments were destroyed. Old Ming walls with their commemorative arches to widows and honored local dignitaries were knocked down to make way for the Communists to build new, wider roads and better housing for citizens."

"Originally," she continued, "the city was laid out into two parts known as the Inner City and the Outer City. The Inner City was constructed between 1409 and 1420 in the Ming Dynasty and was surrounded by a 50-foot wall containing nine gates. Inside this wall were two parts: One part, called the Imperial City, was the site of government offices, palaces, temples and gardens. The other section, called the Forbidden City, is surrounded by a 35-foot wall and a wide moat. Here the former emperors and their entourages lived. The Outer City to the south was built for the populace. It was constructed between 1553 and 1564 in the Ming Dynasty," Helen concluded, as we turned into the driveway of our hotel.

There was the five-star Palace Hotel on Goldfish Lane in the Wangfujing district of Beijing. This structure, very modern in design, was easily one of the finest accommodating guests, not only here in China, but anywhere in the world. A competent, well-trained doorman assisted us inside and pointed to the registration desk. There a bright-eyed young woman greeted us. After we identified ourselves, she escorted us with dispatch to our rooms. It was here we registered. These accommodations had wonderful views of the city, plus everything we might wish in amenities. Maybe we should enjoy being here and simply relax instead of sightseeing. We were tempted.

The next morning, a Sunday, dawned very hot and humid. So much for our anticipation of enjoying cool weather here.

We were going to walk through the famous Forbidden City. After all the stories of intrigue about this place, we approached it with curiosity. Helen guided us to the Gate of Heavenly Peace. In front of this gate, painted a dull red, was a high walled courtyard. A large picture of Mao Zedong hung above the entrance of the gate. It seemed to us this was a cold and unfriendly atmosphere. Probably, this was by design because, in the past, foreign dignitaries were never warmly welcomed to the Forbidden City by the emperors. We felt just as unwanted, as Helen rushed off to a kiosk to buy entrance tickets.

To enter the complex, one walked through a plywood alleyway or tunnel, obviously recently constructed. Why we did not enter through the main gate was not explained, but it was firmly closed. We passed by a few kiosks that were also temporary buildings selling postcards and t-shirts. For fun, I stopped at one and bought a great white t-shirt trimmed with scarlet dragons. At the end of these kiosks, we suddenly walked out onto a huge concrete platform. Here we were looking at a wide panorama of the entire Forbidden City. What an impact this sight made on one! It was an immense compound with many, many pagoda-style buildings. By design, they were all facing south or pointing directly toward us. They sat on 180 acres of concrete, without a tree or bush to soften the scene. Each building faced south on purpose because it was believed this was protection from outside "yin" or bad influences from the north. Those influences might be icy wintery winds from Siberia or enemies who wished to invade the compound. The south brought the warmth of "yang." If we were in awe of this spectacle, that was exactly what it was designed to convey. This was the Court of the Son of Heaven, as every Chinese emperor was known. It was designed to be forbidding to all, but especially to the barbarian foreigners.

These buildings were used by the emperor for formal state occasions, as well as serving as the winter palace for him and his entire entourage. This included his immediate family, plus a multitude of servants called eunuchs who were retained for every sort of task needed to keep the palace functioning. All the buildings were on varying levels and interconnected by concrete courtyards and walkways. That there are no trees or shrubbery anywhere was planned on purpose. Someone might hide in a tree with the intention of assassinating the emperor as he passed. Without any greenery to soften the concrete landscape, the bareness of the entire compound was very severe and, to us, monotonous.

Helen pointed out the middle set of stairs in the staircases. They looked different because these were reserved for the emperor to use. Only the emperor. Sitting in his sedan chair, since he was never allowed to walk anywhere, he was carried from place to place by his eunuchs. The empress, in her sedan chair, always was positioned on his right when she was carried.

Truthfully, to be more believable this place needed the hosts of eunuchs clad in their orange robes and other high officials in their court finery walking around. In the stories we have read, there was always a variety of activities constantly taking place. Now everything seemed unreal and a place more designed for gaping tourists like us instead of serious imperial activities.

There were scads of tour groups and families with their children. It was fun to watch parents lining up their son or daughter for a photograph, to prove they had been to the Forbidden City. Some little ones carried balloons.

Others were wheeled in a stroller by a parent. None climbed on any of the brass pots which were strategically placed everywhere. Those pots were still actively used for fire buckets. Since all buildings were of wood, fires always were and still are a serious threat. A few youngsters stood beside a fierce-looking lion statue to have their picture taken. There were many gilded lions here to scare away bad spirits. The young ones just adored them. Older school children were led by their teachers to various exhibitions inside some of the buildings. They could look in, but were not allowed to enter and neither were we. The exhibitions were very elaborate and stylized scenes of imperial life as it used to be, which makes quite a contrast to the plainness outside. There were beautiful walls of ceramic tiling framing some of the entrances.

Some had beautiful blendings of many shades of blue, from turquoise to the deepest indigo.

The day grew hotter and more humid. Except for some statuary pieces, we were not very impressed with the trappings of the emperors. The far end of the entire complex was the exception. Here, there was a charming little park with interesting shaped trees, a waterfall and fascinating rookeries. Its coolness was welcome. Helen told us this was the home and gardens of the concubines. The park was built for them to exercise outside. Each year, it was the custom for a group of young girls to be chosen as new concubines. They were always the prettiest girl from their district. It was a great honor to be chosen. Once here, the girl's entire life was lived within the confines of this harem, to be in service to the demands of the emperor. Depending on his whim, they might or might not become one of his official concubines, but none were ever allowed to return to their former homes.

The Concubines

Originally, the harem was defined to include as many as three primary consorts; nine wives of the second rank; 27 wives of the third, fourth and fifth rank; and 81 concubines of the sixth through eighth rank. The Manchu emperors of the Ch'ing Dynasty changed this to include only one empress, two consorts and 11 concubines. Quite often, the empress, who was in charge of choosing the concubines for the Emperor, wanted these girls to be levelheaded and amusing companions for the dowager herself, and only then to appeal to the emperor. In addition, she selected girls whom she believed would produce the healthiest heir. She thought the girls should be pleasant, wholesome, well brought up, emotionally stable, small, plump, shapely, with unbound feet, which was a Manchu law, and reaching maturity. Should a concubine give birth to a male heir, she could become a full wife, even if the empress was still alive.

The Eunuchs

Within this harem, the eunuchs resided. They were the only men, with the exception of the emperor, trusted to enter these inner courtyards where the women of the imperial family were housed. Other men, including officials, military guards and even the emperor's male relatives were required to leave the palace grounds at night.

Since the emperor seldom left the inner recesses of the Forbidden City, eunuchs became the intermediaries between the outer bureaucratic world and the inner imperial one. This fraternity of special guardians often masked their viciousness and back-alley politicking with their high voices and soft demeanor. Any senior official who wished to see the emperor had to persuade a eunuch to carry a message to him. Naturally, there would be a fee for such a service. Ambitious officials always tried to flatter and bribe the more powerful eunuchs.

The Last Eunuch

Tuesday, December 18th, 1996 *The International Herald Tribune* ran an article on China's last imperial eunuch, Sun Yaoting, who died in his home at the age of 94. As a young boy, Sun had been emasculated in a crude operation arranged by his family. They were desperately looking for a way out of poverty and, by offering their son to become a eunuch, they hoped to enter into the private world of China's rulers. Only months after Sun's family forced him to go through the ordeal (the anesthetic used was hot chili sauce and the surgical instrument, a sharp curved knife), the Ch'ing Dynasty (1644-1911) was overthrown. Sun never became a part of the fraternity, although he did serve the last emperor, Pu Yi, during the decade that followed. They were allowed to live in a temple in the Forbidden City.

We walked out of the Forbidden City into a parking lot. From there, Helen directed us to a park across the street. We crossed the busy boulevard through an underground tunnel. How cooling that park felt! We wandered on paths with green leafy trees shading us from the sun. What fun it was to watch children as they played on swings and teeter totters, laughed on the merry-go-round and zoomed along the walks, riding electric bikes. All this equipment was provided by the park. Some little ones were not too shy to say "hello" when nudged by their parents.

We missed not having more interaction with the people. Tour guides always stood between us and them, so we had difficulty developing any interesting repartee. Most Chinese in 1993 were still afraid to be seen talking to Westerners, as their government regarded any lengthy interaction with foreigners as dangerous. Most Chinese could not speak any English, and we were not versed in their language and had to depend on our guides for translations.

Developing Computer Land in China

While we and the Chinese could not converse person to person, computers were beginning to become the powerful source of communication for everybody. Their growth in China was already starting and, predictably, would grow through the wide use of the Internet. Once this is firmly established, there will be no way to keep worldwide information from flowing to the people.

The government was making this difficult. For example, on February 1, 1997, State Council Order #195 was enacted. Called the "Temporary Regulations Governing Computer Information Networks and the Internet," and signed by Premier Li Peng, it said, among other things, "Any direct connection with the Internet must be channeled via international ports established and maintained by the Ministry of Post and Telecommunications. No group or individual may establish or utilize any other means to gain the Internet Access." The government wanted to protect its state secrets and worried that the Internet might be used to endanger the nation's security. To them, China's Internet, with its free-flowing information and unauthorized associations, was a profoundly disturbing concept. The Chinese government viewed the computer only as an important new technology to be used for the country's economic growth. Allowing individual citizens leeway to pursue outside information would weaken the government's control of information flowing to the average citizen. Of course, this was a correct assumption.

In 1993, roughly one person in 10,000 was actually on the Net. When a person or business wished to get online, the steps required to use it were as follows: an ISP must be picked from the 32 now in Beijing, which ranged from government-run companies and China Telecom, to start-ups like China InfoHighway. Papers must be filled out and an ID card provided. (For foreigners, a passport will do.) A Police File Report Form had to be filled out in triplicate, a copy for the ISP, one for the local PSB, and the third for the provincial-level PSB Computer Security and Supervision Office. Next, the Net Access Responsibility Agreement must be signed, a pledge not to use the Internet to threaten state security or reveal state secrets. Finally, an application for the ISP which states where one lived and worked, one's profession, home and office telephone numbers, as well as mobile phone and pager numbers. Details concerning the computer equipment used, the modem type, and its permit number must be supplied. But, this is not all. Paying was to be done either by a check or a bank account with its name and number. Credit cards could not be used. News services such as Reuters must conform to the regulations set forth by Xinhua News Agency if they wish to publish anything. In spite of all this red tape, people, particularly foreigners, were lining up to be registered. It was a beginning of the information flow to the average citizen.

For most people, any access to a computer was at the work place or in a university. Internet cafes were just starting to develop and were a new mini-growth industry. In these, people sipped coffee while surfing the Net. There were rules to be observed: no attempts were to be made to visit forbidden sites or download inappropriate material. A person may not change machines during a session, and only one person was to be on-line at a time. The logs of one's activities might be checked. If anything out of the ordinary was discovered, the person using the computer could be fined up to ten times the cost of time on-line used. Data that could be received included updated stock market reports from Shanghai and Shenzhen, discussion groups for parents, a job database, a dating service for young people who met and chatted on-line, an electronic magazine with sports news and a site where art students could advertise their works for sale. A book section allowed users to browse a bookshop and make purchases, and an on-line entertainment center was being developed to let music lovers check the listings of concerts and purchase tickets via computer. Anything political was discouraged.

Returning to our hotel, we passed some low, old buildings painted a medium grey. Their style was atmospheric and handsome so we asked Helen how they were used. She replied this was housing for ordinary people, and the buildings were four or five hundred years old. The residents had small rooms and shared toilet facilities with their neighbors. The people we saw walking around the grounds looked well fed and clothed. I noted many women wore socks rolled down to their ankles or pulled up to their thighs and secured with an elastic band. They were apt to show a lot of bare thigh and emphasized bowed legs. All the men dressed very much like Western men in dark cotton pants with light-colored shirts. No Mao uniforms were in evidence anywhere.

It was inevitable that we would want to learn a little Chinese. Since Beijing was our last stop, it was now or never to start. During the long drive to The Great Wall, Mac asked Helen to instruct us. We started by pronouncing her Chinese name—Huang Hua Jing. I asked her why she chose the name "Helen"? She answered that her instructor said she looked like a "Helen" so that became her Western name. I wondered what a "Helen" looked like. Neither she nor I resembled each other except in size. We were the same height.

"Zao chan hao!" said Helen to us. "Ni hao?" (Good morning. How are you?) "Wan shaw hao" (good evening) "Zai jian" (goodbye) "Xie, xie" (thank you) "Shi" (yes) "Bu" (no). We were speaking Mandarin, which seemed complicated by having four levels of sound. In learning, one must use the proper tonal level that the word falls into. For instance, the word "chi" meant tea only when pronounced with an uplift tone of the second position. One said it like "cha," the "a" is á or aah and the voice sound is up. Said in any other way, the word means something completely different.

Speaking Mandarin

Mandarin is the official Chinese language, but spoken Chinese breaks down into dialects. Every district has its own. Thus, the Chinese spoken in Guangzhou sounds different from the Chinese spoken in Beijing. People with different dialects sometimes have difficulty in understanding each other. There are eight main dialects in total, with many sub-dialects. While dialects can vary from region to region, basically everyone knows Mandarin Chinese. It is the Chinese taught in the schools.

Mandarin Chinese has four tones which are indicated with a mark over the vowel of the syllable. The first tone (known as high level) will be marked with ¯ which above the letter looks like ā. The second tone (called rising level) is marked with ´, for example á. The third tone (called falling and rising) is marked with ˘ or like ă. The fourth tone (called falling) is marked with ` or à. While it is important to use these tones when speaking Mandarin Chinese, the people are quite adept in interpreting improper pronunciations since there are so many dialects in China. Like people of any nation, they are flattered to have the stranger try to speak their language. We felt the same way when someone spoke to us in ours.

In 1979, a system called Pinyin was developed for translating Chinese words into our alphabet by using the phonetic pronunciation of the Chinese word. If one looks up a word in the dictionary, next to it is the Pinyin explanation of its correct pronunciation. Next to this is the Chinese spelling of the word. Finally, there is an explanation of what the word means. In Pinyin, most letters are pronounced as in English. For example, Canton in Pinyin is Guangzhou. The word cough is koff.

The name of stations, streets, and stores appear everywhere in Pinyin, as well as in Chinese characters. For a tourist, with or without a guide, it is a great help to have a grasp of a little Pinyin.

I asked one of our other guides how to pronounce "Qiao." The Q usually sounds like our K, but the vowel which follows determines how it is said. Thus Qi is "key," the a is "aah," and the o is "oh." Key aah oh—Qiao. Like Miao is pronounced Meow.

I liked the idea of the Chinese language. There are no adjectives like the, a, and an, for example and no masculine or feminine or plural nouns. The grammar is simple—subject, verb and object in that order. There are no tenses for the verbs. One said, for instance, "I swim today. We swim yesterday. They swim tomorrow." The verb "swim" is always in the present tense, swim, and never changed to "swam" or "swum." Verbs always use the same tense. Thus sentences are grammatically simple. It is said these features make it easy to acquire a large vocabulary quickly. We never had enough time to even start ours.

Chinese characters are called pictographs. We did not toy with trying to write any. The proper way to write them takes much time and practice to do correctly. Writing is very precise and stylized. Somewhere between 3,000 and 4,000 official pictographs are commonly used. This is reduced down from 50,000 available. We understood Chinese symbols very specifically have one meaning. Conversely, each Japanese pictograph can have several meanings. Pursuing Chinese handwriting would take time and much patience.

Mac asked Helen how to count. One through ten is yi, er, san, si, wu, liv, qi, ba, jiou, and shi. For eleven, Helen uses ten plus one until reaching twenty. Shi yi, eleven; shi er, twelve and so on. Twenty is er shi; 100 is yi biai and 200 is er biai. Contrary to the language, counting seems logical and easy.

The Summer Palace

This was a place we were eager to see. We drove to an approach by Lake Kunming, riding over the beautiful Bridge of Seventeen Arches. The entrance brought us into lovely grounds, full of large leafy trees and beautiful landscaping, and decorated with classical buildings. Everything was so elegant. From the late 1800s, these grounds were used as the summer residence by the Emperors when the weather in Beijing became unbearably hot.

It was the Dowager Empress Tz'u-hsi in the late 1800s who kept developing its style. The atmosphere here was completely different from the starkness of the Forbidden City. The Empress loved beauty and surrounded herself with it. We could picture her strolling around the grounds with her little shih-tzu lion dogs frolicking ahead. The lovely walkways overlooked gorgeous vistas in every direction.

The Dowager Empress and Her Son

The main entrance to the Summer Palace was called the Hall of Well-being and Longevity. The Chinese referred to it as Renshoudian. The throne still was there where the Dowager Empress Tz'u-hsi and Emperor Tung Chih, her son, gave audiences to Chinese officials. The Dowager Empress so disliked foreigners that she would sit behind a curtained wall so she did not have to see them when they presented their credentials. When the Dowager Empress Tz'u-hsi found Emperor Tung Chih unable to rule, she put him under house arrest and took over as the Empress herself. He was placed in the Palace of the Jade Waves, called Yulantang, a building north of here. The Hall of Happiness and Longevity, or Leshou Tang Hall, west of the Great Theater, served as her private residence. She loved the theater and built her own. West from her home was the Long Corridor called Chang Lang. This was a long walkway made of painted wood. Its roof supports 273 columns and was decorated with some 8,000 paintings. There were landscapes, episodes of historical interest and scenes from famous novels of classical literature.

Chang Lang was said to be 796 yards in length. We walked every inch of it. Rain threatened, so we scurried along to reach the car. Although in a hurry, we did look at many of the paintings. They all were different scenes, but painted in a similar technique. Since the walkway followed the coastline of Lake Kunming, we had a wonderful view approaching the famous

Marble Ship, known as Shifang. With its base of marble and upper part of wood, we could see its two stone side wheels. This ship was built in 1888 with funds meant to modernize the imperial fleet, not to renovate the private residence of the Dowager Empress. It did nothing to enhance the image of the navy. She had the ship decorated with several large mirrors and used it for lakeside dining.

The Imperial Dogs

The imperial dogs at the Summer Palace were christened "Pekingese." One was presented to Queen Victoria of Great Britain, who named him "Looty." It was said the Queen put a different ribbon around his neck each day of the week. Looty lived to be 12 years old. We too had favorite Pekingese dogs in our family. I well remember my grandmother's Chou Chou (which we pronounced "Chew-Chew"), and our daughter Helen and I raised two, Pekie and Tarka, with much love and care. Pekie, under the more dignified name of "Louise," even took a cup in obedience training, as well as mothering Tarka. He was a lost soul when she died.

History of the Summer Palace

History says once there were two Summer Palaces. Each was built on entirely different sites. The first, known as the Garden of Perfect Purity, or Yuanmingyuan, was developed in northwest Beijing by the Ch'in Emperor Qianlong. Its architecture was Western style, designed by an Italian Jesuit named Castiglione. Castiglione drew in the same style as the palace of Versailles. During the Second Opium War in 1856-1860, British and French troops burned this park to the ground as a way of forcing concessions from the imperial court. It was never rebuilt, and today there are only a few ruins left.

The second Summer Palace, known as the Garden of Cultivated Harmony or Yiheyuan, was built on 792 acres of land. This is China's largest park. It was the one we were now entering. It began simply as a private garden with a pond. Then in 1153 (Sung Dynasty), the emperor had the land laid out as a park. During the Yuan Dynasty (1271-1368), the lake was enlarged. In the Ming Dynasty (1368-1644), many pavilions were added and it was called an imperial garden. In 1934, it was opened to the public.

Dowager Empress Tz'u-hsi

The Dowager Empress Tz'u-hsi of the Ch'ing Dynasty (1644-1911) had a vivid, if not impetuous, history. When as young girl, her only name was that of her tribe, which was "Yehenara," she became a Manchu concubine in the emperor's harem. While the rest of the harem spent much of their time playing games devised by the eunuchs or inspecting fabrics for new gowns, Yehenara studied in the well-stocked library of the Forbidden City. She read the history of the 24 dynasties and the analects of Confucius and Mencius. She also practiced calligraphy and learned about art to refine her tastes.

In 1851, at the age of 16, Yehenara became an imperial concubine. An imperial concubine, as a member of the emperor's family, enjoyed a luxurious life of great status. It was considered an honor to be an imperial concubine and it definitely was preferable to being an ordinary Chinese citizen. That Yehenara caught the fancy of Emperor Hsien Feng, and produced his only healthy male heir, made her a full member of his family. She was promoted from a concubine of the fourth rank to consort, or concubine of the first rank, giving her the maximum status possible in China for a female and sharing status with Li Fei, another favorite concubine. Their rank meant consort, or wife just below empress. Until Yehenara gave birth to a son, Li Fei outranked her. The baby was born at the Summer Palace on Phoenix Island in Lake Kunming, the traditional setting for imperial births. He was named Tsai Chun and became Emperor Tung Chih.

Later, she would usurp her son's powers after he became Emperor and she became the Empress herself. Known then as Empress Tz'u-hsi, she wielded absolute power in the final decades of the Chinese Empire and was alternately reviled and revered by the Chinese. Empress Tz'u-hsi set a precedent for imperial dowagers by issuing edicts in her own name. Her tumultuous reign lasted almost 50 years. She had only one husband and one son, but 3,000 eunuchs waited on her. She reigned over China longer than all but a handful of male rulers throughout China's long history. She named two successors to the Dragon Throne. It was said she poisoned one of them when he became contrary.

There were only two other women who ruled China. They were Empress Wu in the Tang Dynasty, who ruled from 658 to 705, and Empress Lu who ruled in 170 BC. Over the centuries, occasionally other women were appointed regents, usually during a transitional time, when dethroning an emperor or enthroning a prince or announcing a surrender to an enemy. In the male-dominated Confucian society, a female ruler was feared.

The viewing of the Summer Palace and its grounds offered perhaps the most interesting sightseeing of all the buildings we visited. It had an aura all its own, which we found lacking in the Forbidden City. Somehow, one could imagine people actually enjoying themselves there.

We ended our interesting day of sightseeing with dinner at the Palace Hotel's Szechuan Chinese Restaurant. Remembering our experience in Guilin with the hotness of their Szechuan food, we approached this meal with a guarded attitude and asked our server for mildly seasoned dishes. Our menu included Fungus Soup, described as "sliced chicken soup with rare bamboo fungus and dry fungus" followed by Shredded Beef and green peppers in a mild soy sauce. (All capitals are as written on the restaurant's menu.) Next was Seasonal beans prepared in superior chicken cup. And always, steamed rice. We ordered toffee apples for dessert. On the table was a small dish with chili sauce, another small dish of very hot sliced cabbage and dishes of candied cashews and black olives. We drank Dynasty white wine and ate with chopsticks. Everything was delicious and spiced to our liking. While we ate, there were three performers who entertained the guests with Chinese music. Two played Chinese stringed instruments and the other was a flutist. By choice, we sat far away from them, as we did not enjoy the grating quality of their music.

Mao said, "A man is born with one mouth, but he has two hands to feed that mouth." I think this was what we did that evening.

The hotel had a nice buffet luncheon served in their large, informal, Western-style coffee shop. Every noon after sightseeing, we ate here since this restaurant was the only choice for this meal. Mac insisted on ordering from the menu. He always said to the waitress, who invariably invited us to "look at" the buffet, "No, no, we don't want that. It's much better to order from the menu." Toward the end of our stay in Beijing, we took a look at the buffet, especially the desserts. "Oh, look at what we've been missing," said he, grabbing a plate. Mac served himself a large helping of bread pudding, his most favorite dessert. I spied snow eggs, œufs á la neige, a great favorite of mine. In addition, we saw a lovely bowl of chocolate mousse and delicious looking cut-up fresh fruit. We certainly had been missing the goodies.

The Cuisine of the Chinese Court

A nostalgic little story about food surfaced after we came home. There is a tiny house in Beijing in a small alleyway called Sheep House Lane. Its owner, Li

Shan-lin, age 75, was preserving history here through cooking. His grandfather, Li Sun Ch'in, was the chief guardian in the Dowager Empress' Imperial Court during the last years of the Ch'ing Dynasty. Mr. Li remembered his grandfather's wonderful tales from that era.

For 30 years, as commander in chief of the palace guard inside the Forbidden City, it was Li Sun Ch'in's job to watch over the imperial kitchen. Each day, he sent guards to observe the preparation of the food, as well as eunuchs to taste all the dishes so the Empress would avoid any attempt at food poisoning. (She never was poisoned, but died naturally of dysentery after a feast of crab apples and cream.) Li Sun Ch'in supervised the cooking staff of 128 palace cooks and learned by heart the most intricate and exotic dishes served for the imperial meals. Each chef was allowed to make only one dish, to meet with the Empress' demands for perfection. Li passed along his recipes to his son who in turn passed them to his son, Li Shan-lin. Now Mr. Li's children are creating this food.

Their restaurant, serving Chinese court cuisine, was far from being an ornate banquet hall, as in the Forbidden City. The "restaurant" was actually the family's home. There were just two tables, each in a separate room, and the entire place could seat a maximum of 22 persons. Because of its popularity, reservations must be made weeks in advance. The restaurant attracted diplomats, high-powered businessmen and senior government officials. It was said that relatives of Pu Yi, the last Emperor, came here because the food was just like it used to be in the Forbidden City.

Recipes included a rare whale's tooth and shark's fin soup; a Mandarin fish; a baked version of the traditional Peking duck which was less greasy than the roasted kind; deep-fried lotus root; an imperial pancake and glazed walnuts. Wish we had known about this place while we were there.

Christmas in China

We understood the custom of Christmas started in Beijing as a business ploy for Christian expatriates. It is now a Chinese phenomenon or fad. Chinese families in growing numbers use Christmas as a celebration of prosperity, fun and enjoyment of Western ways. It is not a religious day for the majority of them. Of China's 1.2 billion people, about ten million, or about ten percent of the population, were baptized Christians. (On the day I was born, a Wednesday, I was told my grandmother was busily entertaining a missionary couple who needed funds to continue their ministerial work in China. Three years later a similar experience occurred, when my only sibling, my brother, was born on a Wednesday afternoon. Our grandmother was entertaining these missionaries again. Since she was always interested in their work and did try to help them, I would like to think some of those ten million Christians or their descendants might have benefitted from her generosity. Certainly that was her intention.)

Now one might see Christmas trees in hotel lobbies and shopping malls during December. Along some streets were a few jolly looking Santa Clauses sporting big noses like Westerners and fluffy white beards. The merchants were happy with all the trinkets being bought for the children who, in turn, thought Christmas was a wonderful occasion.

Deng Xiaoping said,
"Rich is good and Western ways are not all bad."

On the other hand, the church authorities found the celebration of this holiday a wonderful way of getting the Chinese into their churches. This past Christmas season, midnight mass was so popular that tickets had to be handed out earlier in the day to accommodate all the people wishing to attend.

The distance to The Great Wall from Beijing was 46 miles. We purposely went on a weekday, expecting there would be fewer tourists. Since the road wound around the mountains and was narrow, we hoped there would be little traffic. Nevertheless, it took over two hours to reach the entrance of The Great Wall.

The driver turned and said something to Helen. "The driver was asking if you want to visit the Panda Bear Zoo now or wait until we return?" Helen asked us. "Oh, let's go now," we answered enthusiastically. He turned off the boulevard onto a nicely paved curving driveway. We circled around a shaded parking square and left the car with our cameras in hand. There were several buildings confronting us. None resembled any zoo we had seen. While we waited to go into the first building, Helen scurried to line up for entrance tickets. Inside was a store selling panda bear paraphernalia in so many varieties of creations that we could hardly absorb everything. Stuffed panda bears in every size, china panda bears, lapel pin panda bears, panda earrings, panda ashtrays, panda lamps, painted scrolls with pandas, postcards with pandas and more. We started to giggle at the amazing variety of ways pandas were used for souvenirs and thankfully were rescued by Helen before we dissolved into outright laughter. "Does anyone buy this stuff?" we asked her. "Oh, yes," replied our guide, scowling. We should not downgrade commerce for the tourist business.

We showed our tickets and entered a building that seemed warm and stuffy. By moving along a railed-off walkway, we soon came to large windows that overlooked the panda cages. These were full of bamboo and other greenery, with a stone cave in the center. The bears had outside access through this cave. There they were—black and white cuddly pandas. I suppose in total there were five or six. They were big fellows, big clowns. Many little children were watching them with us, and we all laughed at their silly antics. The path led us outside, so we walked around the entire yard. It was a big park with trees and shrubs to keep the bears cool. One big fellow sat on his haunches eating a huge bunch of carrots. The zookeeper fed him tomatoes and other greenery too, but he really loved those carrots and chewed big chunks as fast as he could. We did not realize bears were vegetarians. Another bear was a clown. He kept turning somersaults and rolling around on his back. Every time we laughed, he did something funnier. What a cheerful place this was. Thinking about them made the rest of the drive to The Wall seem much shorter than 46 miles.

History of The Great Wall

It was estimated The Great Wall once had a length of 6,200 miles, stretching from the Yalu River in the northeast to Xinjiang in the northwest. It passed through 16 provinces. Today it is 3,750 miles long and stretches from the Shanhaiguan Pass near the Bohai Sea to Jiayuguan Pass in the Gobi Desert.

Undoubtedly, The Wall is one of man's greatest accomplishments. Its construction was a masterpiece of engineering. It is the only manmade object visible from satellites. It far exceeded our expectations in splendor.

The Great Wall's history began during the Chou Dynasty (770-476 BC). The building continued on during the Warring Kingdoms (475-221 BC). Mostly, sections were built in certain strategic areas to keep out the Huns and other tribes who settled in the north and west of China. Following China's unification under the first Ch'in emperor, Shihuangdi (221- 210 BC), 300,000 men, many of them political prisoners, plus 500,000 peasants were ordered to connect the Wall's segments. When finished, it became one huge rampart of stone. Those who died during construction were buried inside its walls. During the Ming Dynasty (1368-1644), the first Ming emperor, Yuanzhang, had the Wall strengthened and lengthened. Watchtowers were erected at intervals of 200 to 300 yards apart. Most of The Wall, as seen today, was built during this period.

Today, there are only three places where The Great Wall is open to tourists. We were taken to one called Badaling, the closest to Beijing. Mutianyu, another section and farther away, was recommended to us as less touristy, but our driver refused to go there. (He gave no explanation. Just shook his head, "no.") Perhaps it was being repaired and would be difficult for walking. We understood it had 22 watchtowers designed by a former Ming general who made them look like the traditional fence design of the region. It was good camouflage. That section of The Wall was built directly onto the mountain with steeper slopes than the section at Badaling. To reach its top, one climbed up 1,200 steps. (A cable car was available, which we certainly would have used.) The view from there was said to be spectacular. The third section opened was called Gubeihou. It was in poor condition. An army unit stationed there from 1970 to 1974 tore apart a large section of The Wall to build themselves barracks. In 1979, a special commission was formed and had The Wall reconstructed by the same army unit.

We arrived at Badaling. This place was like a small village, with kiosks selling cold drinks, postcards, knick-knacks and t-shirts saying "The Great Wall." There were many tourists. To walk on The Wall, one first climbed up a ramp and presented a ticket to the attendant. Then everybody was free to walk in either direction. Most people chose to go up, although some Japanese lady tourists went down. Perhaps they knew something the rest of us did not, for the moment we started up, it was steep uphill climbing. We saw them strolling leisurely downward. Past the first sentry box, the slope steepened considerably. All of us started to pant with exertion. We stopped and took time to look over The Wall into the

countryside, as well as to take pictures and catch our breath. We never expected this walk to be so steep. The views from here went on indefinitely. It was a mountainous, wild-looking landscape. We were awed by the extent of The Great Wall. It rambled over the countryside for more miles than we could see, even on a cloudless day. It was amazing that humans could build anything as complicated and well constructed as this over such an unfriendly terrain. Although a great many tourists were there, none of us was in the least crowded as we explored. We were all too busy taking pictures and being overwhelmed by its immensity.

The structure of The Wall was entirely made up of large cut-stone, including the walkway, steps, high sides and sentry boxes. Since its pathway followed the pattern of the mountain side against which it was built, somehow we never realized it would develop such a steep grade. There were sentry boxes every few yards. Each was a stone enclosure with room for perhaps two, good-sized grown men. The Wall's pathway is wide enough for seven or eight grown people to easily stand abreast. Supposedly, armed soldiers marched along here, as well as horse-drawn vehicles. It must have been an endurance test for all concerned.

Mac wished to continue climbing a little farther up. Helen accompanied him until they came to a series of stone steps with another plateau for viewing. That was enough climbing for Mac. He observed further up was an even steeper climb. Very few tourists were there. Everybody took pictures of themselves to prove they had climbed on The Wall. It was considered a very significant event. While Mac climbed upward with our guide, I watched the crowds huffing and puffing as they went upward. One Scandinavian family, a tall, blond husband with his tall, blonde wife and son and daughter, both teenagers and also tall and blond, came in sight. They had sat near us on our flight to Beijing. We noticed them when the stewardess on the flight served drinks because both the father and mother insisted each child talk to her in Chinese. Apparently the children had been taking Chinese lessons, and the parents thought this was good practice for them. The children were very embarrassed. Here they were now, coming down from their climb, full of vim and vigor and talking to each other nonstop.

The Wall was a fascinating experience, not to be missed.

Our last tourist event was a visit to Tiananmen Square, with the Gate of Heavenly Peace which overlooked and dominated it. Just as the Forbidden City represented China's past, this gate was a symbol of China's openness to the world and the future. First built in 1417 and restored in 1651, it was made of massive stone work and was covered with a wooden roof. A stream flowed beneath it, spanned by five white marble bridges. Today, over the Gate's central portal hung a huge picture of Mao Zedong. To the left was a plaque inscribed with a slogan, "Long live the People's Republic." To the right was another plaque saying, "Long live the unity of the people of the world." It was from the rostrum of this gate that Mao stood to proclaim the People's Republic of China on October 1, 1949. On other occasions, Chinese leaders showed themselves to the public from here, by walking back and forth as they greeted other officials. The grandstand below the rostrum could seat 20,000 people. This was used by officials and their guests to review parades or to participate in national celebrations carried out in Tiananmen Square.

Mao's Tiananmen Square

The Tiananmen Square we saw today directly in front of the Gate was the creation of Mao. Originally laid out in 1651, it was considerably enlarged by him, making it the largest public square in the world. He undoubtedly planned this. Here his people gathered for major rallies during the Cultural Revolution. Squares were marked with numbers so people could find where to stand. The square could hold up to a million people. On its west border was the huge Great Hall of the People. Over 10,000 persons could be in attendance in its main auditorium. Also, there was a large banquet hall where more than 5,000 place settings were laid. We saw all the tables actually were ready to use. So many forks, knives and spoons, as well as glassware and china, waiting for diners. The kitchen or kitchens supplying the food must be massive. When we asked to see them, we were told this was impossible. They were closed to tourists. In addition to this banquet hall, the building had 30 separate rooms, each in the individual style of a province, autonomous region or city. They were available for any of those citizens to use. Conferences were held in the building by the national People's Congress as well as other important political events.

That afternoon, when we walked through Tiananmen Square, there were all sorts of people wandering around. Some were groups of students intent on viewing and being photographed in front of the Gate of Heavenly Peace. To the Chinese, this place was the center of China. A photograph taken here was something to show future generations. Everybody seemed to have a camera. As we started across the concourse, a young male student deliberately pointed his camera at me, intent on snapping my picture. I ducked to the left, then to the right to avoid this, but he followed my every movement. Finally I placed my own camera up to my eye, and while he clicked me, I clicked him. We both smiled at each other, proud of having accomplished photographing each other.

Uniformed guards were posted in various corners and other strategic positions. I tried to take a picture of one of them who was conversing with his friend while still "on duty." Seeing what I was trying to do, the young soldier turned his back. Every time I tried to take a picture, he turned the other way. I knew how he felt.

There were many elderly ambling along, obviously enjoying the afternoon sunshine. Older people headed toward the long line waiting to visit Mao's mausoleum. Parents looked around while pushing strollers or walking hand in hand with a toddler. There were some food vendors, but mostly they sold outside the square.

June 4, 1989

How well many Westerners remember the June 4th incident in 1989, when a mass of students camped out in this place. They were demanding political reform through greater participation of Chinese citizens. Perhaps a million people were involved. Ma Ch'inquo, a student, said, "We want the government to affirm our movement is patriotic, not turmoil, and that they talk to us and realize we are not seeking to overthrow them." They asked for and were granted an audience with government officials. During the session, the government berated the students, saying they were too young to know anything about the Party or state affairs. The students staged a hunger strike to get fuller attention, but the government still paid no attention to any of their requests. The government feared being brought down by the power of the students.

At same time this was happening, Mikhail Gorbachev and Deng Xiaoping were holding a summit. It was the first time the Russian leader had been to China. Some 12,000 members of the foreign press were there to cover the event. CBS, CNN and others assembled with their television cameras and satellite dishes, but it was the plight of the students that attracted the cameras' attention. There was enormous support for the students' cause, even though this got the students no closer to their goal. "Save the Students" became a rallying cry in Beijing and the television cameras focused on hundreds of fainting students being carried off to hospitals, instead of on the Deng/Gorbachev summit. The welcome for Gorbachev had to be held at the airport instead of at Tiananmen Square as had been planned. The press coverage that Deng and Gorbachev sought never materialized because the students' demonstration was of more national and international interest.

Of course, the Party leaders were embarrassed. We watched on television as the army tanks rolled into Tiananmen Square. Mac and I were living in Pontassieve, Italy then, so receiving any television news was important to us, especially news of a happening in China. At seven o'clock each morning, we tuned to Dan Rather of CBS-TV news, who seemed to be the only American reporter describing the incidents live from Tiananmen Square on a daily basis. We well remember the picture of the single student walking up to an army tank and defying it to roll over him. This one picture was beamed all over the world. The demonstration ended when a frustrated government instructed the tanks to open fire on the unarmed students to quell their protests. That happened June 4, 1989. This event is vividly remembered to this day. Ever since, the picture of the student challenging the army tank is used over and over for propaganda purposes.

Back home, I was interested to read that Tiananmen Square had been the site of demonstrations in the past. On May 4, 1919, students protested against the Versailles Treaty. On April 4, 1976, there was one mourning the death of Zhou Enlai, the former prime minister. Neither of these took place without unpleasant incidents.

We had a much more interesting time in Beijing than we had expected. Helen was a quieter girl than some other guides. Being younger than the others, she had not developed a set tourist spiel, so her remarks were fresh and more spontaneous. We appreciated that. It was fun to ad lib with her. She was educated in languages and talked openly about her brother and parents. When we asked, she said boys here study computers and business management. Girls? Languages, mostly languages. If a girl knew a second language, she remarked, her job opportunities were better. Both her parents were scientists working in the field of chemistry. She was curious about us, how we lived and what both of us did. What would be her life's ambition? To work for a foreign company. Many of our other guides expressed the same wish.

Tomorrow, we would leave Beijing. Helen would escort us to the airport and stay with us until we board the flight to Tokyo. There, we will board another flight taking us directly to San Francisco. Although we were ready to go home, we knew a trip back to China was inevitable. This is a nation we shall be watching with great interest.

The China we saw in 1993, Deng Xiaoping's China, seemed very self-assured. It knew where it wanted to be in the world and how it would interact with that world. The Chinese feel very certain they can reclaim their pre-eminent position as a strong, prosperous country. Many of its ideals and principles are bound to clash globally because everything happening in China is not to the liking of everyone in the rest of the world, particularly on the issue of human rights, as led by the liberals in the United States. How China opens up to foreign ideas and still keeps its integrity with its own philosophies remains to be seen. Many Chinese wonder if the issue of human rights is really the major key to being accepted into the world of nations. They question whether it was their way of handling this or the United States' rigid demands on how they should accomplish it that is the crux of the question. On this issue, the Chinese hint that the United States may be the one who is in danger of being isolated from the rest of the world. There is no precedent in history of one nation telling another sovereign nation's people how to behave in the internal affairs of their country.

Since the end of the Cultural Revolution and Deng Xiaoping's rise to power, the last dozen or more years of economic reform and peace was the first period in more than a century when China had been free from foreign intervention, civil war or widespread chaos. We felt the genius of the Chinese people with their intelligence and strength of character remained secure in spite of all the political changes they had gone through. May this always be so. We shall watch with keen interest their growth and development as they become a world power. We wish them good luck.

This trip served to whet our appetite to see and learn more about China—its lands, its people and its history. Our six weeks' stay was a long time for Westerners to be in an Asian culture as tourists. It was exciting and eye-opening. We thoroughly enjoyed ourselves. We left knowing there was much more to be seen and learned, for China is a huge and complex nation. Much needs to be accomplished for the betterment of its people and upgrading of its industries and cities. This will take time and patience. We look forward to traveling there often. And, who knows, someday we really may become "Old China Hands." Certainly we shall be "Old Interested Ones."

A Final Postscript

As this book comes to a close, I reflect on the current feelings in the United States regarding China, and particularly as this was being reported to the public by the press. In October 1997, Jiang Zemin, the Chinese President, made his first state visit to this country. Many diverse American sites were planned for this tour. They first started in Hawaii, viewing Pearl Harbor, then, after landing on the United States mainland, he included among several other localities, Colonial Williamsburg in Virginia and Freedom Hall in Philadelphia, Pennsylvania. To him, these important historic symbols of America would help him understand more clearly what America stood for and what democracy was in this country. It was interesting that he took time during a state visit to learn more about our basic beliefs.

What a media commotion his visit caused! The anti-Chinese forces were out en masse, sponsoring all sorts of demonstrations to protest his even being allowed into the United States. The most touted event took place in Washington, D.C. and was reported to include many well-known Hollywood celebrities. This event occurred as President Jiang Zemin officially met with President William Clinton. Even Congress seemed intent on vilifying this leader with anti-Chinese bills. How convenient that Hollywood "happened" to be premiering two anti-Chinese movies. Both movies supported anti-Chinese sentiments to encourage anti-Chinese emotions from the general public. Most TV commentators and newspaper reporters followed the same theme. The often-used picture from the Tiananmen Square incident, with the single student trying to halt the advance of a tank, was like an icon for the TV and newspaper reporters to reinforce their stories. Such concentrated press efforts seemed to suggest all things Chinese were evil.

How different the press coverage was in February 1972, when President Richard Nixon visited China. His eight-day stay was the longest visit ever to that country by a president of the United States. Also, it was the first time a United States president had negotiated on the soil of another nation that had no diplomatic relations with Washington. I well remember watching his arrival in Beijing on our home television set. After Air Force

One landed and pulled up to the ramp where dozens of Chinese diplomats waited, there were several minutes when an empty staircase was all the cameras filmed. Everyone waited with anticipation. Then, the moment arrived. President and Mrs. Nixon, she in a bright red coat, both appeared at the doorway, waved and walked down the ramp to step onto Chinese soil. President Nixon offered his hand to Premier Zhou Enlai, and both men smiled as they shook hands. Until that moment, no one knew how warm a welcome might be extended to the Americans. No protest voices were heard. The Chinese officials treated the Americans with dignity and respect throughout the visit.

Twenty five years later on October 10, 1997, President Jiang of China and President Clinton of the United States held a joint news conference in Washington, D.C. Jiang so well explained his feelings when he said, "Sometimes noises come into my ears. Naturally, I am aware that in the United States different views can be expressed. Therefore, I would like to quote a Chinese saying which goes, 'Seeing it once is better than hearing about it a hundred times.' The Chinese philosopher Confucius said, 'Isn't it a pleasure to have friends coming from afar?' "

In the light of the United States' negativity to Jiang's visit, it was refreshing to read a report in *Newsweek* written by a Chinese-American man who posed some interesting points about China and its people. His comments were not loudly reiterated in the United States. While living in Beijing, China during the past four years, he stated, "the reality" of the China that he observed every day could not be more different from what he saw in the movies and heard on the media in the United States. The U.S. media would have people believing China was a Communist nation-state, suppressing freedoms right and left. In actuality, he said, the average Chinese person was able to do and enjoy things that were impossible 20 years ago. People were buying TV sets and cellular phones, traveling outside their home districts and switching to new interesting jobs—all unthinkable in the past. There was an improved standard of living, greater ease in communicating with each other, and a declining interest in government propaganda. The public in general no longer believed in Communism.

Frequently, there were candid conversations between citizens about this. Often, Communism was apt to be the butt of a joke, which was unthinkable in the past. The Chinese had never had so many political and social choices as they did now. Millions of Chinese were thriving and cared little for politics. They wanted a comfortable life, to have a job and make some money, to be happy and see their children educated, and to do better than they did. Do these wishes differ from the expectations of Americans?

None of this is to say China does not have its flaws. So too does the United States. When the Chinese are told that all Americans carry guns, that the police abuse criminal suspects, as in the "Rodney King" fiasco, that the fire at Waco was deliberately set and that native Americans are downgraded, they seriously question what democracy is all about and whether democracy is something they really want for their country. They wonder if the racism and violence prevalent throughout the United States is worse than the problems they face in China. China has its share of politicians and writers who would be happy to be isolated from the United States. They fear us, like some Americans are genuinely fearful of the Chinese and their growing dominance in the world.

While acknowledging that both countries have faults, the time has come to put aside these emotions and start learning about each other. Certainly, this was an important reason why the two nations' leaders met in October 1997. Each country has many different opinions and feelings about the other. The people of the United States have as much to discover about China as the Chinese citizens do about America. What better time than the present to break down the barriers of suspicion surrounding both nations and start serious discussions on many issues, especially those in dispute. Hopefully, that would be a positive result from the Clinton/Jiang meeting. How greatly the results could improve the growth and strength of both nations! With the welcome from President Clinton to President Jiang Zemin on his initial visit to the United States, this was the dialogue they were attempting to establish. It was, and is, important that we citizens listen. A healthy and workable relationship between these two powerful countries bodes well for the future of each, as well as for the world at large.

May you have good fortune
as the limitless sea;
may you have life as long as
the mountains are tall.

— A Chinese proverb

APPENDIX A

UPDATE OF CHINESE LEADERS

Results of National People's Congress—March 1998
The International Herald Tribune—March 5, 17, 18, 19, 20—1998

SEVEN MEMBER STANDING COMMITTEE
OF THE POLITBURO

JIANG ZEMIN Number 1 in Politburo
- President of China
- Chairman of the Part Central Military Commission
- Chief of the Communist Party

LI PENG Number 2 in Politburo
- Chairman of the Standing Committee of the National People's Congress, a legislative body
- Former Prime Minister for the past ten years
- Taking over this office from Qiao Shi who was ousted in the fall as being too outspoken on shaping laws and monitoring how they were implemented around the country. Opposed building the Three Gorges Dam on the Yangtze.

QIAN QICHEN
- Deputy Prime Minister
- Oversees foreign policy matters
- Is credited with reviving China's international image following crack-down on the students at Tiananmen and engineering the diplomatic isolation of Taiwan. Said he was too tired and too old to be the Foreign Minister.

HU JINTAO
- Vice President
- Former President of the Cultural Party School in Beijing
- As Vice President of the seven-member Standing Committee of the Politburo, he is the youngest member at age 55, and possibly is being groomed for the top job.

TIAN JIYUN
- First Deputy Chairman
- Wants a party of laws
- Was allied with Qiao Shi and Zhao Ziyang, the former Communist Party head who was ousted when he expressed sympathy for the pro-democracy students.

HE CHUNLIN
- Secretary-General of Congress
- Supervises professional staff

NEW CABINET MEMBERS

ZHU RONGJI Number 3 in Politburo
- Chairman of Cabinet
- Studied electrical engineering at Qinghua University (equivalent to MIT)

1952   State Planning Commission responsible for prices, credits and output targets
1957   Criticized Mao's policies and was exiled to the country
1962   Returned to State Planning Commission
1970   Again exiled to country
1979   Declared fully rehabilitated
1988   Mayor of Shanghai
1993   Deputy Prime Minister—became known as the "economic czar." Chief of the economic policy past five years, steering economy out of a runaway inflation without stifling its growth; trained as an engineer and state planner; he is famous for his frank talk, his brutal impatience with officials and his results-oriented manner. Originally, he was sponsored by Deng Xiaoping.

Vice Prime Ministers:
Li Lanqing; Qian Qichen; Wu Bangquo; Wen Jaibao

Deputy Prime Minister:
Wen Jaibao
- In charge of agriculture policy
- Protègé of Zhao Ziyang, the Communist Party Chief, who told protestors at Tiananmen 1989 that he could do no more to help them. Wen is part of a group of young men employed by Zhao in 1980 to shake up the party and government bureaucracies.

State Councilors:
Chi Haotian; Luo Gan; Wu Yi; Ismail Amat; Wang Zhongyu

MINISTERS IN NEW CABINET

Foreign Affairs: Tang Jiaxuan
- Expert on Japan and Asian affairs
- Replaces Qian Qichen

National Defense: Chi Haotian

State Development Planning Commission: Zeng Huaren

State Economic and Trade Commission: Sheng Huaren and Wu Yi
- Wu, a senior-level woman, a trade negotiator, promoted from Minister of Foreign Trade and Economic Cooperation to State Councilor
- Huaren, formerly manager of China National Petrochemical Corp., an oil concern

Education: Chen Zhili

Science and Technology: Zhu Lilan

Commission of Science, Technology and Industry for National Defense: Liu Jibin

State Ethnic Affairs Commission: Li Dezhu

Public Security: Jia Chunwang

State Security: Xu Yongyue

Supervision: He Yang

Civil Affairs: Doje Cering

Justice: Gao Changli

Finance: Xiang Huaicheng

Personnel: Song Defu

Labor and Social Security: Zhang Zuoji

Land and Natural Resources: Zhou Yongkang

Construction: Yu Zhendong

Railways: Fu Zhihuan

Communications: Huang Zhendong

Information Industry: Wu Jichuan

Water Resources: Niu Maosheng

Agriculture: Chen Yaobang

Foreign Trade and Economic Cooperation: Shi Guangsheng
(Replaces Wu Yi)

Culture: Sun Jiazheng

Health: Zhang Wenkang

State Family Planning Commission: Zhang Weiqing

Governor of People's Bank of China: Dai Xianglong
Protégé of Zhu Rongji

Auditor General of the National Audit Office: Li Jinhu

APPENDIX B

**Log of political happenings in China 1993-1997
during the writing of this book:**

March 15, 1993
The Wall Street Journal
China Expected To Reshuffle Its Leaders
Beijing—National People's Congress meets to begin a new five-year term and ratify a new slate of government officials. 2,977 delegates in total.

Expected to ratify a reshuffle of government units and central power into hands of six men. They will serve on the Communist Party Politburo decision-making standing committee. This is the second step in the reshuffling process that began last October and installed a revised party leadership handpicked by Deng Xiaoping.

In addition, Congress is expected to approve a legal system of government based on institutions rather than on the personal whims of leaders. Deng is fashioning rule by law, not rule of law. All courts are supervised by party committees.

The National People's Congress is the highest authority in China. Its membership is a collection of model citizens who get to the national level by being chosen by their peers in local people's congresses. The roster of senior government officials that these delegates will ratify was finalized at a secret meeting of the party Central Committee just one week ago.

Leaks to the Hong Kong media offer what lies ahead: Deng Xiaoping, 88, remains. Premier Li Peng, 64, will get another term. Party Chief Jiang Zemin, 67, will emerge as party general secretary and chairman of the central military commission. In addition, he will be appointed state president. That gives Jiang the "core" of the current leadership.

Other appointments: Qiao Shi, 68, the party's long-time secret police overlord, as chairman of the National People's Congress; Li Ruihuan, 64, former chief of party ideology as chairman of the Chinese People's Political Consultative Conference, an advisory group made up of prominent people ranging from scientists to movie stars whom the party wants to keep in close political orbit. Zhu Rongji, 64, remains vice premier in charge of the economy. Liu Hua Ch'in, 72, continues as vice chairman and overseer of the central military commission. Hu Jintao, 50, former party party secretary of Tibet, will forego a government post so he can concentrate on party building.

These seven men currently make up the Politburo's standing committee.

There is speculation that Rong Yiren, 76, known as the "red capitalist," and current chairman of China International Investment and Trust Company will become state vice president.

Reformers are concentrating on drafting business statutes to guide China's transition to a market economy. "Under the leadership of the Chinese Communist Party" and "adhere to the people's democratic dictatorship" will remain phrases in the constitution.

MAY 24, 1994
The Daily Telegraph, London
Challengers for the Chinese Leadership Play a Waiting Game
Peking—Jiang Zemin is Deng's successor. He is now China's president, General Secretary of the Communist Party and Commander in Chief of the army.

Hu Yaobang and Zhao Ziyang, Jaing's predecessors as party leader, both fell from grace because of their failure to halt the changes brought by economic reform. Jiang has distanced himself from the controversy in Beijing over how to control a runaway economy that may deal a fatal blow to the Communist Party. Both Jiang and Prime Minister Li Peng are letting Zhu Rongji, the senior premier and potential challenger to both of them, make the decisions. Zhu has been impressing foreign businessmen, but has earned enemies in Beijing and the provinces.

OCTOBER 6, 1994
The International Herald Tribune
Deng Lin, 52 year-old daughter of Deng Xiaoping, opened an exhibition of her paintings in Paris in the presence of Jacques Toubon, France's culture minister, and Pierre Cardin, the designer who sponsored the event. Most of the works in the show are early traditional ones, but some in recent years are forcefully abstract.

OCTOBER 8-9, 1994

The International Herald Tribune

China's paramount leader and most revered living Communist, Deng Xiaoping, has been awarded a special prize for being a "Most Fortunate Old Person." He was one of 600 people awarded prizes for being "Superior Fortunate Old People," but only Deng received the "Most Fortunate Old Person Special Prize," a press report said. Deng, who turned 90 on August 20 (1994), is not only "a man of noble character and high prestige," the *China Times* said Friday, "he is the most beloved among China's elderly people."

NOVEMBER 1, 1994

The International Herald Tribune

How's Deng? The Zhongnanhaiologists Wonder

Beijing—There is a spate of rumors that China's 90-year old leader, Deng Xiaoping, is near death. He failed to make an appearance on October 1, 1994 for China's National Day, the 45th anniversary of the Communist Party victory over the Nationalists.

On October 6, the newspaper *Wenzhou Ribao* quoted Deng's younger sister, Deng Xianqun, as saying that she watched National Day fireworks with Mr. Deng at the government's Beijing guest house. This report was contradicted five days later by South Korea's Yonhap news agency, which claimed Deng was in a coma and had been at Army Hospital No. 305 since late September. It said he was being kept alive by life support systems and had been near death September 26 and 28. On October 13, the Foreign Ministry's new spokesman, Chen Jain, declared at a regular weekly briefing that "Deng Xiaoping is in good health." Pressed about whether Deng was at home or in a hospital, Mr. Chen gave the stock answer used by his predecessor: "Deng Xiaoping is wherever he is."

Last week Deng's daughter and private secretary, Deng Rong, during a visit to Hong Kong, asserted that her father was all right. She is quoted as saying, "His health is not bad. Of course, he is a 90-year old man now."

Each time a rumor starts about Deng's health, the Chinese stock markets go into spasms. Several front page editorials fed the speculation, saying the populace should rally around the party of the national leaders and the spirit of Deng's economic reforms. The *People's Daily* warned "it would be hard for forces from without to topple the party, but the party may collapse at its own hands." Other signs: a newspaper six-year old photograph of

Deng which raised speculation that his current condition was so decrepit that he could not be seen. In February, during the Lunar New Year, he walked unsteadily and appeared disoriented many television viewers said.

Many analysts see signs of a succession battle.

What all this means, in the view of a Hong Kong analyst, is that whatever Deng's physical state, politically he is already finished. That would explain the flood of retrospectives—such as the recent release of his speeches on compact discs—and the eulogy-like tone of recent articles.

NOVEMBER 3, 1994
The International Herald Tribune
Editorial from *The Washington Post*
China After the Emperor
Washington—Deng Xiaoping, who has held the ultimate power in China for the past 16 years, is slowly dying. His grip has failed to the point where open competition has broken out among the many factions vying to name his successor.

The key question for the Chinese is whether the economic reform will continue. Deng relaxed the central government's control over economic life and began to move the country toward open markets. The results have been spectacular. Since 1980, according to the World Bank, the country's output has been rising by more than nine percent a year—three times the worldwide average, and a rate slightly better than Japan's in the steepest phase of its ascent a generation ago.

The choice is whether to maintain traditional political control, meaning a much slower growth, or just continue fast growth requiring further relaxation of the Communist Party controls.

NOVEMBER 16, 1994
The International Herald Tribune
In China, Reasons to Expect a Fairly Smooth Post-Deng Transition
Cambridge, Massachusetts—Yasheng Huang, a visiting scholar at Harvard's Center for International Affairs and Assistant Professor of Political Science at the University of Michigan, contributed this interesting article to the *New York Times*.

His premise is when Deng dies there will be no harsh transition of power like there was after Mao died and the Gang of Four were punished.

Deng is not Chairman Mao. Deng, with a handful of octogenarians, often needs to compromise on key policy and personnel issues. His departure will not leave a power vacuum as gaping as the one Mao's death created in 1976.

Mao had appointed Hua Guofeng as successor only five months before his death. Hua did not have time to consolidate his power base, and soon found himself between the radicals, led by Mao's wife Jiang Ch'in, and the moderate faction, led by Marshall Ye Jianying. The current succession was put in place five years ago when Jiang Zemin assumed party leadership. (He became president in 1993.) Since then Jiang has had time to build up his political support. Knowing that the army holds the key to his survival in the post-Deng era, he has lavished money on the military and promoted his allies in its senior ranks. Jiang has attained a greater status than Hua ever could.

Further interesting points Mr. Huang makes:

In 1976, the leadership was bitterly divided. The Gang of Four and the moderate leaders represented two irreconcilable visions about how China should be governed. The radicals wanted to continue the Cultural Revolution, which ran from 1966 to 1976, when Mao died. The moderates wanted to restore the bureaucratic normality of the 1950s. Now, in contrast, all factions share a commitment to economic reforms and political stability. The disagreements are over the pace and specifics of reform, but they are not close to the kinds of ideological divisions that engulfed China in 1976.

Political life during the Cultural Revolution was nasty, brutish and short. Political opponents were purged as traitors and often their family members were not spared punishment. For example Liu Shaoqi, the former president, died in prison. The punishment of the Gang of Four for perpetuating large-scale persecutions was far milder than his fate or, for that matter, that of Deng Xiaoping, who was sent to the countryside to do hard labor and whose son was crippled by the Red Guard.

The three fallen leaders in the reform era, Hua, Hu and Yaobang were removed from their positions gradually and were allowed to keep most of the trappings of power. Zhao Ziyang was granted considerable freedom and his family's economic interests remain largely intact.

Ending the vicious cycle of revenge and instituting civil rules of the political game are among the great, and underrated, achievements of Deng. Leaders are no longer political enemies but are rivals who negotiate and compromise. This augurs well for a smooth transition of power when Mr. Deng dies.

DECEMBER 9, 1994
The International Herald Tribune
Dengist China After Deng? Not Certain But Likely
Geneva—An article contributed by Zhang Weiwei, a research fellow of the Modern Asia Research Center, University of Geneva.

When Maoism has not outlived Mao, will Dengism survive when Deng dies? This is the focus of this article. The writer's assumption is that Deng's "socialism with Chinese characteristics," which have had such a dramatic effect on transforming China in such a short time, will survive.

Deng's recurring themes are:
Development: A priority to economic development and ultimate "common prosperity."
Market Development: A regard of economic reform as market orientated. Promotes the non-state sector and pursues an open-door policy to attract foreign capital and technology.
Political Rationalization, not Democratization: Urges improving the political system's efficiency without changing its fundamentals. Thinks democracy based on adversarial politics would divide China and make the transition to a market economy more difficult.
Authoritarianism: Wants a pro-business authoritarianism. Defines this as a hard state and a soft economy with an elist party to enforce reforms and resist pressures from specific social groups and partisan interests.
Gradualism: Reforms require strategies and tactics and should produce the highest payoffs at the lowest cost.
Pragmatism: Answers to China's problems cannot be read from a book on Marxism or Western classics. Reform policies should be tried on a small scale before being introduced on a larger scale.
Nationalism: Long term goals for China should restore past glory, catch up with the developed countries and retain China's identity as a major power. This will differ from both Western capitalism and Soviet Communism.

Single-Mindedness: Not interested in an ideological battle with the West. His approach is to mind China's own business, let economic performance speak and laugh last!

The conclusion is Dengism probably will last for some time. The market-oriented development has unleashed people's energy for prosperity. Nationalism has rekindled the dream of the Chinese modernizers for a strong and prosperous country. And authoritarianism, even if contentious, is probably more typical than unusual in Chinese political culture. Mr. Deng's popularity in China today is greater than Bill Clinton's or John Major's in their respective countries.

Deng's ideas are unlikely to be swept under the carpet when he dies. As the country further develops, new ideas and interests will emerge and a political structure to accommodate them must be found. A more democratic China may emerge, but it will be more as a result of gradual reform and greater prosperity, facilitated by Deng Xiaoping's doctrine, than of radical democratization.

JANUARY 10, 1995
The International Herald Tribune
Beijing Denies Deng is Ailing
Following a published report in Japan that Deng Xiaoping is chronically ill, China's government responded with an optimistic bulletin about his health.

The Yomiuri Shimbun quoted reliable sources who said Deng had been hospitalized last month and was so ill that President Jiang Zemin could not see him.

JANUARY 13, 1995
The International Herald Tribune
China's Senior Leader is Healthy
Newspaper Publishes First Photograph of Deng in a Year (It ran on page one in a Shanghai paper Thursday.)

Shanghai—Publication of first picture of Deng Xiaoping intends to counter rumors of the past several days that China's reclusive patriarch had been hospitalized.

Picture shows Deng, 90, sitting in a chair in Beijing's Zhongnanhai leadership compound watching the fireworks display in nearby Tiananmen

Square during the October 1 National Day festivities last year, according to the caption. He was wrapped in a coat and sported a cloth cap.

Deng's failure to appear in public at the fireworks show had sparked rumors that he was either seriously ill or had died. The Shanghai Stock Market plunged as a result. Last week's newspaper report from Japan said he was too ill to receive President Jiang Zemin. A foreign ministry spokesman in Beijing said Thursday that Mr. Deng was well.

"Comrade Deng Xiaoping is healthy," the spokesman said. "Foreign reports to the contrary are without basis."

The Chinese public last glimpsed Mr. Deng in February 1994 when national television news showed him at a Lunar New Year reception in Shanghai.

A Shanghai-based Western diplomat said that Thursday's picture was "an attempt to convince the public that he is not dying. It looks like the same old man we saw 12 months ago," said the diplomat of the fuzzy picture.

JANUARY 14-15, 1995
The International Herald Tribune
Deng Incapacitated, His Daughter Says
Beijing—Xiao Rong, daughter of China's paramount leader, Deng Xiaoping, says her father's health has significantly declined in recent months and he remains at home at the family's compound in Beijing, unable to stand or walk.

His medical care is under the direction of the Communist Party leadership, and there is a debate over whether he will make his annual appearance on national television during the Lunar New Year's celebrations which begin on January 30.

Mrs. Xiao denied reports that her father has entered the hospital, but her unusually frank remarks in an 80-minute interview did little to dispel concern that the leader's death is near.

"His health declines day by day," she said. "People have to understand that at this point he's 90 years old, an old man. And some day there will be a day when he passes away, that's for certain."

Though last year at this time Mr. Deng was able to walk for 30 minutes twice a day, "Now he cannot walk," she said. "He needs two people to support him. He refuses to use a wheelchair to travel. He feels that after he sits in a wheelchair, he won't be able to get up again. It's the natural order." Mr. Deng's decline has left uncertain whether the family will move to its winter retreat in Shanghai. "If there aren't any problems, maybe we'll go to Shanghai," she said. Although she did not provide details of Deng's specific ailments, he is believed to be suffering from advanced Parkinson's disease and perhaps diabetes and kidney dysfunction.

Mrs. Xiao is traveling soon to New York and Paris to promote a biography of her father.

JANUARY 19, 1995
The International Herald Tribune
China's Share Blues—Deng's Health Keeps Foreigners on Edge
Shanghai—The failing health of Deng Xiaoping and the Mexican currency crises are the latest blows to confidence in China's struggling B-share market, brokers said Thursday.

JANUARY 21-22, 1995
The International Herald Tribune
London—David Shambaugh, senior lecturer in Chinese politics at the School of Oriental and African Studies, University of London, and editor of *The China Quarterly*, contributed this article.

The Deng Xiaoping deathwatch is on in earnest.

It can be argued that the succession has already occurred as Mr. Deng and his fellow elders have installed a collective group of advisors since 1992. China's elite today is notable for its relative lack of factionalism and political infighting. This apparent stability may be an illusion, but it is in marked contrast with the Maoist era and much of the period under Mr. Deng.

JANUARY 21-22, 1995
The International Herald Tribune
Deng Reported to Be Unconscious
Hong Kong—China's senior leader, Deng Xiaoping, is unconscious in a hospital, and senior government and army officials had been asked to stay in Beijing to handle any repercussions in case he dies, news reports on Friday.

Although a Chinese government statement on Thursday said Mr. Deng was in good health for a man of 90, several Hong Kong newspapers said he had recently fallen seriously ill. The *Eastern Express*, an English-language daily, said Mr. Deng was admitted to a hospital in critical condition several weeks ago after a stroke.

Quoting sources in Hong Kong and Beijing with close connections to his family, the newspaper said that Mr. Deng's condition had improved and stabilized, but that he remained in "a near-vegetable state" and any recovery would be difficult.

JANUARY 26, 1995
The International Herald Tribune
Deng Reported Unable to Make Any Decisions
Tokyo—China's senior leader, Deng Xiaoping, is no longer able to exercise day-to-day leadership or make decisions on policy issues because of poor health, authoritative sources said Wednesday.

JANUARY 31, 1995
The International Herald Tribune
At 90 and Frail, Deng Lets His Chinese New Year Greeting Slip By
Beijing—Deng Xiaoping failed Monday to make his annual Lunar New Year television appearance for the first time since 1988, in a further sign that the health of the 90-year old leader may be in steep decline.

Mr. Deng has not been seen in public since February of last year when he looked frail and vacant during his annual appearance at Lunar New Year's Eve celebrations in Shanghai, where he traditionally receives Chinese leaders and extends his greetings to the nation.

His failure to appear Monday on the eve of the start of the Year of the Pig heightened speculation that the "architect" of China's economic reforms may never be seen in public again.

FEBRUARY 1, 1995
The International Herald Tribune
China After Deng Called 'Up for Grabs'—
American Interests at Risk, a Pentagon Reports Warns
Washington—The odds are 50-50 of a Soviet-style breakup of China after the death of its paramount leader, Deng Xiaoping, according to a study for the Defense Department. This is according to a report by a group of

university and business scholars. In releasing the study, the Pentagon noted that it did not reflect official U.S. policy.

FEBRUARY 6, 1995
The International Herald Tribune
China's Destiny Not for Deng, Daughter Says
Paris—China's destiny is already in the hands of Deng Xiaoping's successors, according to the Chinese leader's daughter. But she said her father was in good health for a 91-year-old.

Deng Maomao, also known as Deng Rong, said that she hoped foreign nations would shift their attention to her father's successors. She was in Paris to promote her book, "Deng Xiaoping, My Father."

Asked why Mr. Deng had not appeared on Chinese television for the Lunar New Year, as is customary, she said her father had already retired. "The destiny of China is now in the hands of the new team," she said. "I hope our foreign friends can show more concern for the new team."

FEBRUARY 14, 1995
The International Herald Tribune
Voices from Asia
Deng Rong, daughter of Deng Xiaoping, during a trip to Washington to promote her biography of her father: "China practices socialism, not capitalism. The question of distribution is always very important, and we should always see to it that there will not be too big a disparity between the rich and the poor."

FEBRUARY 17, 1995
The International Herald Tribune
Voices from Asia
Deng Rong, a daughter of Deng Xiaoping, on the senior leader of China: "Health permitting, he said he wanted to set foot in Hong Kong in 1997. He would be willing to go in a wheelchair. He still has this hope."

FEBRUARY 17, 1995
USA Today
New York—Deng Rong, daughter of the world's most powerful Communist, is in the United States on a purely capitalist venture: promoting a biography of her father, Deng Xiaoping. The setting for the interview was another capitalist shrine, New York's glitzy Waldorf-Astoria hotel, in a

suite padded from floor to ceiling in thick carpets, rich brocade and fine art. Deng herself is another exception to the image of a drab Chinese in buttoned-up Mao-style blues. At 44, she is strikingly beautiful, with sleek-cut, shiny black hair and ivory smooth skin. She wore a stylish black suit, sand colored silk blouse and chunky gold-and-diamond jewelry. She laughed easily.

Article by Marilyn Greene:
On her month-long tour to promote the biography of her father, Deng Rong says the most questions asked of her are about her father's health. "What really puzzled his doctors was how anyone who smoked for eight decades could have lungs in such good shape. For someone who has reached the age of 90, his health is quite decent. If there is one part of him where his age shows, it's his legs which aren't as strong as they used to be." She discounts rumors that he has Parkinson's disease, suffers from kidney failure, or that he is in a coma or even dead. The incessant inquiries "don't annoy me at all. I think it's inevitable people are concerned about China's future."

She notes that her father ended China's lifelong leadership tradition by bowing out of all official duties in 1989, "precisely to prevent the possibility of chaos erupting in China upon the death of any single person." Now China is run by "a collective" with Jiang Zemin "at the core."

"When the time comes that he passes from the scene, I don't think there'll be instability or disorder. I have absolute confidence." In the meantime, she says, Deng passes his time "the way all retired people do. He is a man of regular schedule. He does exercises he devised himself. He strolls. He reads the papers himself; we don't read them to him. His hearing is not the greatest, but his eyes are excellent." Deng loves television, especially a series on China's Three Kingdoms era. He watches each episode.

The Deng household of 17 people eats together every day at two tables. Her father is "a man of simple tastes," and likes Chinese food from both north and south China, especially the spicy dishes of his native Sichuan province. He drinks a cup of mild rice wine daily with his lunch. He is very disciplined in his drinking. He has it at the same time, in the same amount.

Neither Deng himself nor his eldest son, Deng Pufang, who was crippled when he jumped from a fourth-floor window to escape Red Guards, harbors resentment for their treatment during the Cultural Revolution, Deng Rong says.

MARCH 13, 1995
The International Herald Tribune
Deng's Successor Revealed by China President Jiang to Take Over Power —Emphasis is on Political Stability
Beijing—Prime Minister Li Peng said Wednesday that "the transfer of political leadership has already been completed." Mr. Li disclosed President Jiang Zemin had been confirmed as the "third generation" leader to hold power after Mao Zedong and Mr. Deng. He added that whatever changes may take place "I can assure you that political stability will remain. The political situation is stable."

This is the first time that anyone has heard that the changeover has already taken place. This removes a great deal of the uncertainty and speculation over the stability issue in China.

The announcement came at a conference on China organized by *The International Herald Tribune* and China's State Commission for Restructuring the Economic Systems.

MARCH 22, 1995
The International Herald Tribune
Hong Kong—Article by Philip Bowring about China's new leaders, with emphasis on Jiang Zemin in the weeks before the People's Congress. Jiang took every opportunity to portray himself as the nation's new leader. He made a dramatic eight point statement on relations with Taiwan. He had arrested Zhou Beifang, head of the Shougang Corporation, sending a clear message to the Deng family interests. A Deng son heads a Shougang subsidiary.

Some of the speeches Jiang made at the People's Congress expressed the need to combat corruption and the use of political power to accumulate personal wealth. He was not merely taking a swipe at the Deng family for its Shougang connections, he was also sending a warning to other "princelings," to foreign investors who thought they could buy special relationships in China, and to Chinese entrepreneurs, who thought that "guanxi," or personal relationships, could override the rules of the bureaucracy.

MARCH 23, 1995
The International Herald Tribune
He's No Pinup, But Deng Heir Smiles in Poster
Beijing—Unveiling of a poster showing Jiang Zemin smiling up at Deng Xiaoping as a sign to bolster Deng's chosen heir.

APRIL 25, 1995
The International Herald Tribune
Doubts on Deng's Health as Children Cancel Trips
Hong Kong—The five children of China's leader, Deng Xiaoping, have all canceled trips outside Beijing for at least a month, Hong Kong's *Eastern Express* newspaper reported Monday.

It is uncertain whether there had been any change in Mr. Deng's health, but the Deng children have been advised by the Communist Party Politburo to cancel trips in order to avoid questions about their father's health.

Youngest daughter Deng Rong canceled a trip to Tokyo, scheduled for next month, to promote her book about him. A spokesman for the Japan-China Friendship Association said last weekend Miss Deng canceled her planned attendance at its meeting.

MAY 11, 1995
The International Herald Tribune
Deng's Niece Target of Probe; Paper Says Corruption Inquiry Heats Up
Hong Kong—Chinese authorities are investigating charges that the niece of Deng Xiaoping, the paramount leader, embezzled $12.9 million, a Hong Kong newspaper reported Wednesday.

The investigation of Ding Peng in the southern Chinese city of Shenzhen is another indication that China's leaders may want to purge relatives and associates of Mr. Deng according to the English-language *Eastern Express*.

Ding Peng is the second Deng family member reported under investigation for economic crimes since President Jiang Zemin launched an anti-corruption drive. Hong Kong media reported Deng Zhifang, the youngest son of the Chinese patriarch, was questioned about economic crimes. He denied the reports.

The anti-corruption drive has led to the resignation of Beijing's Communist Party secretary, Chen Xitong, the suicide of a Beijing official who was being investigated, and arrests of several businessmen.

In February, Zhou Guanwu, the chairman of China's largest steelmaker, Shougang Corporation, and an associate of Mr. Deng's since the 1930s, resigned after the arrest of his son, Zhou Beifang, for economic crimes.

Miss Ding is the daughter of Mr. Deng's younger brother. She and a partner, Zheng Lielie, were accused last month by two Hong Kong business partners of illegally diverting $12.9 million to buy shares without their consent, the *Eastern Express* said.

MAY 24, 1995
The International Herald Tribune
Deng is Fine, His Daughter Tells a Paper
Hong Kong—The eldest daughter of Deng Xiaoping, China's senior leader, insists that her father and mother are in good health, a pro-Beijing newspaper here said Tuesday.

"My father's health is good," Deng Lin was quoted as saying in the *Wen Wei Po* newspaper. "My mother's health is good. My brothers and sisters are fine too."

She accused "certain overseas media" of carrying "meaningless" reports about her parents, neither of whom have been seen in public for a year.

Various reports in recent weeks have said that Mr. Deng, 90, has run a fever, gone into a coma or lost the ability to see clearly.

AUGUST 21, 1995
China News
Deng's 1.5 m-tall Shadow Still Looms Large in China

JANUARY 2, 1997
The International Herald Tribune
Deng is Said to Be in Intensive Care
He fell unconscious briefly and was placed in intensive care in his house in Beijing after he recovered consciousness later that night.

JANUARY 9, 1997
The International Herald Tribune
Rumor Mill on Deng Shifts Again to High Gear
A documentary is shown on television each evening, summing up Deng's life and achievements. This is a sign his days are near to an end. Since details of his health are kept secret, it is difficult to know whether he is seriously ill or near death.

*JANUARY 20, 1997
The Wall Street Journal–World Wide
Deng Xiaoping Died, Leaving China Economically Free but Still Authoritarian
Deng's Death Isn't Expected to Lead to Reversal of China's Political Policies—Kathy Chen

Deng's Contradictory Legacy

Rule Without Law—Martin Lee

A True Leninist Capitalist —David Shambaugh

*This article was printed, but was incorrect about Deng's date of death. Deng died February 20, 1997.

FEBRUARY 18, 1997
The International Herald Tribune
China Leaders Rush Home as Deng's Health Deteriorates

**FEBRUARY 20, 1997
The International Herald Tribune
Deng Xiaoping, Who Transformed China, Dies
**This is the correct date of Deng Xiaoping's death.

FEBRUARY 21, 1997
The International Herald Tribune
China Looks to Next Generation
A Great Reformer Who Brought China into the Modern Age
Editorial: After Deng Xiaoping

FEBRUARY 22, 1997
The International Herald Tribune
After Deng, the Real Power in China Rests with the Army—
    Richard Halloran

Dissident Exiles in U.S. See Chance for Change in Post-Deng China

Jiang Vows to Pursue Deng's Reforms

FEBRUARY 24, 1997
The International Herald Tribune
Editorial Opinion—China After Deng: What Should Washington Do?

Paramount Leader Was No Saint—Jim Hoagland

Don't Make It an Evil Empire—Robert J. Samuelson

FEBRUARY 25, 1997
The International Herald Tribune
Beijing Seals Off Students' Means of Protest in Aftermath of
    Deng's Death —Seth Faison

China's Course in the Post-Deng Era—Winston Lord

In China, the Interim Won't Necessarily Be Peaceful—William Pfaff

Albright, in China, Upholds Rights

Mourners Line Route to See Deng

Differences 'Made Clear' By Each Side

FEBRUARY 26, 1997
The International Herald Tribune
At Memorial for Deng, Jiang Appeals for Unity

FEBRUARY 27, 1997
The International Herald Tribune
As Mourning Ends, Beijing Turns to Work
After Deng, Different Problems Invite Novel Solutions—Philip Bowring

APPENDIX C

BIBLIOGRAPHY

BOOKS

Arnold, Eve **In China**
    Alfred A. Knopf—New York 1980

Chang, Jung **Wild Swans—Three Daughters of China** – quotes on pages
    190-194—Flamingo, London 1993

Diamond, Jared **Guns, Germs, & Steel—The Fates of Human Societies**
    W.W. Norton & Company—New York 1997

Duncan, Robert L. **China Dawn**
    Delacorte Press—New York 1988

Durant, Will **Our Oriental Heritage**
    MJF Books—New York 1935
    Chinese chronology

Eastman, Lloyd E. **Chiang Kai-shek's Secret Past Memoirs of His Second Wife**
    Westview Press—Boulder, Colorado 1993

Fairbanks, John King **China—A New History**
    Belknap Press of Harvard University—Cambridge, Massachusetts 1994

Finer, S. E. **The History of Government—Volumes 1-2-3**
        Chinese History
    Oxford University Press, Inc.—New York 1997

Kristoff, Nicholas D. & WuDunn, Sheryl **China Wakes**
    Times Books—New York 1994

Lachs, Lorraine **Flowers for Mei-Ling**
    Carroll & Graf Publishers, Inc.—New York 1997

Larsen, Jeanne **Bronze Mirror**
   Henry Holt & Company—New York 1991

Lau, Theodora **Best-Loved Chinese Proverbs**
   Harper Perennial, New York 1995

Liu, Aimee E. **Cloud Mountain**
   Warner Books—New York 1997

Lord, Bette Bao **Legacies—A Chinese Mosiac**
   Middle Heart
   Alfred A. Knopf—New York 1990 and 1996

McCune, Evelyn **Empress**
   Fawcett Columbine—New York 1994

McCunn, Ruthanne Lum **Chinese Proverbs**
   Chronicle Books—San Francisco 1991

Rius & Friends **Mao for Beginners**
   Pantheon Books—New York 1980

Seagrave, Sterling **Dragon Lady**
   Vintage Books—New York 1992

Seagrave, Sterling **Lords of the Rim**
   G.P. Putnam's Sons—New York 1995

Seagrave, Sterling **The Soong Dynasty**
   Harper & Row, Publishers—New York 1985

Sinclair, Kevin with Iris Wong Po-yee **Cultural Shock—China**
   Graphic Arts Center Publishing—Portland, Oregon 1994

Tan, Amy **The Hundred Secret Senses** – quote page 194
   G.P. Putnam & Sons—New York 1995

Webster's New World Encyclopedia
   Prentice Hall General Reference—New York 1992

TRAVEL GUIDES

Baedeker's **China**
    Prentice Hall 1994

Berlitz Country Guide **China 1990-1991**

Buckley, Samagaishi, Storey, Taylor & Lindenmayer **China**
    Lonely Planet Publications —Australia 1994

Insight Guides **China**
    APA Publications—Singapore 1990

Kaplan, Sobin, de Keijzer **The China Guidebook**
    Houghton Mifflin Company—Boston 1993

Malloy, Ruth Lor **Fielding's China**
    William Morrow & Company—New York 1993

Odyssey **Illustrated Guide to Xi'an**
    Sing Cheong Printing Company, Ltd.—Hong Kong 1993

Peh T'l Wei **Old Shanghai**
    Oxford University Press—New York 1993

Passport Books:
Sing Cheong Printing Company, Ltd.—Hong Kong
    Xi'an—China's Ancient Capital 1993

    The Yangtze River 1995

    Nanjing, Wuxi, Suzhou 1988

Summerfield, John **Fodor's China**
    Fodor's Travel Publications, Inc.—New York 1991

Newspapers & Periodicals:

China Daily

China News (Taiwan)

Encarta 98 Encyclopedia CD Rom

Far Eastern Economic Review

Harper's Bazaar

NBC & ABC News on Internet

Newsweek

Shanghai Star

The Financial Times

The International Herald Tribune

The New York Times

The South China Morning Post

The Wall Street Journal

Town & Country

Vogue

Wired

Acknowledgements

Several people have helped me shape this book.

Ned Brandt, Mac's and my friend, always finds the time to read my manuscripts no matter how long they may be. His critique of this writing encouraged me to keep going.

Katherine Wright kindly read the text and found the story as interesting as my Midwestern terms were amusing.

Provost Catherine Chen's calligraphy is an elegant addition to the book.

The people who work at Typographics in Hailey, Idaho produced this beautiful volume. Tinka Raymond and her staff are a skilled and professional group with whom it was my pleasure to work. Besides Tinka's fine editing, Evelyn Phillips developed the maps, Laurie Skinner composed the text into a book form on her computer, and Craig Orison scanned my photographs into the computer so Laurie could position them in the chapters. And special thanks to Norma Douglas who meticulously proofed the entire document.

My thanks to each of them.

Last, but hardly least, was the fun of exploring a new culture and interacting with its citizens, which we both enjoyed so much. You have been a partner in all of this, Mac.

360

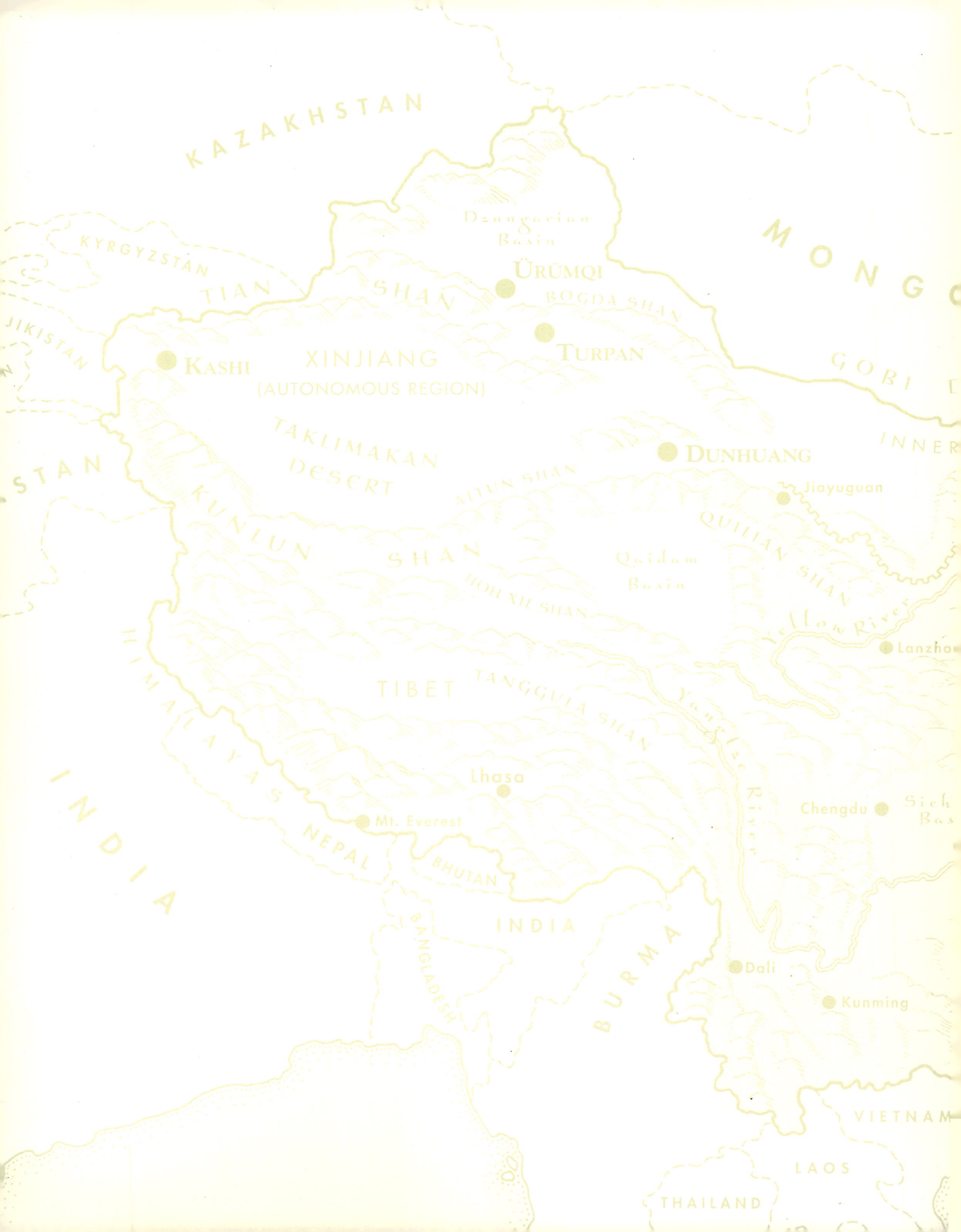